Recent Directions
in the Military History
of the
Ancient World

Publications of the
Association of Ancient Historians

The purpose of the monograph series is to survey the state of the current scholarship in various areas of ancient history.

Continued publication of the series is made possible through the efforts of the AAH publications committee, W. Lindsay Adams of the University of Utah; Lee L. Brice of Western Illinois University, chair; Eugene Borza of Pennsylvania State University; Mark Chavalas of University of Wisconsin La Crosse; Kenneth Harl of Tulane University; Timothy Howe of St. Olaf College; Jennifer T. Roberts of City College – City University of New York; and Carol Thomas of University of Washington. Readers with questions about the series or topic suggestions for future volumes or manuscript questions should contact the current president of the Association of Ancient Historians.

RECENT DIRECTIONS
IN THE MILITARY HISTORY
OF THE
ANCIENT WORLD

PUBLICATIONS OF THE
ASSOCIATION OF
ANCIENT HISTORIANS 10

SETH F. C. RICHARDSON
EVERETT L. WHEELER
SARA E. PHANG
DOUG LEE

EDITED BY
LEE L. BRICE
AND
JENNIFER T. ROBERTS

Regina Books
Claremont, California

Book design: Mary Stoddard

ISBN   1-930053-70-3 // 978-1-930053-70-0

Co-published by arrangement with the
Association of Ancient Historians

Regina Books

Post Office Box 280
Claremont, California 91711
Tel   909.624.8466
Fax   909.626.1345

Manufactured in the United States of America

PREFACE

This volume is the tenth in the series *Publications of the Association of Ancient Historians*. The mission of these volumes has been to survey the state of current scholarship in various areas of ancient history and provide a resource for historians and students seeking guidance on particular topics.

Our volume arose out of a collaboration several years ago between the then presidents of the Society of Ancient Military Historians and the Association of Ancient Historians. We felt that the current pace of publication in military history and the obvious popularity of military history panels at the AAH conference (and military history classes at our institutions) demanded a survey of recent approaches. Military history is not a fad; however, it remains not entirely fashionable in some circles. The days of doctoral candidates avoiding military history topics or being told by a potential employer that they are "too military" for academe, or departmental colleagues denying the value of military history are not entirely past, but the state of the field is much improved over the last two decades. The current topical and methodological growth demonstrate that it remains a vibrant, vital field. This expansion of directions for inquiry has led in turn to more research initiated, more papers submitted for conferences, and more publications on a wide array of military history-related topics. There is simply too much material for any individual to analyze and discuss it all. We quickly realized the need to find scholars who were up to the task of reviewing the state of the literature. Our authors rose to the challenge and smote the charge set before them. We would like to thank our four authors, Seth Richardson, Everett Wheeler, Sara E. Phang, and Doug Lee for their contributions to the volume and their patience with our numerous requests.

In addition to our contributors, numerous others deserve our appreciation for their assistance and encouragement throughout the process. We are grateful to W. Lindsay Adams, current president of the AAH, and the members of the AAH publications committee, Eugene Borza, Mark Chavalas, Kenneth Harl, Timothy Howe, and Carol Thomas, for giving us a free hand and their unwavering support of the project from its inception. Additionally, we thank Steven Garfinkle, Christopher Fuhrmann, and especially Georgia Tsouvala for their aid in bringing the project to a successful close. We would also like to express our thanks to the anonymous readers who helped enormously to improve the volume. Any errors that remain are entirely of our own making.

    PAAH 10 will be the last volume on which we collaborate with Richard and Glenda Burns; we would like to recognize their superlative efforts over more than a decade in support of the *PAAH* series. They will be much missed.

    Now that the book is complete there will be much rejoicing; we look forward to the next *PAAH* volume.

LEE L. BRICE
Western Illinois University
Macomb, IL

JENNIFER T. ROBERTS
City College of New York – CUNY Graduate Center
New York, NY

To:
Georgia Tsouvala,
   carissimae uxori (L. L. B.)
   optimaeque discipulae (J. T. R.)

Contents

ABBREVIATIONS

Except as noted in chapter one, abbreviations of journals and works employed in this book are those from *L'Année Philologique* and the *Oxford Classical Dictionary*, in addition to the following:

ANRW   Temporini, H. and W. Haase, eds. 1972-. *Aufstieg und Niedergang der romischen Welt. Geschichte und Kultur Roms im Spiegel der neueren Forschung.* Berlin: W de Gruyter.

CHGRW   Sabin, P., H. van Wees and M. Whitby, eds. 2007. *The Cambridge History of Greek and Roman Warfare,* 2 vols. Cambridge: Cambridge University Press.

CRA   Erdkamp, P., ed. 2007. *A Companion to the Roman Army* Blackwell Companions to the Ancient World. Malden, MA: Wiley-Blackwell, 2007.

JMH   *Journal of Military History*

INTRODUCTION

LEE L. BRICE
Western Illinois University
JENNIFER T. ROBERTS
City College of New York – CUNY Graduate Center

It would be difficult to overstate the importance of warfare and military institutions in the ancient world. Beyond the prevalence of warfare itself, nearly every facet of life in the ancient world—art, literature, music, religion, athletics, agriculture, manufacturing, gender roles, architecture, trade, education, and science—influenced, and was influenced by, warfare and the military institutions tied to it. Little surprise then that warfare and the military have been important components of historical narratives for as long as they have existed.

Throughout the ancient cultures of southwest Asia and the Mediterranean world, various types of ancient texts as diverse as boundary inscriptions, king lists, celebratory reliefs, religious hymns, poetry, art, inventories, and historical prose touch on warfare or ancient militaries in varying degrees. The historians Herodotus and Thucydides followed a long tradition of discussing warfare in a literary format. That these two authors have long been seen as the font of the western historical narrative tradition means one can reasonably argue that history focusing on warfare is the oldest or one of the oldest varieties of history.

Despite its age, military history is remarkably difficult to define with precision. Each era and culture defines it in its own terms. Over time military history has been seen as a vehicle for: entertainment, nationalist propaganda, military education, self-justification, the recounting of valorous deeds, and the recording of events related to warfare. The definition of military history as describing what happened (and sometimes analyzing why) in war was limited and relatively constant throughout much of the nineteenth and early twentieth centuries, even as new methodologies emerged for the rest of the historical field. When other fields of history went through methodological and topical changes post-1918, so too did this one. Military history of the ancient world is no exception, having experienced in less than a century an immense blossoming in approaches and topics. Practitioners of the field, many of whom would not call themselves exclusively military historians, employ methodologies as diverse as any field in the Humanities. At present military history can properly be said to include history of war, warfare (waging of war), and all historical aspects of military institutions. Current realities have jarred many in the field to realize, as ancient authors did, that we must think of war as including many kinds and scales of organized violence besides state-level conflicts. At the same time, we must accept the fact that it is difficult to understand the sharp end of battle if we do not understand the military institutions engaged in it.[1] If this broad definition means that the modern field overlaps with other varieties of history, then we can be pleased that military matters are now better appreciated in the discipline of history than they were in recent decades.

Military history has not always been so valued by other academics. It has become a commonplace for military historians to complain of the "gulf" between their field and those of other historians and the lack of sensitivity to the importance of military matters.[2] The reasons for this gap are numerous, but in part are anchored in the opposition to militarism and war that developed in the post-World War II era, a feeling that gained further traction in America during the controversial war in Vietnam. A sense among other academics that the field was methodologically obsolete and too popularized contributed to the distance.

This yawning intellectual gulf within the discipline remains, but since the 1980s new American attitudes toward conflict, a more mature understanding of the connections between war and culture, and the related openness of the field to interdisciplinary approaches have led to some easing of the academic ostracism that military history has

---

1   For discussion of this broad, modern definition and the blossoming of new approaches see James 2002, 7-14; Black 2004a, 17-18; Morillo 2006, 1-4; Citino 2007. Defining war remains a topic of debate; for the ancient world, Hanson (1999c and 2007) maintains the limited state-based definition of warfare worthy of military historians' attention; cf. below chapter two.

2   The literature on this topic is too numerous to cite in its entirety but for ancient historians see Hanson 1999c; and James 2002, 1-7 and 12-14. More recently for the field as a whole see Black 2004a, 1-22 and 26-7; Citino 2007; and especially Shy 2008, 1033-36.

endured.[3] Despite this mixed academic reception, military history has not lacked for modern audiences and authors employing a variety of methodologies.

Much of what has been written about warfare and militaries has focused heavily on three interrelated and well-worn threads: battle narratives (including operational histories and discussions of tactics and strategy), consideration of famous military personalities, and military manuals. Battlefield narratives have served a wide variety of functions since their ancient origins, growing to include campaigns and even entire wars.[4] Although it would be easy to dismiss military biographies as hagiography, the way in which some authors use these to push contemporary historical agendas means that we cannot discount them entirely. Most biographies, however, serve more limited entertainment and profit functions.[5] Emerging in ancient Greece as a means by which an author could instruct readers in his views on the proper conduct of military matters, manuals based on historical examples remain important and show no sign of incipient extinction.[6] Sharing ancient antecedents, these methods long fulfilled all the needs of military history.

Modern historians refer to these traditional types of military history as "drums and trumpets," even though the name more properly belongs to battlefield narratives and operational histories. For some critics the label pokes at the militaristic or nationalistic fervor with which such narratives are identified, but for other authors the label simply evokes the repetitiveness and vacuity of these works at their worst. The strongest criticism against the "drums and trumpets" approach is that the way it is often done is insufficient—it tells us nothing new—communicating

3   James 2002, 12-14; Shy 2008; Rosenstein 2009b; Kaegi 2009.
4   On traditional military historiography for ancient studies: Hanson 2007, 3-10; discussion of traditional approaches in the entire field see Black 2004a, 26-34; Morillo 2006, 11-37.
5   In 1999 Victor Hanson observed (1999c, 398), "The nineteenth-century practice of personal military hagiography has now passed out of style." A visit to any bookstore and a recent review of military literature on the ancient world reveal, however, that this approach shows no sign of fading away. Tucci's disappointing recent review of ancient military history includes (2010, 879-883) hagiographic comments about several ancient leaders and bibliographic works. On biography in the field see Black 2004a, 37-49; and Morillo 2006, 11-37.
6   Lonsdale 2007, is a recent example. On manuals as a genre, modern: Morillo 2006, 26-37; ancient and medieval: Bliese 1994; Hanson 2007, 5-6; Wheeler 1988a; idem 2010.

little about warfare, its history, and its place in the larger culture and historical context.[7] Despite these drawbacks, traditional approaches still dominate much of the military history written every year.

Partially in response to frustration with how little "drums and trumpets" history often tells us about battle, John Keegan published in 1976 his re-visioning *Face of Battle* to refocus attention on what battle was imagined to be like for soldiers. He inspired as well as initiated a steady stream of studies cast in a similar methodological mold including in the field of ancient studies.[8] Although his methodology appeared new, because of its focus on battle narratives, even if told from the bottom up, face-of-battle method should be categorized as either a new manifestation of traditional approaches, or a blending between tradition and the next methodology to make an impact on the field.

Although various new historical approaches appeared after World War II, it is only since the early 1970s that military history began to embrace the "new military history," or "war and society" approach. A key point proponents of the "new" school made is that organized violence has always had an impact on societies, something we need to explore to be able properly to understand and explain warfare.[9] Also, given that evidence is uneven, "war and society" approaches with their use of theory and modeling can, when done with care, be useful in opening up ways of explaining the past. That is not to suggest that the new military history is unproblematic, but that despite continued critiques it has become one of the dominant 'schools' among academic historians.[10] New military history, now more than forty years old, was not the only solution sought for all the field's problems.

A more recent approach to military history that has become increasingly popular among both historians and the public is grounded in a technocentric approach to analysis and explanation of the history

---

7   Black 2004a, 26-29; contra Showalter 1975; Citino 2007, 1079-81.
8   For discussion of works that follow a "face of battle" approach see chapters two to four, below.
9   For recent discussions of the European (primarily French) precursors to "war and society" approaches see Wheeler 2007b, xiv-xix; Paret 2009.
10   The Anglo-American literature on the History field's reception of "war and society" or "new military history" is voluminous, but see Chambers 1991; Black 2004a and 2004b; Spiller 2006; Citino 2007, 1071-76; Shy 2008; These authors agree that more work needs to be done, but that "new" approaches are not just a fad imposed on the field nor have they resulted in a "paradigm shift" as one might think from hostile treatments like Hanson 2007, 8-13.

of war and warfare. Such works tend to treat technology—its invention, adoption, development, impact, or failure to be open to it—as key to the history of warfare. Because it is (or seems) newer than "drums and trumpets" it has been popular among academic as well as non-academic authors and analysts. Seductive to readers familiar with technology, this approach is nonetheless no panacea. Technological determinism— the argument that technology is what drives all history and determines success in war—is the biggest pitfall of this approach. Also, because they ignore much of the society that creates and uses such technology, technocentric approaches and arguments, even those that are not deterministic, tend to present history in mono-causal terms.[11] Given its entrenchment, the technologically-centered approach shows no sign of dissipating, so there is need for continued vigilance.

Since the late 1980s military history has continued to grow along with the rest of the historical discipline as a new generation of historians seeks new topics as well as new methods (and improvements in older methods) to shed new light on previously explored topics. In some cases the new approaches have been tied to explanation, and in others analysis has been the goal. The "Military Revolution" thesis, for example, after stewing for several decades, came fully into its own in 1976 with publication of Geoffrey Parker's re-examination of the concept and has since become nearly a cottage industry, having an impact even in ancient history.[12] An element of the "Military Revolution" discussion that is indicative of the recent wave of military history is the increasing use of global comparative history. In ancient military history such work has recently appeared in comparisons of the mechanics of ancient empires in West and East, and military changes in ancient Rome and China.[13] In other cases, military historians have expanded on their methodologies for analysis by drawing on other fields (e.g., gender studies and physiology), and theoretical approaches (e.g., chaos theory

---

11 Black 2004a, 33-35 and 104-27; idem 2004b, 1218-25; Spiller 2006. Fernando Rey recently concluded (2010) that technological determinism is as insidious a problem for scholars of the ancient world as it is for modern military historians.

12 Parker 1976; for the historiographical context Rogers 1995; Morillo 2006, 75-81; Citino 2007, 1077-79; a recent reconnaissance of the topic, Brice 2011b.

13 Morris and Scheidel 2009; and Rosenstein 2009a. On comparative military history as related to entrenched Eurocentrism see Black 2004a and 2004b. On the strengths of comparative approaches see Walter Scheidel's introduction in Scheidel 2009a. cf. chapter two below.

and game theory) with mixed results.[14] In the discussion that follows it will become apparent that military historians of the ancient world, open to ways of making sense from limited evidence, have shown in the last decade a marked openness to these methodological waves. While these trends are a far cry from old school or "drums and trumpets," military history has nonetheless not abandoned its roots.

By now it should be clear that military history written currently is a combination of the traditional and the new. The various new methodologies and new ways of interrogating old evidence help keep the field fresh and vigorous. At the same time there is a place for "drums and trumpets." There are some tasks that operational histories can still do well. As the steady annual production of them suggests, there will always be battlefield narratives, many of which tell us nothing new, but good works that synthesize new methodologies into their analysis without sacrificing narrative are being produced and will continue to be welcome additions to the field.[15] Despite those who carp about work "no one reads," there will always be a need for new specialist studies based on hard evidence and current trends in research to stimulate growth in the field and in popular military historical works.

Although one might think our title, *Recent Directions in the Military History of the Ancient World*, would be entirely self-explanatory, it seems best in the case of such an expansive title to discuss the limitations and goals of this collection. Our primary aim is to make available to members of the Association of Ancient Historians as well as to interested teachers and students of ancient history who are not specialized in military history a short volume to which they could turn for a quick review of recent topics and arguments as well as a sense of

---

14   On expansion in the field as a whole: Black 2004a; idem 2004b; Morillo 2006, 42-43 and 61-70; Spiller 2006; Citino 2007; Shy 2008. On expansion among ancient historians: Hanson 2007; Wheeler 2007b; Rosenstein 2009b; Kaegi 2009; Fagan and Trundle 2010, 1-16.

15   Showalter 1975; Citino 2007, 2079-81; and Shy 2008. For the ancient world there have been numerous battlefield studies recently from the Persian wars and the Punic Wars. No doubt some of the former are due in part to the 2500th anniversary of Marathon as well as the film *300*. These studies have been of decidedly mixed value (see the limited discussion in chapters two and three).

the current state and recent bibliography of certain trends in the military historical field. A secondary goal was to provide those specializing in military history (e.g. Greek, Roman, Modern, etc) a resource that gathers some recent directions of research in ancient specializations both for review of recent historiography as well as demonstrating the health of the field. We expect this small volume will be a useful tool for teachers and students in various fields in need of class preparation, advising, and bibliographical searches in the military history of the ancient world. Of course, the limitations on a volume such as this can be formidable, but our organizational strategy overcomes the most serious of these issues.

Gone are the days of Thomas Carlyle. No longer is it possible for any one person to read everything written in any field during one's career, much less synthesize and evaluate trends and developments in several fields over an extended period. Similarly, reviewing all the military historical literature for the entire ancient world would be too much for a book of the size we have envisaged.[16] In order better to focus on new approaches our authors have restricted their review largely to works produced in the last fifteen years and those reflecting newer approaches in military history. This choice means that we eschewed more traditional works in preference for works in the face-of-battle or war and society 'schools' or employing new methodologies to explore military-related topics of our authors' choosing including economics, women, gender, culture, technology, identity, demographics and recruitment, ideology, or military and politics. Since the intended audience for AAH publications tends to be primarily Anglo-American, the bulk of the works considered are in English. A single, complete bibliography of all works cited will enable readers to explore titles of interest in more detail at their leisure.

---

16 As will become obvious in the chapters and bibliography below, publication in military history topics is not in serious decline. In addition to a steady stream of monograph and academic journal publications over the last decade the significant increase in publication of "Companion" volumes and anthologies from academic and trade presses has become a gift and curse. While many of these volumes contain military history-related articles even when the volumes themselves are not primarily military, there is more material getting into press so there is ever more publishing to track and evaluate. That said, given the poor state of military history publishing in the mid-late twentieth century we are pleased to see the field so active right now. Fortunately, the production of useful companions shows no sign of abating (e.g., Tritle and Campbell 2011).

A pattern too common in collections such as ours is a tendency to ignore the Ancient Near East entirely and treat Late Antiquity as an afterthought. This habit of regional or chronological omission, while handy for organization, can make it more difficult for readers to identify regional parallels and connections that were important.[17] We accept it as an axiom that the geographic entirety of the ancient world is too great for meaningful coverage of every inch in so small a book as this one. That need not require us to ignore much of the ancient western world when organizing our chapters.

In an effort to give the fullest coverage possible the four chapters include the Ancient Near East, Greece, Rome, and Late Antiquity. Discussions of recent work on military history of the ancient world east of Susa (the Persian empire), in North Africa (including Egypt), and a more thorough treatment of naval combat throughout the ancient world are much needed, but are beyond the scope of this collection.

Our team of contributors consists of four ancient historians selected for their recent experience writing about the military history of one of the four areas on which the volume is focused. We chose them not only for their recent publications, but also because of the diversity of their approaches and points of view. After giving each author a sense of our broad goals we gave them free rein to tackle the chapter as best they saw fit. The result is that each chapter has a distinctive authorial voice that reflects the writer's own experience, vision, and approach to the field of military history. Since each chapter is intended to be a stand-alone resource, this array of authorial views will not impede the success of the volume as a whole. Readers will find that repeated readings reveal additional insights and gems from each contributor.

We start at the beginning of the historical record with Seth Richardson's review of the Ancient Near East (ANE). After discussing the basic background and problems (e.g., mixed quality sources, a huge span of time) that contribute to making it difficult to wrangle the disparate threads of ANE military history, Richardson provides a case study within military history. He sets forth his parameters and goals clearly and then examines a variety of military and 'war and society' issues of importance. In the process he highlights a number of the primary sources available and cites the key relevant recent work. By

---

17   Hanson 2010. Garrett Fagan and Matthew Trundle (2010) provide a needed corrective regionally and topically.

the conclusion the reader should have a sense of recent trends and problems in the military history of the Ancient Near East.

Taking as his goal a cautionary historiographical review for graduate students, Everett Wheeler's whimsically titled chapter on Ancient Greece treats the cleft in scholarly trends between traditionalists and "eager adventurers" who ignore historicism and seek guidance from social science methodologies. Although his use of Alice in Wonderland as a motif to tie the wide-ranging discussion together may come as a surprise, do not be put off; readers will find much of value in this learned and provocative chapter. Not everyone will agree with his evaluations, but Wheeler builds his discussion on extensive breadth and familiarity with the literature. In the process he covers recent trends in the military history of Ancient Greece (and occasionally Rome too) and the antecedents of some of these historical movements as well. This chapter will be useful for readers seeking a more developed sense of historiography underlying "war and society" and "face of battle" approaches.

Roman military history often leaned towards the jingoistic and triumphalist. Modern authors, steeped in the success of contemporary 'empires' often fell (and still fall) into habits similar to those of the ancients in writing about Rome. In chapter three, Sara Phang brings her affinity for cultural approaches to bear on her broad examination of how modern historians go about reconstructing a more nuanced picture of the Roman military and the warfare in which it engaged. Not surprisingly given her prior work, battle narratives, biographies and weapons analysis do not figure prominently in her discussion. Phang highlights recent trends in a wide variety of military historical topics connected with Rome as late as the Severan dynasty.

Late Antiquity, the four hundred or so years from the early third to the early seventh century AD, is the shortest of the periods any of our authors had to review. Its brevity in comparison to the other periods covered herein did not diminish the turbulence and thus the importance of this period for the Roman empire. Doug Lee tackles this deceptive period with aplomb in chapter four. He conveys to readers the complexities that historians must take into account and the diversity of recent work. Although some authors might choose to focus exclusively on west or east in the period after AD 312, Lee continues to cover both as appropriate in covering the later Roman Empire as late as the reign of Justinian. Readers will find that Late Antiquity, too often tied up in responses to Edward Gibbon, is the recipient of much new research in a variety of aspects of military history. As with the other regions, much remains to be done.

We are pleased with the breadth and depth of this volume and with the erudition and panache of the authors who have worked so hard to make it possible. We thank them for their patience in fielding our frequent requests for revisions that would lend coherence to a collection of disparate essays and enable us to join them profitably together rather than fitting them to a tortuous procrustean bed of homogeneity. We are confident that many of our readers will profit from their labors as they go on to do their own work in the many subfields of military history and others will simply take pleasure in learning about new developments in this exciting and important area of scholarship.

1

MESOPOTAMIA AND THE "NEW" MILITARY HISTORY[1]

SETH F. C. RICHARDSON

University of Chicago

1. FROM PRE-MODERN TO "OLD" TO "NEW"

For a moment, let us leave aside the "new" military history: Assyriology already had venerable theological and civic-historical purposes for military history when the "old" variety first came along in the nineteenth century A.D.[2] Fusty as it may seem today, the "old" military history was born out of the then novel early modern premise that war, like politics and statecraft, was a rational science which could be studied, mastered, taught, and distilled, not the enactment of destiny or the will of the divine. To our eyes, that "old" military history seems theoretically underdeveloped—focused on political elites, pedantic in its attachment to detail, and not-so-subtly fetishizing mass violence. Yet it was radical in its day, married to the civic-historiographic needs of emerging bourgeois nation-states, and not to the theological and classist ideals of Church and nobility. Most branches of historical study

---

1   Bibliographic note: Abbreviated citations throughout this essay conform to sigla cited by the *Chicago Assyrian Dictionary* (=CAD; Chicago: The Oriental Institute of the University of Chicago, 1956-). Specific texts cited by sigla include: AbB 2 = Frankena 1966; AbB 10 = Kraus 1985; AbB 11 = Stol 1986; AbB 13 = van Soldt 1993; ABC = Grayson 1975; Mari texts denoted as ARM, F, or A = Heimpel 2003; SAA I = Parpola 1987; SAA IV = Starr 1990; SAA V = Lanfranchi and Parpola 1990; SAA XI = Fales and Postgate 1995; SAA XII = Kataja and Whiting 1995; SAA XIII = Cole and Machinist 1998; SAA XV = Fuchs and Parpola 2001; SAA XVI = Luukko and Van Buylaere 2002; SAA XVII = Dietrich 2003; SAA XVIII = Reynolds 2003; EA = Moran 1992; CH = Roth 1995; RIME 1 = Frayne 2008; RIME 2 = Frayne 1993; RIME 3/1 = Edzard 1997; RIME 3/2 = Frayne 1997; RIMA 1 = Grayson 1987; RIMA 2 = Grayson 1991; RIMA 3 = Grayson 1996. Electronic resources include references to ETCSL = http://etcsl.orinst.ox.ac.uk; BCHP and Walker Chronicle = http://livius.org.

2   All dates are BC unless otherwise noted; absolute chronological dates prior to 1300 follow the so-called Middle Chronology in which the accession of Ḫammurabi of Babylon is dated 1792.

busily professionalized themselves in these terms by the mid-1800's, but perhaps none was more resistant to civil-military history than Ancient Near Eastern studies.

Professional and popular historians in these fields continued to carry forward pre-modern Judeo-Christian and Classical historiographic traditions for generations. Under these formulae, the military histories of "Oriental despots" closely mimicked those of the ancient sources: armies and wars were either the instruments of a now wrathful, now redeeming god, or embodiments of the Oriental ruler's lust for power, his innate cruelty, his hubris. To muddy these lofty themes with discussion of mere tactics, strategies, and weaponry would have confounded nineteenth-century Assyriology's moral obligations to a) rescue the Bible from a creeping secularism and b) demonstrate relevance to Greek and Roman history.

The production of a "history of events" that old military history required, however, remained obstructed by basic issues of translation and chronology still being worked out well into the twentieth century. Only by that time did sufficient progress with respect to evidence open the floodgates of interpretation; only then did Ancient Near Eastern disciplines come to foster the study of the "old" military history no less than other fields, and these topics quickly took strong hold in the popular imagination.[3]

Like any other quarter of human history, the primary record of the Ancient Near East abounds with famous battles, marches, and military leaders: Sargon of Akkad's twenty-fourth century conquests of all lands from "the Upper Sea to the Lower Sea," Mursili I's lightning double-raid on Aleppo and Babylon in 1595, Ramses III's 1178 stand against the invasions of the "Sea Peoples," etc. Campaign accounts were among the earliest (though, significantly, not *the* earliest) forms of royal literature, beginning with terse reports of victories in third millennium inscriptions and gradually developing into lengthy and monumental literatures in annalistic, epic, and summary genres, each with its own rarified stylistic and narrative conventions. But warfare was hardly limited to royal sources—it leached out topically into every textual genre known to us: letters, hymns, economic documents, ritual-magical texts, administrative rosters, stories, poems, and date lists.[4]

---

3   The most successful social-historical treatment of the Mesopotamian military remains Sasson's (1969) short study of Mari.

4   For a discussion of sources and their historical use, see Van De Mieroop 1999; two recent compendia of sources in translation include Hallo, 2003 and Chavalas, 2006.

The militaries of early states were ubiquitous in non-textual media as well. Defense architecture was a highly visible element of the archaeological landscape, from the fortified site of eighth millennium Jericho to the real and fabled eleven-mile defensive walls of sixth century Babylon.[5] War was a central subject in symbolic and representational art, best known from the mural reliefs of Egyptian and Assyrian palaces and temples, but also from battlefield stelae, divine symbols used as unit standards and weapons used as cult objects. Some artifacts seem to have the "whiff of gunpowder" still upon them: the mass of ivories and treasures pitched down a well during the destruction of Nineveh; the cuneiform letter containing desperate pleas for help from Ugarit's king shortly before the city's utter destruction ("the enemy's ships ... did evil things in my country");[6] the skeleton of a mother clutching her child (*une tableau-vivante véritable*) found under the burned debris of the sacked lower town at Hasanlu.[7] These and a thousand other details make clear that wars were not only the formal window-dressing of royal rhetoric and ideology, but also a nasty and brutish experience for those who lived through them.[8]

Histories of the Ancient Near East seem eager to demonstrate the quality and quantity of their evidence. Some military actions are enshrined in scholarship as much for their blow-by-blow particularity as for their historical significance. The Battle of Qadesh (May 12-13, 1274), for instance, is known for the Egyptian sources' detailing of field maneuvers of identifiable units: advance guards, mercenaries, infantry and chariotry, and a list of no fewer than eighteen contingents of Hittite allies.[9] In a few cases, the sources are so numerous as to produce the kind of "thick description" necessary for *histoire événementielle*, as with the 1765 siege of Razama accounted for in the Mari letters. Some clashes are known from dual-accounts, such as the multiple sources for the fall of the city of Larsa in 1763, the historical and literary accounts (biblical, cuneiform, Greek, and Latin) of the "siege" of Jerusalem in 701, the divergent Assyrian and Babylonian claims about the Assyro-

---

5   See Burke 2008.
6   Nougaryol 1968, 87-90 no. 24.
7   Muscarella 1966.
8   See Vandkilde (2003) on violence as a theoretical problem for scholarly observation.
9   The Egyptian "Poem" and "Bulletin" describing the event are known in more than a dozen copies, with a few disparate Hittite sources adding small bits of information.

Elamite engagement at Halule in 691.[10] But cases which demonstrate that the sources *could* be as detailed as we might want are in the minority. In the overwhelming majority of cases, we are forced to rely on singular, official, and laconic royal inscriptions concerning warfare. I have attempted partially to remedy this bias by drawing heavily in this essay from Mesopotamian letters, notably those of eighteenth century Mari and seventh century Nineveh, documents more reliable for their non-idealizing voice. There are methodological pitfalls in the use of letters as well, though, and these we should bear in mind: a) letters were problem-solving documents and usually described atypical predicaments, b) they often overstated problems in order to obtain resources from central authorities, and c) they tended to accentuate anecdote over context.

Royal inscriptions in the meantime have undergone scrutiny on theoretical grounds in the wake of the linguistic turn: it is not merely doubted whether such texts are accurate, but whether their intent was to produce narratives of historicity at all—rather, narratives of authority. Thus, although warfare was the beating heart of royal literature—if predictably inaccurate where it can be checked—even the enthusiasm of "drums and trumpets" historians has waned as the value of their "facts" has shifted like so much sand under their feet. For these reasons, a true military history of events will not emerge. Important work on Ancient Near Eastern military economies and strategies continues to be produced,[11] but one senses that new directions are necessary if we are to make much headway in understanding the social place and purpose of these earliest state militaries.

I will look at four areas of interest: two are social-historical (the military and society, the military *as* a society), and two are political-historical (the military and the state, the military and ideology). A proviso: though the pristine civilizations of the Ancient Near East provide just about the earliest forensic, structural, locational, artifactual,

---

10   On the Larsa episode, see Van De Mieroop 2005; on the latter two episodes, see Laato's (1995) critical (if somewhat simplistic) essay.

11   E.g., the new volume edited by Vidal 2010, which aims "to consolidate the studies on Ancient Near Eastern warfare," but is essentially a set of essays on disparate issues of military tactics and technologies; cf. de Souza ed. 2008. On sieges, see now Eph'al 2009 and Melville and Melville 2008. The important anthology by Raaflaub and Rosenstein (1999) unfortunately did not include a chapter on Mesopotamia. See Abrahami's useful bibliographies (2005, 2009).

epigraphic, and iconographic evidence for warfare[12]—this abundance must be balanced against the enormous time span of three millennia of historical change, amidst which it is difficult to say anything normative or definitional. Given that comprehensive coverage is an unrealistic goal,[13] I hope to proceed on five premises throughout a thematic study:

- Militaries and polities were mutually structuring and productive of cultural change, through ethnolinguistic contact, professionalization, gender construction, military means of production, and imperialism. I will touch on points of change including state formation, political economy, specialization and scale, ritualism, material conditions of soldiering, and political agency.

- The military historical issues which concern Assyriologists today relate mostly to state produced historiography and the role of ritual in warfare, placing less emphasis on social- and economic-historical questions.

- Though the possibilities for historicism regarding ancient Mesopotamian warfare are abbreviated by the types of written sources, they offer rich opportunities for social history studies.

- We should adopt a deep skepticism that royal literature touching on our topic reflects the concerns of civil society; mono-vocal state claims about political unity or security needs were not necessarily shared or culturally representative.

- Any definition of "the military" must account for the absence of any ancient, emic distinction between permanent states of war and peace. I understand a "military" to be a distinct, organized and permanent (though not necessarily "standing") force of men, materiel and emplacements at the disposal of the state or its ruler or both. I will think of both "the nexus between armies and the societies that spawn them" and the "memory and culture" of war.[14]

- Our contextualization of war violence need not shy away from

---

12 Cioffi-Revilla 2000, 64-70.
13 It also seems unproductive to dilute this essay by covering other Ancient Near Eastern culture areas, such as Egypt or the Hittite lands. Among "old military" topics, I will not be addressing military technologies (especially as they regard metallurgy, fortifications, equids, etc.) or field tactics, as studies of these already abound in the secondary literature.
14 Citino 2007.

modern social-historical questions regarding the morality of violence and terror in warfare or the politics of the body.[15]

2. THE MILITARY IN THE TIME OF STATE FORMATION

Mesopotamia boasted one of the world's earliest state civilizations.
Since Weber's famous axiom runs that states were entities maintaining
a monopoly on legitimate violence, the development of the Sumerian
city-state would presumably emerge at an historic juncture between
feuding and warfare, between armed kinship groups and a true military.
Insofar as the selection of permanent war leaders has been seen as the
institutionalizing moment of early states, state formation and military
organization seem inextricably bound up at the nexus of who sought
legitimacy, how, and why.[16] Yet Weber's definition has not stood the
test of time very well: it is probably anachronistic to typologically
differentiate "the military" from other purveyors of social violence in
antiquity,[17] since at no point did early states fully hold (or perhaps even
wish to hold) Weber's talismanic monopoly.[18] From the side of legal
history, self-help under the law included recourse to private violence
down to very late periods,[19] and from the political science side, it
has been doubted whether "legitimacy" necessarily distinguishes
war-making from criminal violence in kind in any period.[20] A debate
on the existence of prehistoric warfare has continued for more than
forty years now,[21] but in that time the Syro-Mesopotamian region has
not produced unequivocal evidence for either widespread warfare

---

15 As Bahrani (2008) argues, warfare was an extension of the mechanics of state punishment,
    and its practices and representations informed one another on all cultural levels.
16 Cioffi-Revilla 2000, 71, "the protobellic period precedes the protopolitical period, but
    often not by much."
17 Though I will not address "warfighting as such," "warfare" could refer to everything
    from "small wars" to the "armed peace" of empires (e.g., the so-called *pax Assyriaca*),
    to the roles of and effects on non-combatants, to all processes of preparation, support or
    and prosecution of combat, the deep historical causes for war, and its long-term effects
    long after the shields were laid down.
18 Richardson 2011. Neither is this pattern confined to deep antiquity: as late and as
    centralized an empire as eighth/seventh century Assyria still saw the building of private
    armies not under state authority: see SAA I 11, and the prevalence of feuding and
    non-state force in the letters of SAAS IV, *inter alia*.
19 Whitman 1995.
20 Tilly 1985.
21 Anthropologists have extensively questioned both the categorical helpfulness and the
    evolutionary distinctiveness of legitimized, organized violence: Otterbein 1999.
    Hobsbawm (1959) already argued that the very concept of an internal "monopoly of

or state control of violence. One may point to possible examples of military architecture and perhaps military activity in the Chalcolithic,[22] but the larger record points to early Mesopotamian state ideologies de-emphasizing warfare.[23]

A comparison to early Egyptian civilization may be useful, since the formative role of the military there differed considerably from Sumer.[24] The Narmer Palette, one of the earliest Egyptian royal objects, depicts an almost fully formed visual repertoire: the pharaoh victorious in war along with military attendants, standard-bearers, conquered towns, and killed or captured enemies. It might be noted, however, that only the king is shown as dispensing violence. The highly conventionalized representative strategies and historical issues of the palette are typological for much of Ancient Near Eastern art-historical evidence: the central role accorded to the ruler, a focus on his (singlehanded) victory over the docile bodies of the enemies, with a minor role for the king's actual fighting force. The Narmer and Scorpion mace-heads of the Dynasty 0 period (c. 3100-3000) also symbolically link early kingship to military power, and war thus seems virtually synonymous with state unification.[25]

Uruk-period Mesopotamia (c. 3400-3000), however, was virtually devoid of symbolic evidence for military power, its rulers presented as priestly elites or hunters, its records focused on agricultural administration and scribal training, its urban architecture focused on temple complexes—walled, but not overtly fortified.[26] Not until a half a millennium later, around the twenty-sixth century, did Mesopotamian rulers begin to appropriate military symbols for themselves, including inscribed mace-heads, chariot burials, and objects bearing scenes of warfare, such as the "Standard of Ur" and shell plaque figures depicting soldiers and bound, nude captives. The largest known monument from

---

violence" never existed until the formation of early modern nation-states, thus a pure anachronism for pre-modern societies. For a review, see Simons 1999.

22 Reichel 2009, citing fortification walls at Mersin (ca. 5000) and both Habuba Kabira and Hamoukar (fourth millennium); his discovery of hoards of "sling bullets" in a destruction layer at the latter site have not met universal acceptance as evidence for warfare, see Oates et al. 2007, 593; Clare et al. 2008, 77.

23 On the relatively low incidence of warfare claims in early Sumer, see Richardson 2011.

24 Yoffee 2005.

25 See also Sanders (2006, 7) on early writing on weapons in Levantine contexts.

26 A lone seal impression from fourth millennium Uruk levels may depict a ruler figure supervising the execution of prisoners by soldiers, Dolce 2004, 124 and Fig 5.

the period depicting warfare, the "Stele of the Vultures," stood less than six feet tall. The Royal Cemetery of Ur, dating to about this time, indeed contained elite and royal burials with a wide variety of weapons—spears, daggers, war-helms, and axes—but these were almost entirely made of gold—symbolic and ceremonial, and not functional.[27] The objects include the famous gold "Helm of Meskalamdug," but even this supposed war-helm is modeled to appear as a royal coiffure, not a piece of armor. The military seems to have grown only gradually more central to kingship ideologies in the Sumerian case, which in its earliest symbology articulated the king's role as a priestly figure, as fructifier of the land, and as hunter.[28]

This slowly emerging military ideology coincides with an apparent expansion of interstate warfare in the Early Dynastic period (2900-2334). In their royal inscriptions, the kings of Kiš, Lagaš, and other city-states spoke of warfare commissioned by the gods for the protection of local lands and borders,[29] and boasted of the personal heroism of the kings.[30] Combatants were depicted in massed ranks, whether as advancing victors, as carpets of corpses of vanquished enemies underfoot, or heaped up in burial mounds; in all cases their compactness evoked the image of the city itself.[31] Regionally, there is some evidence as well that city-states coordinated military forces to satisfy joint needs of defense and trade protection, such as the so-called Kiengi League, a confederated force of soldiers from 10 cities—as much forces of collaboration as of competition.

---

27 Weber and Zettler 1998, 163.
28 It is commonly assumed that the various hunter motifs alluded to the king's function as war-leader, but this is a) hardly clear, and b) an allusion which is not clearly demonstrated until much later times, and may thus be entirely anachronistic to deep antiquity.
29 In Lagaš monuments, the tutelary god was depicted on the field of battle engaged in combat.
30 The motif of the king as battlefield hero unsurprisingly remained a staple of royal literature from earliest times, e.g., Šulgi's boast that "I go ahead of the main body of my troops and I clear the terrain for my scouts," etc. (ETCSL šulgi B, Text 2.4.2.02). This remained the image well into Neo-Assyrian times, when the annalistic accounts were often written in the first-person. While there is no doubt that the kings routinely went on campaign, their own prowess is less verifiable: one letter of that time, however, suggests the reality of the situation, as an exasperated general writes the king, saying: "Just as your royal fathers have done, stay on the hill, and let your magnates do the battle" (SAA XVI 77).
31 Compare to the war dead strewn across extensive landscapes in Neo-Assyrian times, more evocative of the lands of empire (Richardson 2007, 193-96).

But over-attention to any of this evidence would obscure the statistical rarity of warfare as a *topos*. Of 191 Early Dynastic royal inscriptions, only 28 mention 24 inter-city conflicts in a period of ca. 250 years; only nine of the conflicts involved bordering states, and only two did not involve Lagaš.[32] Both representationally and topically, military action only moved closer to the center of state ideology and individual action in the succeeding Akkadian period (2334-2193).[33] A scholarly emphasis on military activity would overshadow the more urgent need of the early state to call up able-bodied males for corvée labor on public architecture and civic projects, such as canal digging, more routinely than for defense.[34] Even professional soldiers of later times could still be levied to carry out emergency harvests or other public works projects.[35] Sumerian and Akkadian terminology did not normally differentiate soldiers from workers in any case—both were just $eren_2$/*ṣābum*, normally non-agentive third-person subjects— even into the first millennium. This lack of distinction in manpower may have been matched on the technological side, since bronze weapons were unlikely to have been much more battle-worthy than agricultural tools made from the same metal. Thus, outside of the few elite, professional units—as certainly there were in Late Bronze and Iron Age states—the military in the Early Bronze Age was mostly made up of primary agricultural producers called away from their lands temporarily for war or defense.[36]

However militarily unimpressive this might be, these occasional reprieves from the boredom of grueling subsistence fieldwork, supplemented as they were by guaranteed distributions of food, were crucial public exercises in polity building. The massive circumvallations of Mesopotamian cities in the Early Dynastic, for instance, enclosing areas as large as 400 hectares, were projects by which militias built their city-states in literal, visible, and performative terms. Since levied

---

32 Cooper 1986.
33 Even in Akkadian royal inscriptions, one is struck by the prominence of non-military themes such as piety before the gods and a focus on movement across wide patches of geography, not necessarily in connection with warfare.
34 On the low frequency of Early Dynastic warfare, see Richardson 2011.
35 E.g., ARM 26/362, "troops of the headpad contingent" drafted for earthworks building; ARM 27/27-37, an emergency draft of soldiers to harvest the lands of the palace and of "commoners"; AbB 11 116.
36 See, e.g., FM 269, in which a king is reminded that his commoners need to be provided with their seed-grain before they are sent out on campaign.

forces were formed and rewarded through clientage to the ruler, they also doubled as his (armed) political constituencies, and so the interests of the ruler and the polity gradually became indistinguishable. Later references in Sumerian literature to an "assembly of the able-bodied young men," distinct from an assembly of city elders, may reflect this early and inchoate phase of military formation.[37] It is remarkable, at least, that Mesopotamian states seem to have been substantially formed well before they emphasized or even possessed large militaries.

3. Land Tenure and Pay: Tilth and Wealth in Territorial States

How then were men induced to endanger their lives through military action on behalf of the state? As we see Mesopotamian polities changing from proto-historic urban communes into territorial states, their militaries become most profoundly socially integrated through the land-tenure regimes which tied primary producers through service obligations. The economies of these states remained overwhelmingly agrarian no matter how large they grew, their redistributive administrations harnessed to the incessant conversion of harvests into goods and services, of which defense was one. At their inception, state claims on military service were thus secondary benefits of a wider program to grow their base of agriculturally productive clients. For the soldier, the benefits of these arrangements included not only land-holding, but access to irrigation, community membership,[38] draft-animal power, and economic security and mobility,[39] not to be underestimated in a time and place in which landlessness or dependent status were less palatable alternatives. For the state, the distribution of service-land had the benefit of installing clients and promoting loyalism by making soldiers political stakeholders.[40]

---

37 Jacobsen's (1943) contention that such assemblies formed the earliest democratic insti-
    tutions has been widely questioned but even more widely quoted. In his view, though,
    the military constituted only one of several consenting state bodies.

38 There even existed a specific term for administrative lists of service-land tenants,
    mudasû-tablets: settlers on these tracts of state lands formed a community of property,
    at least in administrative terms.

39 At Mari, soldiers from poor families were provided with "good positions in the palace,"
    while well-to-do soldiers were expected to provision and quarter themselves in their
    paternal households (Sasson 1969, 24); notwithstanding, "only a free man (*awīlum*)
    was considered worthy of entering the military" (ibid., 22).

40 cf. the description of soldiers as **keš₂** / *riksu* (the semantic root of which is "to tie, to
    bind") is sometimes translated as "pledged," connoting a military oath, but the appli-

Service-lands were known by different names according to period and region, and tenure regimes were only gradually integrated into the Mesopotamian political economy. "Ration" (**šuku**) and "leased" (**a p i n - l a**₂) fields held by soldiers are known as early as the end of the Early Dynastic period at the city of Girsu, but it is not clear that military service was expected in exchange instead of corvée labor;[41] most such allotments were for palace staff rather than soldiers.[42] In the Akkadian period, **šuku-** lands were also allotted for soldiers, but in no especial concentration and under no terminology differentiating their tenancies from those of others,[43] though one surviving letter from a captain suggests that the state already protected the tenure-land of soldiers at this early time: "Luzah, the son of Azuzu, is serving in the army; Dada, the son of Nigar, has seized his estate, but he is to release it!"[44] Certainly by the Ur III period (2112-2004), the practice was well established.[45]

The best-known of these forms of tenure was *ilku* (from *alāku*, "to come, to go"), a term from not only Mesopotamia proper, but Alalakh, Ugarit, Mari, and even exported to the Hittite realm. The term *ilku* survived well into the first millennium to designate arable plots of land given to soldiers, even when more specific names were developed to designate plots of service-lands for the specific types of soldier they supported. Soldiers' land holdings in any event may be distinguished from other types of feuds (*ṣibtu*) and subsistence allotments (*šukūsu*) for which tenancy was either dependent on regular payments or as awards for certain classes of officials and priests. Although occasionally communal or corporately held lands of soldiers are known, the predominance of individual holdings suggests a general

---

cation of the term in most other contexts points towards something less political and more legal, e.g., "contracted."

41   E.g., VS 25 70 and VS 14, 170, both from EDIIIb Girsu, list both types of fields held by the soldiers (**aga₃-us₂**) Ur-Ninmu and Di-Utu, but their plots sat alongside many more held by non-military personnel.

42   Nissen et al. 1990, 64.

43   E.g., Foster 1982, 17-18, who noted around 84 acres of "good land" given to soldiers (**aga-us₃ aga-us₂**) under the authority of **a nu-banda₃** captain, around 3% of a local royal estate's holdings. Other references (Foster 1977, 32 n. 10, 35) suggest that soldiers detailed to imperial provinces were also given rations in bread or grain, and perhaps some pay in silver as well.

44   Michalowski 1993, 26 no. 20.

45   Studevant-Hickman 2008; Michalowski 1993, 118 no. 240, though the letter may be a "late fabrication."

dispersal of soldiers throughout city-state communities. Service-land holdings near Old Babylonian (2004-1595) city of Sippar were typical of these arrangements, averaging around six hectares per soldier, in theory enough to provide basic subsistence for around 20 people.[46] These tenures were thus lucrative and desirable in general terms, and the state protected fields and obligations against alienation through legal sanctions and regular administrative inventories, sometimes tracking tenancies for centuries at a time, periodically reclaiming and reassigning fields.[47] Most of the contexts in which soldiers appear in the Code of Hammurabi have to do with the disposition of their *ilku*-lands, mostly prohibiting their sale or transfer, but also protecting them from seizure.[48] But in the generations after Hammurabi, service-lands were often treated as heritable and salable in practice, and the obligations as transferable by hire. The alienation of service-lands to non-military holders through inheritance, marriage, adoption, sale, and leasing created secondary markets for service substitutes, and further diversified the military's economic benefits well beyond the ranks of the soldiery.[49] The death of a tenure-holder in wartime, however, could spell economic disaster for his family.[50]

The meaning of the term *ilku* was also as protean as it was durable: in different contexts, *ilku* could refer to the service-land itself, the work done on that land, the delivery of the yield of that land, the service obligations attached to it, the tenure-holder himself, or goods, animals, and services used to support *ilku*-service.[51] In all periods, it is difficult to assess the degree to which *ilku*-tenancy in practice obligated actual military service instead of payments by the tenant to support the hire of troops by central authorities or provide substitutes (prohibited by the Code of Hammurabi, but well-honored in the breach).[52] The further thorny question of how royal authorities came by land for distribution

---

46   See De Graef 2002, 155 n. 35, on plot size; Richardson 2005a, 21, for calculations of subsistence areas.

47   See Ellis 1977; DeGraef 2002.

48   CH ¶¶ 26-32, 36-41.

49   Charpin 2004, 371, however, implies that the increasing tendency to pay *ilku* in silver as the period went along also deteriorated political-economic relations between Crown and clientele.

50   For the forced sale of a family estate by a woman widowed in wartime, see Westbrook 2001, 25-26, 31.

51   For Old Babylonian *ilku*, see Stol 2004, 736-42, 747-57; for Middle Assyrian *ilku*, see Postgate 1982.

52   Charpin 2004, 371; see also CH ¶35.

in the first place cannot be tackled here; one may compare Old Babylonian administration of *ilku*-lands, for instance, which entailed reallocations of specific state lands, to the Middle Assyrian state, for which Postgate concluded that *ilku* intersected with a system of lots and shares in common land funds of the community: "it would not have entailed large-scale re-assignment of land-ownership, merely the acknowledgement ... of the *status quo*."[53] If that was the case, then the Assyrian military was deeply integrated, if not identical to, the village community, and quite different from a two-sector economy of village and palace lands prevailing in Babylonia.

The ensuing Kassite and Middle Babylonian periods (c. fifteenth to eighth centuries) saw the development of a rural manorial system, under which land tenure tied to state service was mediated through local grandees.[54] The existence of their large estates or fiefs has often given rise to a rubric of "feudalism" for these times. This view has been criticized by scholars of these periods, but it is still true that military organization became diffused throughout Babylonia in these centuries by an overlap of estates and provinces which redistributed political identities formerly exclusive to contending city-states.[55] Perhaps because of this geographic dispersal, less is known about the military from the few central archives we possess. New terminologies— *ḫurādu, sakrumaš*[56]—were added to older ones for types of soldiers— while some professional names related to equine care were borrowed to designate military offices (e.g., *kizû, kartappu*, both loosely meaning "groom"). This emphasis on heavy and then light cavalry in post-Ḥammurabi Babylonia generally increased over time,[57] with chariotry

---

53 Postgate 1982.

54 I have argued elsewhere (2005a) that the fortress communities developed by the end of the Old Babylonian period were the basis for the next period's manors.

55 See Richardson 2005a 25-26: of more than 20 Kassite provinces, a minority were centered around cities.

56 *ḫurādu* was a type of soldier; *sakrumaš* was a title specific to chariotry; see Sassmannshausen 2001, 52-56.

57 Chariots had been in use since Early Dynastic times (really early war carts, probably drawn by donkeys rather than horses), but only began to assume real offensive capability towards the end of the Old Babylonian period, when light cavalry also emerged on the field (e.g., AbB 2 67, 10 150, 11 77, and 13 60; ARM 4/79; see Hamblin 2006, 145-47); for the Neo-Assyrian situation, see Dalley 1985 and Postgate 2000. But the denotation of chariots as "heavy cavalry" in all periods may be a misnomer, given that their principal offensive capability was to permit mobile archery fire, not the charging of massed enemy ranks.

rising to the forefront of battle forces and charioteers emerging as a top officer class. This required ever greater costs for specialists andstable staff—bowmen, drivers, "third men," etc.—a military corps divorced from agriculture and anchored to palace centers.[58] Scholarship of chariot and horse technology is heavily trammeled by a long historiography which trots onstage innumerable diffusionist postulates about Indo-European languages, peoples, and cultures which cannot be critiqued or treated here.[59] The importance of equine corps is reflected in the political and economic cultures of the day.

The Amarna correspondence between the Babylonian king and the Egyptian pharaohs reflects the prestige in which chariots, horses, and charioteers were held, since they were included among royal wives, households, and children in greeting formulae ("For you, your wives … etc. … your horses, your chariots, may all be well.").[60] Consignments of gifts between the kings of Egypt, Babylon, and Mitanni included wooden chariots overlaid with gold, golden and bejeweled whips, bridles, reins, blinkers, and other tack.[61] Chariot officers formed the core of the Babylonian feudal nobility, important enough to have been the subjects of monuments and heroic literary material. Such was the case of one Šitti-Marduk, celebrated by Nebuchadnezzar I as "he whose chariot did not lag behind the king's right flank … he feared no battle but went down to the enemy and went furthest in against the enemy of his lord."[62] For this, Šitti-Marduk was granted rights to lands and villages, and exempted from providing taxes, including military ones.[63] At this time (c. twelfth century), the King of Babylon required the voluntary participation of his nobles to form large armies. The Neo-Assyrian state later used similar practices, granting tax exemptions

---

58   ABC 22 (=Babylonian Chronicle P III 2'-4') makes one mention of the size of such forces, numbering horses captured by Kurigalzu II of Babylon at least in the several thousands.

59   See, e.g., Cline's (1997) review of Robert Drews' work on this and related subjects.

60   Military forces had a prominent position in greeting formulae for letters in all periods.

61   EA 14 and 22, *inter alia*; Morkot (2007) argues for these exchanges as part of an "international arms trade"; I do not, however, see the numbers of weapons traded as economically significant in scale.

62   Foster 1996, 297-98.

63   Granting relief from required military service was considered a kingly virtue, as when Išme-Dagan of Isin bragged "I have exempted [Isin's] labourers from carrying earth in baskets, and I have freed its troops from fighting" (ETCSL, Išme-Dagan A, Text 2.5.4.01).

not only to the lands of military officers (many as absentee landlords), but often to dozens of client families holding smaller estates.[64] The soldier's field, however, remained the bedrock subvention for the Babylonian military. Designations of service-land once again proliferated as Babylon regained political prominence after 600 Native Babylonians, colonies of foreign mercenaries, and tribal groups were all settled with military lands, some designated as chariot, horse, bow, or quiver fiefs (*bīt narkabti / sisê / qašti / azanni*), with much flexibility built into the range of types of military service.[65] It does not play too much on semantics, I think, to point out that these fiefs were denoted as "households" (*bītu* = "house") rather than simply "fields" (*eqlu*), legally constituted to refer to the families who occupied the lands rather than simply the lands themselves. Many arrangements continued to exist from Kassite times as well, when larger fiefs granted to governors or other officials in exchange for providing military contingents gave them *de facto* rights over the inhabitants on those lands. The principle of land-for-service only intensified in Persian period Mesopotamia, when *ilku* obligations were extended to military colonists from other lands, e.g., Carians and Egyptians—resettled in Babylonia on military estates called *ḫaṭrū*.[66]

4. FOR SILVER, LOOT, AND FAME: WAR ECONOMIES

As suggested above, land-tenure was not the only form of remuneration for military service, which could also be compelled through mechanisms other than land holding. An increasing reliance on professional soldiers, for one thing, bred a class of soldier with little connection to the life of the farmer. "Since being a child," one eighteenth century soldier wrote his king, "I lived the life of a soldier; I was not able to hold the front of a plow."[67] Professional soldiers were procured from allies, vassal kings, and tribal contingents, and sometimes even by state purchasing

---

64 *passim*, SAA XII, but for examples of grants on a smaller, everyday scale see, e.g., SAA V 109, fields for garrison troops, or SAA XI 36, the exemption of taxes on the estates of a cohort commander and his clientele.

65 See especially van Driel (2002, 226-73) for an exhaustive treatment of terms and forms.

66 Briant (2002, 75-76) feels that the *ḫaṭrū* system was more intensive than preceding Babylonian forms of service tenures, but the basis for this assessment is unclear.

67 ARM 26/333; see ARM 26/345, in which one Uštašni-El complains that he has been stuck in the same garrison for five years.

agents.[68] Foreign mercenaries also joined on to Mesopotamian militaries, alluded to (albeit disparagingly) as early as the twenty-fifth century.[69] Limited numbers of hired, professional soldiers were kept under garrison regimes as early as Akkadian times, provisioned by the state through rationing or with silver. The Mari letters of the Old Babylonian period then reveal a dizzying array of ethnically-denoted contingents, often billeted together with men of radically different backgrounds. A significant intensification of this practice only came under the Neo-Assyrian empire, when foreign military technologists were targeted for deportation and resettlement in Assyria, bringing with them families, slaves, and pack animals.[70] To choose just one example, Sennacherib boasted of incorporating 61,000 archers and shield bearers into his army from conquered lands, terming them "booty" (*šallatu*).[71]

Yet provisioning was hardly an uncomplicated affair: under-provisioning soldiers could lead to revolt or desertion,[72] but over-provisioning could just as easily lead to theft of supplies or honest services.[73] Two Babylonian commanders had to caution a superior, after their troops had demanded a whole year's ration "or we will not take anything," that "if [you] give them their whole year's barley ration, the troops will leave our control … let them give it to them elsewhere … either for one month or for two months."[74] Letters tell us that troops could negotiate for better or worse quantities or qualities of rations. Provisioning systems also had to anticipate that unknown numbers of soldiers might need to be provisioned at multiple locations or on the move (or both) depending on the course of campaigns, and provide for both soldiers on the march and families left at home.[75] Even when

---

68 Neo-Assyrian treaties with vassals and allies lack provisions for the supply of troops, so we can assume that their access to these did not result from legal obligations as such, but simply as tribute due a hegemon. ARM 26/363 and 488 both refer to merchants supplying soldiers for the state.

69 RIME 1 9.4.2 viii 1 and 9.5.1 iii 1, "hired mercenaries of foreign lands."

70 See SAA XI 174 for a sample list of military deportees; see also Dalley 1985.

71 The practice was as old, however, as Middle Assyrian times, e.g. when Šalmaneser I tells us that after his campaign against Uruaṭri, "I took a selection of their young men and I chose them to enter my service" (RIMA 1 0.77.1).

72 In ARM 26/29, unpaid troops looted the granaries holding their rations.

73 On desertion in the Mari letters, see Sasson 1969, 45f. Desertion was also a persistent drain on manpower in Neo-Assyrian times: see, e.g., SAA XV 294, XVI 105, and XVII 149.

74 AbB 11 194; see also ARM 27/1 and 44-45.

75 ARM 27/78, 80, and 81; 27/129 calls for 100 donkey-loads of provisions for men on the move. Postgate 1992, 241-44.

soldiers remained stationary and worked plots of land, accounting, political relations, and even translation issues complicated oversight of garrison towns by central authorities.[76] One long missive from a provincial governor to Zimri-Lim of Mari complains that he could not find men he was supposed to have; had men he did not know about; was accused of "oppressing" his troops; and did not have sufficient interpreters to speak with his men—none of which prevented him from assuring his king that he was doing a outstanding job as commander.[77]

General levies (Sum. **z i g**, lit. "to rise") are not documented until the twenty-second century,[78] when men could be called up under the banner of individual towns, clans, or gods. Literary references to levies retrospectively refer to the time of Early Dynastic Uruk and its hero-kings, such as in the Sumerian tale called Gilgameš and Huwawa B. Here, the king's levy is characterized as calling to war only able-bodied young men without families:

> O city! He who has a wife, to your wife!
> He who has a child, to your child!
> Warrior or not,
> He who has no wife, who has no child,
> Let such men fall in by my side, (as the companions
>   of) Gilgameš.[79]

A lack of contemporary references suggests, however, that early states were slow in actualizing their ability to compel wartime service on a mass scale; note that Early Dynastic references to "obligations" on the citizenry are made only on the occasion of their cancellation. The corpus of eighteenth century Mari letters make clear that the logistics of assembling, keeping track of, and even dismissing troops was a persistent challenge to authorities,[80] even though extensive service-rolls

---

76 ARM 27/107.
77 ARM 27/116.
78 RIME 3/1 1.1.7.Cyl A, xiv 7—xv 10, though this levy was for building, not war. One exception might be from the Late Early Dynastic inscriptions of Urukagina; see RIME 1 9.9.1 and .2, both **lu₂-zi-ga**, translated variously as "attendant" and "conscript." For obligated landholders, however, the **kingal**-official called up service levies on Crown land as early as the twenty-fifth century.
79 Foster 2001, 117.
80 E.g., ARM 26/25-27 (Heimpel (2003, sub. ARM 26/27) proposes that long-range expeditions had trouble keeping troops together because they would disperse to visit relatives along the way); 26/266, on dismissals; 26/286, a soldier who had been AWOL

existed to track compliance. Long-term furloughs, runaways, deaths, and substitutes made human resources systems extremely difficult to administer,[81] while tribal units were left to muster themselves clan by clan.[82] An exceptional early case was Ḥammurabi's apparently total conscription of his population in the gathering storm of an Elamite war:

> The conscripts of Ḥammurabi have positioned themselves for battle against [the enemy]. Brother looks at brother. The day I sent this tablet of mine to my lord, Ḥammurabi has set a total mobilization in his land. He called up troops of any merchant, any male, including releasing slaves, and they are ready.[83]

Despite occasional and isolated references in earlier periods to drafted men or the like,[84] what few levy officers (e.g., *dēkû, kallû*) we know of were primarily responsible for levying corvée labor, not soldiers. It remained in most times a difficult or even dangerous business for state officers to compel service in peripheral communities.[85]

Pay bonuses are attested as early as Ur III times, pointing towards avenues of meritocracy and competition.[86] A letter concerning Ḥammurabi of Babylon shows that he honored officers and regulars by taking meals in their company, bivouacking among them on campaign, and rewarding them with golden rings and fine garments;[87] even squads of common soldiers received silver medallions from him.[88]

---

for two years; ARM 27/116. Even literary letters echo this bit of reality, as when a letter to Šulgi of Ur sheepishly admits, "I was levying troops for the expedition, my lord; but when Aba-indasa had inspected the troops, 2000 men of those troops were missing" (ETCSL, Text 3.1.05).

81   E.g., ARM 26/33, 126, 314 and 408, on furloughed and runaway (**b a - z a ḫ₃**) troops; 342, on dead troops; 353, on furloughs and troops seconded from their original stations; 147, in which a unit of troops is simply reported to have "quit."

82   ARM 6/28.

83   ARM 26/363; note also ARM 26/515, in which bonfires are lit "to assemble the entire land (of Mari)." A thousand years later, Assyrians also imposed a general levy in antici- pation of an impending Elamite attack (SAA XVII 120).

84   In Ur III times, there were indeed, the **lu₂ -nig₂ -dab₅**, "requisitioned men of the army," which may have amounted to the same thing; see also Lafont 2009, 12-13 §§4.19-.21.

85   E.g., AbB 10 150, in which Babylonian recruiters are scared off by reports of nearby hostiles watching the village they hoped to draw troops from, and SAA XVIII 183, in which an Assyrian recruiter is killed by "deserters" from the city of Dilbat—who then don his clothes and headgear to mock him.

86   Lafont 2009, 12 §4.19-.20; at Mari, pay in silver was termed *qeršum*.

87   ARM 27/164.

88   ARM 25/815, 23/435, 24/94, 25/815; similarly, for Ḥammurabi, ARM 26/366 and 369, 27/161, and A.486+; see Van De Mieroop 2005, 23-25. Note also ARM 26/38, in

The familiarity of high officials with their troops was a necessity: one was scolded by King Šulgi of Ur: "You have made yourself too important! You do not know your own soldiers!"[89] Later Assyrian kings also rewarded individual battlefield valor with gold bracelets, jeweled scabbards, and distinctive military dress,[90] though praise for the army as a whole is spare throughout the large corpus of Assyrian royal inscriptions. Occasional epithets credit the army as "valiant warriors, who wage relentless war to the finish;" "[my] foot soldiers, who are mighty in battle;" "my battle chariot and cavalry, who never leave the place of danger(?) at my side;" "[who] expose themselves to the risks of battle." Less often, specific acts were credited to the army: Adad-nirari II said that he leveled a city wall in Hanigalbat "with the help of my warriors," and Tiglath-Pileser III credited his troops with "smiting the Aramaean contingent."[91] The credit extended to common soldiers in Assyrian texts was matched by the visual repertoire: palace reliefs across the ninth to seventh centuries showed a dramatic expansion of the space given over to images of common soldiers fighting, working, and parading, a presentation indicative of an expanded sense of military life as a collective imperial ethos.

The distribution of booty (*šallatu*, *ḫubtu*[92]), which in all periods included captive prisoners of war (though it could also mean everything from sheep to divine idols), was also a staple of entrenched war economies such as that of the Ur III and Neo-Assyrian states. The Ur III king Šu-Sîn, for instance, reported that, of the prisoners from his eastern campaigns, he blinded the men and set them to fieldwork, and offered the women to the weaving mills, in both cases as gifts

---

which Zimri-Lim of Mari is urged to appear among the troops to "calm their frightened hearts"; but cf. ARM 26/176, in which he is warned away from walking amidst armed troops without his shock-troop bodyguard. For Ur III examples of direct rewarding of soldiers with war booty, see Lafont 2009, 4 n. 20.

89 Michalowski 1993, 66.

90 http://www.ucl.ac.uk/sargon/essentials/soldiers/warheroes/; note the image from the Ninevite palace featuring a soldier receiving a commendation from an officer for his service. A land grant given to one soldier by the Assyrian king Aššur-nirari V praises him for his combat action, "by means of stairs and scaling ladder(s)" in capturing a city (Dalley 1976, 107). A letter (SAA XVII 121) discusses a silver sword to be made for an official; see also SAA XVI 207. See especially Postgate (2001) on Assyrian uniforms and Radner (2011) on the role of fame and rewards.

91 Luckenbill 1927, I 76, 113, 275, II 9, 32, 333.

92 Also *būšu*, "valuables," but this term excludes human captives.

to the temple institutions of Nippur.[93] The public distribution of war
booty as prestige wealth is attested as early as the twenty-second
century, the Akkadian king Rimuš, who distributed vessels, lapis
lazuli discs, shells, and other objects inscribed with his name to at
least nine Mesopotamian cities, probably to celebrate his eastern
victories.[94] One letter from eighteenth century Mari makes clear that
the distribution of POW's to soldiers was a normal and ordinary post-
campaign procedure, and that economies of scale were produced by
warfare with human booty as their chief product.[95] Without doubt, this
was true for Assyria as well: Šamši-Adad V gave "captured warriors
... to the soldiers of my land like grasshoppers," Tiglath-Pileser III
apportioned "horses and mules among my artisans ... like sheep,"[96]
Sargon II boasted "in Assyria, people bought things at a price in silver
like that in copper" and Aššurbanipal that "in my land a camel was sold
at ½-1 shekel of silver."[97] The Assyrians also practiced something like
triumphal parades, publicly displaying war wealth, at least implying
that the regular influx of war booty benefited the entire population: "I
passed in review," Esarhaddon exclaimed, "without cessation all the
steeds, mules, asses and camels, arms and other implements of warfare
of all the hosts of the conquered enemy."[98] On the ritualistic aspects of
these triumphs, see below (Ritualism and Intelligence).

Free looting was also among the incentives used to attract
expeditionary soldiers as well as to destabilize enemy lands, especially
under the Neo-Assyrian state: numerous images in Assyrian palatial art
show soldiers carrying off weapons, metal goods, and jewelry, as in
the burning of Muşaşir shown in Sargon's Khorsabad palace, or the
sack of Hamanu depicted in Sennacherib's Nineveh palace. Without
doubt, throwing open a city to full looting was satisfactory reward to
ancient armies; Sargon II of Assyria, on conquering one enemy city,

---

93 RIME 3/2 1.4.3.
94 RIME 2 1.2.20 and B. R. Foster, pers. communication (2010).
95 ARM 26/408; 26/421 refers to an elaborate treaty scheme to profit from the ransoming
    of POW's; 27/16 refers to POW's kept in handcuffs and "(neck)-ladders," a form of
    stock depicted in Akkadian art.
96 Luckenbill 1927, I 259, 273, II 20, 98, 133, 137-38.
97 Ibid., II 13, 152, 338.
98 Luckenbill 1927, II 267. Sennacherib claims to have needed to "enlarge the outer
    courtyard (of my Nineveh palace) in order to review the vast booty taken from enemies"
    (CAD s.v. *šallatu* A s. 1b-2'). The so-called "letters to the gods" may have in effect been
    the transcripts of such parades.

boasted, "Its filled-up granaries I opened and let my army devour its abundant grain, in measureless quantities. Its guarded wine-cellars I entered, and the wide-spreading hosts of Aššur drew the good wine from the skins like river water."[99] Yet it is difficult to distinguish with certainty in any given image or text passage when soldiers were looting on behalf of the army and the king, or filling their own pockets.[100] Though Mesopotamian kings probably had some interest in reducing military predation on civil populations, their ability to police these kinds of problems was quite low. One Assyrian official moaned to his king that "whenever the bodyguard sees the prospect of booty, he neglects [his work]."[101] The great conqueror and lawgiver Ḥammurabi seemed to spend most of his post-conquest years sorting out claims and appeals from occupied cities in which Babylonians had appropriated local properties—yet there is no sense that confiscations were *a priori* unacceptable, only that the conflicts they produced were undesirable. On the contrary, it is clear in some instances that it was Ḥammurabi's policy to license free looting, at one point complaining of a failed raid, "How can 5,000 troops return empty-handed to camp?"[102]

Neo-Assyrian divinatory queries presuppose that looting and plundering of civilians was a regular option for military expeditions,[103] but this practice was not without its problems. One Neo-Assyrian letter, for example, complains that "the king's bodyguard took advantage of the [Tabalean deportees'] oxen, sheep and women"—but the complaint was lodged only because the official writing the letter was responsible for settling those deportees in the first place, and wished to avoid being blamed.[104] In another case, one outraged official writes to another, "The king our lord says: 'You must not take booty from them.' But you are

---

99 Luckenbill 1927, II 16, 76, 77, 87, 90, 91. One Old Babylonian omen predicts that an army would be "sated with booty," *šallatum šebûm*.

100 Some portion of booty was often redistributed to high officials, post-accounting, e.g. SAA 11 36, in which war booty is given to a wagon master, a scribe of the treasurer, a palace supervisor, and others.

101 Waterman 1930, 85.

102 ARM 27/141; raiding was enough of a regular practice at Mari to warrant a distinct verb, *sadādu*. However, one text (ARM V 72) outlines financial damages to be paid by a soldier convicted of illegally appropriating war booty, Ziegler 2000, 21-2.

103 See, *passim*, SAA IV, but, e.g., 271, a query asking whether Assyrian troops should loot and plunder the Gambulu tribe.

104 SAA XV 54.

assuredly coming and taking booty from our city!"[105] It becomes clear that both the king's order and the official's complaint have to do with the responsibility efficiently to allocate resources between units, not to protect civilians from soldiers.

The Code of Hammurabi addressed a similar concern in protecting, rather, soldiers from their captains, who might "oppress" them, hire them out, use them as scapegoats in legal proceedings, or "take a gift that the king gave to a soldier."[106] A similar edict of Šamši-Adad I of Assyria at Mari warned, "the general, captain, or sergeant who deprives a soldier of his booty has committed a sacrilege against (the god) Dagan."[107] The central authorities, of course, also intervened when abuses extended to outright insubordination and military indiscipline, as when an official complained to the king of a cohort commander, a "third-man," and a bodyguard: "These three men are drunkards! When they are drunk, none of them can turn his iron sword away from his colleague!"[108] In another case, troops in the capital city of Kalḫu were reported to be "loitering in the center …riding [their] horses [around] like … common criminals and drunkards."[109] Looting on foreign campaign was one thing, but discipline and the orderly division of spoils was to be preserved among the imperial ranks.

Recourse to all these incentives—land, rations, pay, promotion, and loot—reflected the fact that Mesopotamian militaries drew on manpower reserves from different sectors of society, and the military economy and the social order of the army were diversified accordingly. Can we then speak of a first-millennium "military economy" when endemic warfare and military land-holding had long been central features of the political landscape?[110] The answer, I think, is yes,

---

105 SAA XVIII 72. Appeals against looting as problems of insubordination include ARM 26/436, 27/57, and SAA XVIII 175.

106 CH ¶34. Sasson 1969, 14 and 37.

107 V. Matthews 1981, 143; see also Sasson 1969, 48-49.

108 SAA XVI 115.

109 SAA I 154; see also SAA XIII 33, in which officers of mercenary troops are reported for goldbricking, eating stores, drinking wine, stealing toll monies, and "molesting" anyone who called them to account.

110 cf. Cioffi-Revilla's (1996, 10-11) conclusion that Mesopotamia had very high onset rates for protobellic warfare in comparison to modernity: 871 wars in 2,190 years, about one every two and a half years. However, this is not appropriately considered in light of the multi-polity landscape. Even for the two cities most intensively identified (and actually prosecuting) regular warfare—Babylon and Larsa in the Old Babylonian period—we still find only an average of one conflict documented every 10.8 years:

insofar as military elites had increased influence on state policy and ideology, state economies were reorganized around tributary modes of production and economic rationalization, and where the performance of war became an indispensible function of kingship. "Militarism" denotes the point at which war was no longer the instrument of policy, but the policy goal itself, and a "military economy" where the mode of production pertained not just for soldiers in one economic sector, but at the level of the state as a whole. By these standards, the Neo-Assyrian empire following 745 (under Tiglath-pileser III) qualifies, for instance, since it was no longer possible for the state to do without the financial and ideological incomes produced by the execution of warfare—an "addictions model" of imperialism.[111]

The consequences of this "addiction" are less clear. Some scholars tend to see Mesopotamia's first-millennium empires as militarized political realms with a steadier diet of warfare with obviously negative consequences for millions of people. Others tend to see them as ushering in a period of armed peace under which local wars occurred less frequently and surpluses accrued in all sectors of society under a generalized security. It is often suggested that the Neo-Assyrian, Neo-Babylonian, and Achaemenid empires merely represented phases of a single process of imperialization—that the Assyrians did the heavy lifting in breaking the back of localism, with subsequent empires enjoying the fruits of those labors.[112] The resolution of these positions are based on unequal evidence, and the question of which state was "kinder" or "more violent" seems inherently wrongheaded— but it must at least be said that the insistent refrain of institutionalized violence continues to compromise the legacy of the millennium's imperial floruit in comparison to previous epochs.

---

common, but hardly endemic. On the other end of the spectrum, the Ur III period, most frequently identified with bureaucratic institutionalism, in fact documented foreign warfare in most years of its existence. It is, among these observations extremely difficult to draw firm conclusions.

111 See Fuchs 2005 for a closer inspection of this issue. Melville (forthcoming) presents a compelling argument that the Assyrian empire collapsed so quickly in the face of invasions because it had become so habituated to offensive warfare that it had virtually forgotten how, why, and when to fight defensively.

112 This point lays behind much of what is examined in the papers assembled in Lanfranchi, Roaf, and Rolling 2003.

5. SPECIALIZATION, SCALE, AND DIVERSITY

In third millennium contexts, warfare was prosecuted by and for elites and the retinues of palatial estates, for whom we have evidence in the form of ration-lists and a basic hierarchy of titles (chiefs, subordinates, and ration holders).[113] To the best of our knowledge, the early military was a relatively small segment of society and economy, and manpower units were often not functionally distinguished between civil-engineering work and military action—mostly termed e r i m, either "people" or "troops"—let alone by rank or military specialty.[114] Neither was any soldier-class reflected distinctly in institutional documentary regimes, where military personnel often appeared in ration and personnel lists mixed in with priests, civil servants, and craftsmen.

The overall scarcity of military professional names and the rarity of their attestation in Early Dynastic times reflects the indistinction between soldiering and other types of mass labor. Among the Early Dynastic "Lu"-lists, enumerating hundreds of professions and titles, only a scant few are military in nature—the š a g i n a ("general"), u g u l a ("overseer," but more often a workers' "foreman" in usage), the n u - b a n d a ₃ ("captain"), the l u ₂ - e n - n u ("guard"), and n i ğ i r ("herald")—among many more titles for priests, food processors, and shepherds. This distribution of evidence within these (at some level) idealized lists is more or less matched by the prosopography of early account texts. Thus in practice as well as in theory, military personnel were a distinct minority of the payrolls of early state institutions. Some sort of elite unit may be referenced in Lagaš inscriptions which speaks of an army's "vanguard" (s a g   m u - g u b - b a) and equid drivers (a n š e   e r e n ₂). There was always, however, a sizable gap between title and function with regard to military function; one of the rare Early Dynastic letters mentioning Elamite attack notes that the leader of the counteroffensive was to be a temple administrator.[115] This situation altered only gradually, with full-scale professionalization emerging

---

113 The u g u l a, š u b - l u g a l, and l u ₂ - k u r ₆ - d a b ₅ - b a, respectively; other known ranks in the Early Dynastic period included the n u - b a n d a ₃ (a "lieutenant"), and, quite late in the period, the š a g i n a ("general"). The personal quality of military loyalty is alluded to in the twenty-first century text called "The Death of Ur-Namma," in which the king's soldiers weep for their dead ruler.

114 The craft specialization may be attested as early as the ED in the professional names i l l a r - d i m ₃ and p a n - d i m ₂, probably "weapon-maker" and "bow-maker."

115 Michalowski 1993, 12.

under the empires of the first millennium. Thus, despite its military ideology, the Akkadian conquest state (2334-2093) introduced only a modest degree of military institutionalization, preferring relatively few innovations in titles and control through temple and private households where it directly administered annexed cities.[116]

Only with the advent of the Ur III state do we begin to find a wider array of references to specialized functions related to the army (**ugnim**)—not only soldiers, either, but military scribes, administrators, potters, attendants, and female food workers—the personnel of permanent army camps in the home provinces.[117] The murky chain of command of the Akkadian state becomes clearer in this twenty-first century scene, since generals clearly served the Crown chancellor (**sukal-maḫ**) directly, and not as subordinates of the civil governors (**ensi₂'s**). Out in the conquered peripheries of this empire, the military had even more free rein: the system of taxation required all ranks of soldiers to deliver in-kind goods—probably with no questions asked—from the ten oxen and 100 sheep due from generals, down to the common soldiers, who delivered animals collectively in varying amounts.[118] By this time, the permanence of military establishments produced communities of various kinds—households in the imperial core, and armed tax offices in the periphery—and service was no longer necessarily of the temporary kind. Old Babylonian states in turn could distinguish an even wider array of specialized troops, and the first references to *kiṣir šarrūti*, the "royal army," a term which distinguished professional soldiers from regulars or occasional troops.[119]

The number of persons involved in these enterprises also grew over time, but probably attained a plateau by Old Babylonian times. Warfare in the Early Dynastic was occasional and seasonal, socially- and politically-formative with a lesser interest in the permanent destruction of enemy manpower or acquisition of territory.[120] Notwithstanding, the circumvallation of Early Dynastic cities indicates that large reserves of

---

116 Compare, e.g., Visicato 1999, 23-26 to Foster 1982, 36-38.
117 Lafont 2009, 4.
118 Maeda 1992.
119 Lafont 2009 refers severally to Ur's "royal army," but it is not clear what ancient term implies it; perhaps 11, the **eren₂ aga₃-us₂ lugal**. On the other end of the spectrum, one notes that even at the height of the Neo-Assyrian empire, fortress commanders could still complain that they were only supplied with young farm-boys, and not professional soldiers (SAA V 200).
120 Richardson 2011.

manpower could be mobilized for temporary, domestic projects. The modest scale of early forces can be appraised based on the boast of Sargon of Akkad that 5,400 men—apparently an impressive number—"ate before him daily."[121] By the Ur III period, units in the range of 5,000-10,000 men are attested at Girsu,[122] and the eighteenth century Mari texts convincingly refer in many contexts to individual corps of 3,000-5,000 men,[123] and coalition forces numbering up to 60,000 troops.[124]

Invariably, questions arise as to the dependability of such references, but the consistency of references in functional documents such as letters —i.e., not in propagandistic royal inscriptions—lend the weight of truth to their use of large numbers. This is not to say, of course, that writers always had a perfectly accurate count of troops at their command— several letters refer to the difficulty of estimating troop numbers, but it is clear that name-lists, censuses, and enlistment rolls existed as the basis for these numbers.[125] A thousand years later, Assyrian officials struggled to achieve results with essentially unchanged technologies.[126] What is remarkable in the Mari corpus, in fact, is the great amount of administrative oversight given to the disposition of smaller forces—400, 50, 25, or even a single soldier[127]—in a pre-modern context in which personal identity could be almost impossible to verify.[128]

In almost every case, these forces were identified by ethnonyms or cities-of-origin, not as belonging to the state; the forces were multi-ethnic and multi-national, yet not quite, one senses, a public institution.

---

121 RIME 2.1.1.11.

122 Lafont 2009, §§4.7 and 8.2.

123 E.g., ARM 26/29 permits the calculation of a force of ca. 3,928 men from allotted rations (Heimpel 2003, 193). Other references are more explicit of large numbers: 26/35 mentions 2,000 lance troops; 26/128, an ambush by 2,000 Turukkeans; 26/131, 4,000 "good troops" from Babylon; 26/171, "one or two thousand troops"; 26/217, 5,000 troops; 26/254, 1,000 men; 26/320, 2,000 troops at Šeḫna; 26/355, 5,000 troops at Šubat-Enlil; and so forth.

124 The high number of 60,000 is derived from an expected levy of troops by Šamši-Adad I of Assyria (Sasson 1969, 8). Enough other instances show that such high numbers were not at all fantastic: ARM 26/379 (40,000 men); 440 and 479 (20,000); 503 (34,000 total); 27/18, 145, 147 (all 30,000); see Van De Mieroop 2005, 35, 93. See also ARM I/42, describing the assembly of a 20,000 man force by various means.

125 E.g., ARM 3/19, 26/408, 26/500, 27/25, 46, 151 (for an overview of the registration system) and 153 for a glimpse of the system's specificity.

126 See SAA XV 181 and the many census documents of SAA XI 123-40.

127 26/316, 260, 353, and 286, respectively.

128 Note the troubles with "imposters" in ARM 14/104+ and 26/515.

The size of and terms for forces suggest that the military by the Middle Bronze Age had become a public institution identified with individual *poleis*, rather than belonging to single rulers or palaces. Accordingly, soldiering took on the aspect of a mass experience without reflecting a national identity.[129] One is struck, for instance, by the fact that in the Code of Hammurabi, if a soldier was captured while on campaign for the king, the state would only pay the ransom for his return if merchants, the soldier's family, and the city temple (in that order) could not.[130] The Assyrian army was not so different in this regard. Although Assyrian kings could claim to control forces as large as 120,000 as early as the mid-ninth century[131] —and total manpower reserves probably grew at least commensurately with the expansion of the empire over the next two centuries—such troops remained geographically dispersed and deliberately compartmentalized. Radner has written:

> The Assyrian army was in reality many armies, each with its own command structure; its composite character can be seen as the intentional product of a royal strategy which aimed to neutralise the military's otherwise unbridled power vis-à-vis the king in order to protect his sovereignty—a useful and successful approach that significantly contributed to Assyria's internal stability and the

---

129 In the Mari letter A.4515, the writer urges the recipient to mix contingents of soldiers from different cities to promote a sense of common purpose on campaign.

130 CH ¶32; cf. the Neo-Assyrian letters SAA V 32 and 115, on negotiating for abducted soldiers.

131 Dezso 2006 has treated this question exhaustively, but it is worth a long note to give a sense of the problem. Šalmaneser III famously reported in 845 that he deployed 120,000 men against the so-called "Damascus coalition," which itself put at least 50,000 troops in the field: RIMA 3 102.6 iii.24f. De Odorico 1995, 111 terms this a "marvelously high number [and] roaring in its roundness," but still a "theoretical or conventional size of the Assyrian army" and, though unlikely for a single battlefield engagement, "after all possible." Other individual references in royal inscriptions to troop strength rarely mention large corps of Assyrian troops—no larger than 50,000 and often smaller—but two factors argue in favor of a massive overall army: #1, consistent and believable references to enemy dead and captured, routinely numbered in the tens of thousands (though indeed inflated sometimes to "high-exact" numbers, e.g., 200,150); #2, a ubiquity of references in Neo-Assyrian letters to substantial forces of men in the individual contingents scattered in probably more than a hundred places throughout the empire (e.g., SAA XV 25, an expedition of 3,000 men in Zabban; SAA XV 142, a requisition for 2,000 men to man fortresses is deemed insufficient; SAA XVII 70, 20,000 archers in Babylonia; etc.). One large and fragmentary account (SAA XI 126) accounts for at least 33,700 troops; SAA V 250 is an order for a little over 7 million liters of grain to be stored for troops in Kār-Aššur, the equivalent of annual subsistence rations for about 10,000 men.

longevity of its royal dynasty. The different contingents which constituted the Assyrian army were allowed and encouraged to preserve and develop their own customs and idiosyncrasies: rather than being forged into a unified army, its individual components found themselves in intense competition with each other for royal recognition and favour.[132]

The inertia of localism, however, came under centripetal pressures, too. Barron, for instance, has concluded that despite some differences, Assyrian weapons and armor reveal "a basic homogeneousness throughout the empire"; in terms of fortress-building, Parker has pointed to building corps that constructed emplacements on a common template empire-wide; in terms of ethnic contingents, Postgate showed the composition of Assyrian forces in Zamua to be of a mixed makeup, approximately 25% Qurraean, 31% Ituean, and 44% Assyrian, though the Assyrians clearly occupied the more elite positions of that unit.[133] Thus unit autonomy and idiosyncrasy was not an absolute rule.

It is worth pointing out that, in purely economic terms, an army of this size, stationed throughout the territory of the empire, would have obligated the empire to support costs normally dwarfing the investments made in its imperial capitals on preciosities and palace building. I estimate that the cost of basic subsistence provisioning for the army—i.e., its grain rations alone—would have required an input of 20.5 million labor-days per annum—more than five times the annual labor invested in building Aššurnaṣirpal's Kalhu palace (maximum 4.7 million labor-days per annum). The investment in standing forces across a wide geographical area would de facto have redistributed imperial resources of all kinds away from imperial centers and out towards peripheries.

Imperial states also had to police, defend, and expand ever-larger borders, but they found their home populations numerically insufficient to the task, and looked to unhitch their military staffing needs from the confines of the agricultural cycle as military action became not only an annual, but a year-round obligation. Empires turned to admixtures of professional soldiers, mercenaries, and vassal armies of ethnically and linguistically diverse composition. From the time of the Ur III state, troops and even high officers bore Hurrian,

---

132 Radner 2010; cf. idem 2011.
133 Barron 2010; Parker 1997; Postgate 2000, 93.

Elamite, and Amorite names, and this diversity only expanded as time went by. By the time of the high Assyrian empire, the army included units from Nubia, Egypt, Samaria, Hamath, Ellipi, Kummuḫu, Urartu, Karkamiš, Arabia, and other conquered places, though in many instances, these remained purely provincial forces, never brought to the capitals in any numbers.[134] The process was aided by programs of mass deportation and recolonization, which had been practiced by the Hittite and Assyrian states since the middle of the second millennium, and ultimately relocated millions of people across those empires.[135]

The military was, through deportations, thus visibly associated with the death and birth of entire political cultures, through the wholesale destruction of cities, temples, and even gods—the entire cultural undergirding of targeted polities. These practices as much as the military itself have been credited with social mixing, economic mobility, and multilingualism, but also produced broader social disaffection and political instability at all levels as it became less clear by and for whom empires were built and maintained. This pattern included the imperial metropole, too, where substantial social distance was created between imperial militaries and the civil societies they served. One can discern the withdrawal of metropolitan elites from direct engagement in building and maintaining the empire, ceding some avenues of political advancement, and a corollary vertical and geographic integration of peripheral non-elites (arriviste, pluralist, *novi homines*?) into imperial structures. The price of building up an "imperial citizenry" or the like was the destruction of the mytho-ideological bases on which all local cultures were founded, to which the imperial cores were no exceptions.

6. RITUALISM AND INTELLIGENCE

The military was both the subject and site of ritual action. The theological dimension of Mesopotamian warfare is well-established and needs little elaboration here: the gods demanded and guaranteed military success for the king.[136] Royal ideology styled almost every war to some extent as a "holy war." The successful prosecution of warfare was the crucial performative and constitutive act of kingship by the

---

134 Dalley 1985.

135 Oded 1979.

136 For issues related to monumental depictions of war, see Bahrani 2008; the book does not comprehensively treat, title notwithstanding, military rituals *per se*, as does, e.g., Beal 1995 for the Hittite world.

Neo-Assyrian period, and failure in this endeavor had always been accounted for as the withdrawal of divine favor—the historiographic rationale of major compositions from city laments[137] to restoration apologias.[138] Cosmological and theological problems were also narrativized by having war play out on the divine plane—in curses, omens, and most famously in Marduk's triumphant campaign against an army of demons in the Babylonian *Epic of Creation*.[139]

Within this context, a wide variety of ritual symbols and practices were deployed to signal the favor and protection of the gods. From earliest times, the divine weaponry of kings and gods were fixtures of song and legend: battle nets, axes, bows, spears, and three-, five-, and even fifty-headed maces with epithets of their own, such as "Mows-Down-a-Myriad" and "Floodstorm Weapon."[140] Such weapons made their appearance on campaign as emblems carried before the troops (šu-nir giš-tukul), and were the subjects of offerings and rituals in their own right.[141] Sumerian hymns saw the entrustment of such weapons to the king before campaigns;[142] an Old Babylonian letter speaks of ritually "opening" weapons before battle;[143] armies which reached the Mediterranean or the sources of rivers often symbolically washed their weapons (or themselves) there. With divine weapons in hand, the conception was no less than, as one Assyrian letter put it, that "the king's gods are ready to march into battle,"[144] processions accompanied by singers and musicians, with ritual performances

---

137 Michalowski 1989, 4-8.
138 E.g., the heroic literature surrounding Nebuchadnezzar I, Foster 1996, 290-301.
139 See Foster 1996, 350-401 for an accessible translation of this famous text.
140 A study of weapons in Sumerian literature has yet to be undertaken, but see Salonen 1966.
141 Lafont 2009, 6. Akkadian *kakkum* does not distinguish between "weapon" and "emblem" (not to mention weapon-shaped divinatory marks) except by context, and thus the extent of military symbology in ritual is not always clear.
142 ETCSL sections 2.4-2.5, *passim*, though note also an equally strong *topos* of kings' puissance with weapons in non-ritual contexts, especially Šulgi's proficiency with the mace, spear, bow and arrow, throw-stick, sling, lance, and the battle-axe, while his person, his luster, his city, and his words are also said to be his "weapons."
143 ARM 26/205.
144 SAA XVI 132.

preceding[145] and following[146] battles. Images from obelisks, gates, and reliefs suggest that there may have developed a single comprehensive set of rituals to celebrate success in war upon the king's re-entry into camp (*madaktu*) and city (*ēreb āli*), including animal hunts, re-enactments of tribute receipt, and the shooting of an enemy or his image with an arrow.[147] Rituals of protection also guarded campaign routes, city-walls, and gates,[148] and celebrated the fallen, including an Assyrian ritual close in spirit to the remembrance of the Unknown Soldier.[149] Weapon-emblems were used locally, too, in judicial and tax-collection contexts, the latter known at Old Babylonian Sippar by the practice of the "journey of the weapon of Šamaš."[150]

The sacralization of battle, however, was not the most emphatic aspect of ritual activity surrounding warfare; for this point, pride of place must go to the practice of divination, especially liver divination. Since divination was used to assess everything from the welfare of the army, to the efficacy of its weapons, to the suitability of rations and the availability of water—and since the army and things military form the single most common subject of divinatory inquiries—it may be said that the craft was essentially one of military intelligence. In the Old Babylonian period, divination was already an indispensable step in planning a campaign:[151] "If the troops," queried one diviner from Mari, "whom [Zimri-Lim] dispatched to Hammurabi, (arrive), will Hammurabi not catch, not kill, not cause to kill, not detain for evil or

---

145 Preparatory rituals at Mari, according to Sasson (1969, 36-37), included letters to gods, sacrifices, consultations of omens and prophecies, anointing of officers, gift-giving and pledging.

146 On the ritual cycle of Neo-Assyrian victories in both camps and capital cities, see May, forthcoming; ARM 26/391 discusses an *eššeššamma*, a shrine service for coalition troops.

147 May, forthcoming, on the so-called Field War Ritual K. 9923; elements of the ritual are depicted or described on the White Obelisk, the Balawat Gates, in the Nimrud palace of Aššurnaṣirpal II, and in inscriptions of Sennacherib, Esarhaddon, and Aššurbanipal (also in room XXXIII of his Ninevite palace). She notes that one of Esarhaddon's descriptions of the ritual included supposed passages of direct speech by the soldiers, nearly unique among the corpus of royal inscriptions.

148 E.g. SAA XVIII 164: "The Babylonians have several times performed the ritual on the city gate, and on the xth day they have locked it."

149 Assyrian "letters to the gods" all include homage to "one charioteer, 2 cavalrymen, and three infantrymen."

150 Harris 1965; Richardson 2010c.

151 ARM 26/96, 100, 101, and *passim*.

peaceful intentions those troops? Will those who went out through the gate of Mari alive enter the gate of Mari alive?"[152]

By the Neo-Assyrian period, this procedure had been ornamented by further ritual procedures, but remained fundamentally geared towards gaining military information down to the smallest tactical detail—at what point an enemy might breach a city wall, whether the avant-garde or the rear guard was more vulnerable on the march, what were the prospects for booty at a campaign's conclusion.[153] Given the extensive network of spies, informers, and diplomatic specialists the Assyrians used to gather and verify what we might think of as actionable, i.e., "on the ground" intelligence,[154] however, it remains an unsolved question as to how they balanced these two sources of information, from both gods and men.

One unique historical problem related to ritual and warfare is the role of troops in the destruction of tombs, temples, and divine images in the first millennium. Accusations of depredations against the gods were sometimes leveled by Babylonian sources, as in the chronicle charging Assyrians with setting fire to the temple in the city of Šaznaku,[155] but most often Assyrian sources are informative about their own role in these cases. Assyrian campaigns resulted not only in the deportation of people, but also in that the deportation of divine images.[156] In these episodes, the gods were carted off—not destroyed—and presumably stored in Assyria. This practice began at least as early as the late Middle Assyrian period, when Tiglath-pileser I laconically reports of a conquered enemy king, "I carried off his wives, his natural sons, his clan, 180 copper kettles, five bronze bathtubs, together with their gods, gold and silver, the best of their property."[157]

Assyrian royal inscriptions account for not only the abduction of divine images—depicted among the reliefs of Tiglath-pileser III's palace, among others—but their destruction by fire (most famously

---

152 ARM 26/100; this query, which received a favorable reply, has the distinction of having proven demonstrably false, since Ḫammurabi subsequently detained the army of Mari and later attacked that city. See Jeyes 1989; Richardson 2010a, 245-48.
153 Starr 1990.
154 On espionage in this period, see: Durand 1991; Dubovsky 2006.
155 ABC 2. The Judicial Chronicle (BCHP 17) accuses soldiers, among others, of having stolen from the garden of Bēl-Marduk; Hanean troops who had slaughtered civilians were said to have "not feared the gods" (BCHP 11).
156 Bahrani 1995, also on the abduction of royal images.
157 RIMA 2 0.87.1.

in the burning of the temple of Haldi at Muṣaṣir by Sargon II) and dismemberment, and their anticipated destruction through burial, drowning, or trampling by animals.[158] The number of abducted gods grew over the centuries and finally culminated in instances of deicide, reported with an equal lack of reflection. Consider, for instance, the unintentionally dark satire of Aššurbanipal's description of his soldiers' experiences in Elam, when he sent his troops into "… the sanctuaries of Elam …. their secret groves into which no stranger (ever) penetrates, whose borders he never (over)steps—into these my soldiers entered, saw their mysteries, and set them on fire."[159] Aššurbanipal's Ninevite palace also shows, in parallel, the execution of an Elamite king by foot soldiers—and in front of Elamite troops—a measure of the public exposure to these previously unthinkable acts. These cases may have engendered a disenchantment with representations of the divine, though at this early stage, kings tended to distance themselves from such acts by most frequently "crediting" them to their soldiers.

7. "I DON'T WANT NO MORE OF ARMY LIFE": COLD, HUNGER AND HARDSHIP

"My troops are scarce," one Assyrian commander wrote, imploring his king for help; "(even) the horses of the king, my lord, had grown weak, so I let them go up to the mountain and graze."[160] Another wrote that his troops would "die of hunger … (they must be released) lest they starve … (and yet) they cannot depart because of snow."[161] Conditions in one fortress on the Zagros frontier were so bad it was nearly deserted: "There is nobody there except 200 rounded-up soldiers, and no food except for the travel provisions which they carry with them. Moreover, (enemies) have cut off the water between us and the land…"[162] From the extreme south of Babylonia, another fragmentary letter tells of dire conditions: "[The men] do not eat bread … they have contracted …

---

158 See Bahrani 2003, 174-84.
159 Luckenbill 1927, II, 310; in this campaign alone the king carried off nineteen divine images of named gods and 32 unnamed royal statues from Susa as well as destroying the royal tombs.
160 SAA I 241.
161 SAA V 126. The problem is echoed in an Old Babylonian letter (ARM 2/24+), pleading with Ḫammurabi to dismiss troops before winter: "A soldier must reach his house before the cold season!"
162 SAA XVII 152.

have not rested ... [The warriors of the] king, my lord, have pains in their legs ... and their eyes have become dark."[163] These letters were all written during the years of Assyria's greatest power, yet the many letters concerning the hardships of garrison life are enough to want for a Mesopotamian Bill Mauldin. In this respect, they form a welcome tonic to the interminable and untroubled narratives of victory purveyed by Mesopotamian royal inscriptions and images of happy and orderly camps (*madākātu*): Assyrian palace reliefs of this same period from Kalhu and Nineveh depict soldiers and even deportees under guard contentedly baking bread, grooming horses, cooking food and drinking wine by open campfires.

The Assyrian letters of discontent echo earlier Old Babylonian ones. In one town, an agent replies testily and sarcastically to a king who has breezily written repeated orders to distribute flour freely to the troops that the garrison commander "has become tired of all that writing" and that food was so low that "the division commander ... and the lieutenant under my authority receive grain rations like the (common) soldiers ... Now, from this day on, (why not) let the soldiers receive 21 liter grain rations, (and) I and the general will eat animal fodder."[164] The incessant warfare of the early eighteenth century saw campaigns lasting far beyond the agricultural season, with troops absent from home for as long as three years and more.[165] Middle Assyrian letters from the lonely western fortress of Dūr-Katlimmu present a similarly bleak picture of garrison life. One letter back to Aššur reveals that grasshoppers had eaten what little food there was; then the troops had survived for a while on chickpeas; but finally they had reached a point in which they had to choose between food for themselves and food for their hundred prisoners; in a later communiqué, the same letter writer admits disgustedly that "all soldiers have made their provisions out of the dust."[166] It was under such conditions that the Assyrian kings of the twelfth to tenth centuries spoke repeatedly of "rescuing" Assyrians who had long since gone native in their borderlands communities, melting back into the village-scape to farm as settlers.

---

163 SAA XVII 201.
164 ARM 26/314.
165 Ziegler 2000, 21.
166 Cancik-Kirschbaum 1996, Nos. 2, 3; notwithstanding, this was a place which nobles and foreign kings might visit periodically (No. 10).

It seems an eternal truth of army life that the tents should be too thin, the postings far and lonely, and the sergeants foul-mouthed and harsh. Mesopotamians were no strangers to the experience of battle trauma, either: In one Sumerian lament poem, low morale on the battlefield resulted in despair and flight, when "war veterans gave up, their brains were muddled."[167] One should note, it is true, the occasional burst of *élan*: "It is all laughter and play [among the troops]," writes one captain. "Their hearts are content as if they were staying in their own houses. The(ir) hearts ... tell of their zeal for doing battle and killing the enemy." (This zeal for battle was idiomatically known as the "dance of Inanna," the battle goddess.) But mostly our letters provide a steady antiphonal response to the idealizing images of royal inscriptions on almost every conceivable topic. Where kings boasted of their triumphs over high mountains and raging rivers, commanders complained that the terrain was too difficult and the troops could not swim.[168] Where kings claimed that their troops would defend widow and waif against enemies, captains asked, "Who would go out to the rescue and face a raider to save boys and girls?"[169] Against the image of the seemingly boundless puissance of the king's troops, one Assyrian officer has to explain to the annoyed king why a temple wall was peppered with the arrows of inept troops.[170]

The boredom of military life, the seeming ubiquity of incompetence, the thematic refrain of insufficiencies are all here, but the emphasis in Mesopotamian letters is clearly on problems with the food supply. What is revealed by the insistent concern for food is that there seems to be a relatively low expectation on the part of commanders that other kinds of supplies—armor, weapons,[171] wagons, etc.—were to be supplied to them by the central authority. This is not to say that arsenals did not exist—there is plenty of evidence to the contrary[172]—but only that

---

167 ETCSL, Lament for Unug, text 2.2.5, l. 61.
168 SAA V 200.
169 ARM 26/171.
170 SAA XVII 158. Mari letters referred to incompetently-led armies as "blind snakes" (ARM 26/491).
171 In one Middle Assyrian letter, a frustrated commander asked to produce arrows disgustedly wrote his superior that "the little piece of iron my lord gave me is unfit for the manufacture of (so much as) a whip handle" (Cancik-Kischbaum 1996, No. 16).
172 See, e.g., Ziegler 2000, 17-18; and Richardson 2005b; see also, *passim*, the numerous mentions of supply depots and central arsenals in Middle and Neo-Assyrian royal inscriptions.

these were occasional provisions, and that the true economic boundary on military costs was in sustaining manpower, not technologies (a boundary which has only relatively recently changed anyway).

In any event, one should not confuse reports of thin rations in garrisons for the genuine famines visited on besieged cities, in which starvation and even (according to Assyrian royal inscriptions) cannibalism resulted.[173] Even when sieges were unsuccessful, investing armies would steal supplies, cut off the water supply, burn growing crops,[174] or—perhaps worst of all—destroy orchards, economic products which took decades to rebuild.[175] The aftermath of raids found settlements licking their wounds, and enumerating the killed and captured.[176] Of course, situations existed in which the arrival of troops provoked joy and celebration,[177] but by and large most civilians were chary of men with weapons then as now.

This is hardly the place to consider all the potential directions in which an analysis of the Mesopotamian horror of war could be directed, so I will use just one example to suggest the profitability of such a study. Probably the most iconic literary depiction of war and its brutality in cuneiform literature is the Akkadian poem conventionally titled "Erra and Išum." The text describes the rage of the god Erra and his war against mankind; it contains not only a critique of warfare violence (amidst a vivid narration thereof[178]), but an almost ritually prophylactic conclusion. One aspect worth emphasizing is Erra's deployment of seven terrible warrior-monsters, themed on terror, fire, a fearsome lion, a mountain, blasting wind, a deluge, and a viper.[179]

---

173 ARM 27/156; Zaccagnini 1995; and see examples in CAD B s.v. *būru* C s., "starvation." Notwithstanding, strongholds were seen as safe zones for civilians: ARM 26/515, 27/113.

174 A.3669, ARM 2/50, 27/141; cf. Richardson 2005b. Curtis and Reade 1995, 47 shows an Assyrian soldier cutting down a rope with a bucket meant to draw water into a besieged city.

175 E.g., ARM 2/33; for Neo-Assyrian examples, see CAD K s.v. *kašāṭu* v., "to cut down orchards"; the act is depicted in the reliefs of the Aššurnaṣirpal II palace at Nimrud, among other places. See Oded 1997; cf. Aufrère 2005.

176 For a rare and detailed look at such a history "written by the losers," see Maidman 2008.

177 E.g., SAA XVIII 142.

178 E.g., of prisoners: "I cut the clothes from the bodies of men, the young man I parade naked through the city street, the young man without clothes I send down to hell" (Foster 1996, II 774); see ARM 27/151 for just such a display of naked enemies.

179 One might compare these monsters to the band of demons sent to seize the young god Dumuzi in the early Sumerian poem "Dumuzi's Dream." These demons take on the aspect of soldiers: "Those who come for the king are a motley crew, who know not

Their semblance as allegories of misery to the medieval "Four Horsemen of the Apocalypse" should be clear, but what is specific to the Mesopotamian conception of these forces is a) that they were charged with destinies, i.e., to perform their functions of warfare, but also b) that these functions were potentially reversible—by the gods, by ritual—precisely because of their written nature.[180] War, like so many other evils of the Mesopotamian world, was ultimately perceived as a construct which could be modified or averted; it was not, at its root, an unalterable fact to be endured.

8. ARMY POLITICS: ASSEMBLY, AGENCY, AND IDENTITY

Perhaps the most intriguing windows into military life afforded by episodes of hardship are the instances in which they provoked the non-compliance or rebellion of troops. Innumerable reports of desertion and malingering—not hard to find—could, by themselves, already be counted as a kind of exercise of agency. These kinds of discontent were incessantly corrosive of authority by their ubiquity, but their specific causes are not always clear: one garrison commander wrote to his king that his men were simply fed up, their "hearts are angry, and they will rise up and depart for somewhere else."[181] But Mesopotamian armies were not only responsive to authority and lapses thereof along the axis of obeisance/dereliction; they exercised political agency through clear examples of assembly, deliberation, and decision-making.

Explicitly political behaviors in military groups can be located in the record: the occasion of muster as a form of assembly, cases of persuasive speech, independent negotiation, appointment to office, and even mass defections. Part of these independent behaviors were underwritten by the exigencies of communications in the pre-modern world: down the chain of command, officers and troops had to make decisions in the field without recourse to advice from above. Armies had to accept or reject terms of surrender in the field without specific

---

food, who know not drink, who eat no sprinkled flour, who drink no poured water, who accept no pleasant gifts, who do not enjoy a wife's embraces, who never kiss dear little children, who never chew sharp-tasting garlic, who eat no fish, who eat no leeks." ETCSL, text 1.4.3. See also Ziegler's (1997) contention that the parts of Mesopotamian armies—its forehead, wings, navel, and tail—were part of a metaphorical system designed to terrify enemies by imparting to armies the qualities of monsters.
180 See J. Cohen 1996.
181 ARM 26/356.

royal orders and on their own judgment.[182] "Our troops were about
to do battle with the Numḫeans," the governor of Qaṭṭunan wrote
Zimri-Lim, "but the Numheans retired, saying 'Our brothers! What
do you have against us? We are searching for our enemies...'"[183]
Another letter seems to presuppose that armistices were agreements
involving all participants: the oracle of the god Dagan asks "Have the
kings of the Yaminites and their troops made peace with the troops of
Zimri-Lim who came up?"[184] The delegation of authority is reflected
in an early literary letter in which Šu-Sin, King of Ur, excoriates one
of his generals: "Why did you not act as I ordered you? You were not
(previously) empowered to kill anyone, to blind(?) people or to destroy
cities, but I gave you authority to do so."[185] The principle of command
presupposes delegation of authority, and thus some degree of the
heterarchy of power.

Our cases go beyond this, though, since political pressure emanated
from the bottom up, too. Old Babylonian fortresses, for instance,
are known to have developed some aspects of civic life over time—
families, dependents, elders, and cult emplacements.[186] A sense of
community developed over the decades: one garrison captain writes
the king that he cannot punish two local criminals, or his troops would
leave, prompting the commoners to rebel;[187] in another case, it was
feared that the entry of troops into a city would spark a rebellion.[188]
Even appointments from above had to take the political temperature into
account: one high general wrote confidentially to his king that he had
to defer to an inferior on the appointment of 12 division commanders
instead of the 10 he thought necessary: "I considered it and said to
myself, 'Once I take away two among the division commanders, who
were assigned, it will cause lips to turn against me.'" [189]

In some instances, troops would hear speeches of potential
commanders in assembly and accept or reject their leadership:

---

182 ARM 2/26, 26/385, 405.
183 ARM 27/68.
184 ARM 26/233.
185 ETCSL, text 3.1.16, ll. 24-7.
186 On elders, see AbB 13 107; on dependents, see Richardson 2010c, Texts 16-20; on
    institutional, family, legal, and religious life at a Babylonian fortress, see Joannès 2006,
    27-33.
187 ARM 26/408.
188 ARM 26/155.
189 A.486+.

"Assemble the troops and hear their words (lit., 'lip'): If the troops are willing to accept [their officer], he may keep his troops."[190] After a lengthy denunciation of enemies in the assembly of troops at Qaṭṭara, an agent of Zimri-Lim's reports: "These things and more Kakkutanum told the assembled men and caused the troops to change their minds. And he caused the opinion of the commoners to turn [as well] .... and the commoners turned to the side of Kakkutanum."[191] One among a number of verbs for the gathering of an army for expedition in all periods was *pahāru*, "to assemble," the same used for the gathering together of decision-making assemblies in Mesopotamian cities. Esarhaddon played quite deliberately on this coincidence in one inscription; of the surrender of an enemy army, he wrote that Ištar broke up "their compact line of battle, and in their assembly they proclaimed 'This is our King!' By her illustrious command, they joined themselves to my side."[192] The elective principle of the army-as-assembly suggested in the Gilgameš Epic seems thus to find some reflection in practice.

Sources for political voices other than the king's are precious few; we cannot follow this thread about the soldier's political agency too far. Yet we can note that Neo-Assyrian armies in several instances backed rival candidates for king—against Šamši-Adad V, against Aššur-nerari V, against the accession of Esarhaddon. Throughout the tumultuous centuries of the Neo-Assyrian state, field marshals rose to act as *de facto* rulers of large parts of the empire, and schemed against monarchs to whom they owed nominal allegiance. Of Esarhaddon, a Babylonian Chronicle laconically reports the suppression of a *putsch*: "The eleventh year [of Esarhaddon]: In Assyria the king put numerous officers to the sword,"[193] and we are aware of other successful army plots.[194]

---

190 ARM 26/322-3.
191 ARM 26/412-3; the troops who remained loyal in this case were later re-assembled and forced to swear an oath of allegiance; similarly, ARM 26/344,
192 CAD Q s.v. *qabû* 1e-3'; see also Richardson 2010b on the ubiquity of Assyrian royal language delegitimizing speech and assembly.
193 ABC 14. Whether Esarhaddon's death the following year was, as reported, due to illness, cannot of course be confirmed. Nebuchadnezzar II also put down an officers' rebellion (as distinct from others blamed on rival lords, nobles, or the general populace); ABC 5 reports: "With arms he slew many of his own army."
194 These include the assassination of Tukulti-Ninurta I (ABC 22), the seizure and delivery of Enlil-kudurri-uṣur (Walker Chronicle), and perhaps another seventh century revolt (ABC 15). Babylonian officers' plots include the overthrow of Karahardaš (ABC 21, and the appointment of the new king, Nazibugaš); late period examples include a supposed army rebellion against the Median Astyages (ABC 7) and an apparent reference to the

We may say this: professional soldiers and imperial officers were probably better traveled than many palace elites, and familiar with foreign people as deportees and auxiliaries, while residing apart from the traditional culture of the Assyrian heartland. Assyrian royal inscriptions make for colorful travel brochures of military life: the king's soldiers had climbed high mountains, seen far valleys, tasted the waters of distant rivers. The linguistic melting pot of camp life acquainted soldiers with peers from distant lands and with different social identities.

There have been arguments that the Mesopotamian military sustained and produced concepts of masculinity as well.[195] A Mesopotamian conception of "manhood," on the one hand, could be said to have included the idea of man-as-warrior; on the other, one could note in the Neo-Assyrian context that eunuchs fought alongside bearded men on the battlefield.[196] Images of women in palace reliefs, Bahrani has argued, "signify the humiliation and destitution of the conquered land through the bodies of women"—while victory was always masculine.[197] In a few instances, it seems likely that the accusation that a fleeing enemy king "fled on a mare" was intended to strike at his masculinity by allusion to his feminine mount, but this specific image is restricted to a few cases in the late eighth century.[198] Be this as it may, it would also be impossible to maintain that defeat was marked among the same period texts and images as exclusively feminine—male bodies were in fact the much more common subjects of graphic abuse to the extent of producing a deliberately titillating pornography of violence.[199] What is all the more remarkable is the low incidence of feminizing metaphors in characterizing defeated enemies. For those who failed their essential duties as men in warfare, the much more common metaphors were borrowed from the animal world: an enemy who fled the battlefield "flew like a bird," "escaped like a fox through a hole," "like a crawling creature," "like a mouse through a crack"—enemies fled like pigs, bats,

---

assassination of a Seleucid monarch by "generals with their troops" in BCHP 9 (time of Seleucus I Nicator).

195 E.g. Chapman 2004; Bahrani 2008, 107.

196 See Chapman 2004 on the construction of male identity in the context of Assyrian warfare; for a depiction of eunuchs in battle, see Curtis and Reade 1995, 67.

197 Bahrani 2001, 124-30.

198 Tadmor 1994, 101, 133-35; Luckenbill 1927, 8, 82.

199 See especially Bersani and Dutoit 1985, 52-56.

pelicans, and sheep.[200] One can think that many elements common to all military experience—deindividualization; participatory violence; the celebration of the fit body—were also constructive of masculinity in Mesopotamia. Yet when one seeks out what seems particular to this culture's sense of personhood with reference to the military, the dyadic divide is more strongly drawn along the divide of human or non-human than masculine or feminine.

Decades, even generations of garrison life would have imparted senses of community and identity to multi-ethnic, "borderlands" military units, with their own cultures of hierarchy and merit. It is not hard to see in Assyria's insistent militarism the recasting of the empire as a whole along the lines of these nascently political communities. The era of city-states had ended in Mesopotamia around 1600, followed by the rise of so-called "national states" down to ca. 900, when an age of empires arose. This imperial period also saw the development of urban Chartism—legal exceptionalism—that emerged by the fourth century as a newly-dominant era of localism, largely conditioned by the cellular character of imperial military rule.

9. CONCLUSION

I have barely scratched the surface of what has been examined. Many more research areas remain under-explored: wartime trauma and the habituation to violence;[201] the production of gender identity through military life;[202] the economic analysis of war and "armed peace."[203] Other areas remain almost untouched: the long-term effects of war; its frequency; the role of non-combatants; treatment of the dead and the missing; the functions of the military's police. Clearly, more studies are needed. It is true that military life is so thoroughly suffused throughout the sources and periods that it seems at first quixotic to consider it as a separate historical problem. Yet its ubiquity being a clear indication of its importance, we can look forward to ever-newer scholarship on this oldest of historical problems.

---

200 RIMA 1-3 and Luckenbill, *passim*. In a unique passage, one tribute-paying people is said to "do their hair like women" (RIMA 2.101.1 ii. 72b-76a), but the aside seems devoid of gendering intent.

201 On post-traumatic stress disorder and (literary) evidence, see Ben-Ezra 2004; idem 2010; on state promotion of violence, see Bonneterre 1997; Bersani and Dutoit 1985; Crouch 2009.

202 See especially Kuhrt 2001, but also Hammons 2008 (esp. Ch. 3); Philip 2002.

203 Spek 1993; Aperghis 2000.

2
GREECE:
MAD HATTERS AND MARCH HARES

EVERETT L. WHEELER

Duke University

1. INTRODUCTION

As the studious Alice trod the path of ancient military history in the Wonderland of contemporary scholarship, she spied a grinning Cheshire-Cat lounging on a bough above her and inquired:

"Would you tell me, please, which way I ought to go from here?"

"That depends a good deal on where you want to get to," said the Cat.

"I don't much care where—" said Alice.

"Then it doesn't matter which way you go," said the Cat …
"In *that* direction … lives a Hatter: and in *that* direction"… lives a March Hare. Visit either you like: they're both mad."

"But I don't want to go among mad people," Alice remarked.

"Oh, you can't help that," said the Cat: "we're all mad here. I'm mad. You're mad."

"How do you know I'm mad?" said Alice.

"You must be," said the Cat, "or you wouldn't have come here."[1]

The Cheshire-Cat's enigmatic grin conceals an overly-simplified bifurcation of scholarly trends between the Mad Hatter traditionalists and the March Hares, chasing "new approaches." Hatters generally represent some type of historicist doing biography, campaign or battle studies, and institutional, social, economic, or cultural history within the framework of an acknowledged limit to literary, documentary,

---

1 Carroll 1960, 62-63. Dates for all ancient events are BC unless otherwise indicated.

and material sources, whereas Hares, frequently shirkers of battle studies, are eager adventurers, denouncing the limits of historicism for the promise of gains from theories and methodologies in the social sciences, and often addicted to self-generated "new evidence" from modeling. Neither type can escape the *Zeitgeist*, as historiography commonly mirrors the social and political concerns of the generation that writes it. Both types can be ideological with agendas not always subtly concealed. Indeed, the Hares, so zealous to expose the foibles of both earlier and contemporary "old-fashioned" work, often tend to swing unabashedly farther to the Left with due reverence to nineteenth- or early-twentieth-century icons like Max Weber, Emile Durkheim, and not least Karl Marx; they eagerly succumb to (or exploit) the latest scholarly fads. Both equally seek new interpretations, even if the Hares seem more impatient to produce dramatic "results." Nor can comparative history and use of *comparanda* be counted the exclusive property of either Hatters or Hares, although the latter often display fewer qualms about rules of evidence (from an historicist's perspective) and arguments by analogy.

Yet the real Wonderland of current ancient military history also features "war-gamers," "numbers-crunchers," the "how-they-must-a-dun-its" (excessively fond of *comparanda*), and (not least) the "cutting-edgers." Hybrid practitioners combining some or all of these characters also appear. The "face-of-battle" phenomenon, a "new approach," precludes any facile distinction between Hatters and Hares, as it has been "cutting edge" with elements of war-gaming and "how-they-must-a-dun-it," even if some of its proponents are often characterized as traditionalist Hatters. Distinguishing Hatters and Hares can be messy.

Indeed, in recent decades the very definitions of "history" and "historian" have become murky. Many from other academic disciplines are called "historians" and the slim, if not bizarre, selection of new works in "ancient history" for discussion in the venerable *American Historical Review* confirms the identity crisis—or at least the editors' biases about which works to showcase. Historical training in any technical (History Department) sense no longer seems a prerequisite for claiming the label "historian." Certainly interdisciplinary studies are *au courant* and merit applause when done well. A useful anthology on killing in war reflects the new field of "historical anthropology." Its scattered geographical and temporal coverage ("timeless" New

Guinea and East Africa, combined with papers ranging from Antiquity to WWII) betrays its universalist anthropological origins—incoherent to an historicist.[2] Much work published as "ancient history" might be more accurately called (from a Hatter's perspective) sociology, anthropology, or even political science. In the current interdisciplinary rage many young scholars may no longer be able to recognize the differences between disciplines and, more significantly, the distinctions in rules of evidence and argumentation derived from each discipline's theoretical bases. An anthropological or sociological "fact" may not be true for a specific situation from a traditional historian's perspective, but Hares often cannot be bothered with such trivial scruples.[3] Adventurous interdisciplinary and comparativist forays can also become embarrassing.[4]

For the sake of completeness, cultural studies and postmodernist literary theory should also be noted. The former, a radical stepchild of cultural anthropology and (usually) not to be confused with an historian's cultural approach, can disguise itself as "history," although Hatters readily recognize the ruse. Hares expediently use or ignore this perspective. If, after at least two decades, the postmodernist turn in literary interpretation is becoming passé—historiography has its own fads—its influence on making even Hatters think of sources as "texts" cannot be denied. Its extreme relativism and reduction of issues to an epistemological *aporia* are less commendable, or, as recently remarked: "the idea of post-modern too often serves as a label for little real substance."[5] Excessive jargon and obscure argumentation may sometimes conceal a naked emperor. Nevertheless, as the field of ancient historiography, often slippery and subjective, has become

---

2   Stietencron and Rüpke 1995; cf. a non-anthropological volume on the same theme: Sordi 1990.

3   Note Henk Versnel's reflection (2002, 37-38) on participation in a conference on "social control," as a confession that he did not know what "social control" was led to his enlightenment on the non-existence of this practice: "As a bonus I also found out that having a *wrong* definition is far worse than having *no* definition, the first being unforgivable, the latter only unimaginable." Cf. Linderski's views of the influence of sociology on the current practice of ancient history: 2007, 175, 178, 288, 583, 585; note also Keegan (1987, 1), "[M]ethods of social scientists ... condemn those who practice them to the agony of making universal and general what is stubbornly local and particular."

4   See Knauf's review (2009) where several prominent Graeco-Roman historians are caught with their bibliographical pants down on current biblical scholarship.

5   Philip Hammond, quoted in Dandeker 2007, 35.

increasingly more literary and (in a sense) less historical, space requires its sacrifice to the greater good here.[6]

Such is a preliminary reconnaissance of the Wonderland of current scholarship in ancient military history with all its quirks and whimsical scholarly types. A conventional and straightforward assessment, given academia's penchant for novelty and constant re-invention of its subject matters, would politely nod at the Hatters and glamorize the Hares. Everyone would feel good, but the state of the field would lack critical assessment. After all, the Cheshire-Cat is quite right: much depends on where Alice wants to go.[7]

2. RECENT ASSESSMENTS

This chapter emerges from the shadow of the massive two-volume *Cambridge History of Greek and Roman Warfare (CHGRW)*, nearly a decade in the making, to which this writer confesses contribution of a chapter.[8] Moreover, a panel at the 2009 meeting of the American Philological Association treated "New Approaches to the Political & Military History of the Greek, Roman, and Late Roman Worlds."[9] Two brief surveys by Sidebottom and Burckhardt are also of note: the former, largely a polemic against some views of Victor Hanson; the latter, a straightforward overview with few factual errors or controversial interpretations and (*mirabile dictu!*) no axes to grind.[10] Here Burckhardt wins the palm.

---

6   I also forego inclusion of the never-ending parade of "picture books" and "coffee-table" tomes on ancient warfare, even if by reputable scholars, and the ceaseless torrent of "battle books" aimed at the general public. This paper's scholarly gaze is generally limited to works appearing through summer 2009.

7   The target audience of this paper is primarily graduate students, whose training may lack sufficient exposure to the intellectual and methodological roots of all the "novelties" appearing in the current "publication explosion." Indeed the author prefers to stress the problematic nature of various views rather than to endorse specific works. Selection of texts depends on not only availability and costs but also an instructor's own predilections and how much she or he wishes to teach against or correct a selected work, especially as undergraduates tend to view the contents of assigned texts as "the truth."

8   Wheeler 2007a, 186-223.

9   Perhaps the best offering is the Late Roman discussion of Walter Kaegi (2009), who in part reprises his earlier general assessment (1981), and justly notes the perpetuation of many of the same shortcomings noted in 1981, although his apology for apparent criticism of the pervasive influence of the *Annales* school was hardly necessary.

10 Sidebottom 2004; Burckhardt 2008; a French assessment of work 1985-2005 on Greek warfare at Corvisier 2005 and 2006.

The *CHGRW* meritoriously includes both Hatters and Hares. A close reading of the first volume on Greek and Hellenistic warfare soon reveals the diversity of opinions on numerous issues, as a standard reference work should. Michael Whitby, for example, targets the problems of reconstructing ancient battles and campaigns more accurately than Philip Sabin's innovative "war-gaming."[11] Yet seekers of the *status quaestionis* on various specific issues must wade through multiple chapters with a discerning eye, since a "structural" approach to categorizing the material produced numerous overlaps between the chapters. Nor do all the Greek and Hellenistic chapters strive to balance opposing views. Some contributors are riding the hobby-horses of their previous publications. Hanson on the modern historiography of ancient warfare and Hornblower on war in ancient literature are so Greek in orientation that Romanists should complain about neglect. In particular, Hornblower's ready acceptance of various dubious assertions minimizing the role of war in Greek civilization invites debate, if not rebuttal, nor does he seem to understand ancient military treatises.[12] Creation of written military theory—essentially a Greek invention—involves much more than a Greek love of "the technical" and has a specific historical context, which Hornblower ignores.[13]

Predictably, the *CHGRW* editors justify their enterprise with praise of present progress: they contrast "narrowly focused studies … before the First World War," identified with Hans Delbrück, Johannes Kromayer, and Georg Veith, with richer text analysis, new archaeological discoveries, and the Hares' agenda of social, economic, political, and cultural *structures* (a key word), whereby "our understanding of ancient warfare has been transformed."[14] Unless twentieth-century ancient historians have been wasting their

---

11 Whitby 2007, 54-81; Sabin 2007a, 399-433.
12 Hornblower 2007, 22 n.4, 27 n.18, 50-51. On war and Greek society see further below.
13 Two recent discussions of the origins of Greek military manuals, Tejeda (2004) and Whitehead (2008), suffer from bibliographical myopia and offer little that is new or at times even accurate: see Wheeler 2010a, 19 n.50 with references.
14 *CHGRW*, 1, xv. Surprisingly, the statement is factually inaccurate: Volume IV of Delbruck's *Geschichte der Kriegskunst* only appeared in 1920 in the third edition of the collected work and Kromayer and Veith's classic was published in 1928. The work of these historians only partially antedates World War I. On the publication history of Delbrück's *Geschichte*, see Bucholz 1985, 175-76. I am not convinced that the *CHGRW* renders Kromayer and Veith's handbook totally obsolete, especially for Greek, Hellenistic, and Roman (Middle and Late Republican) tactics; seekers of basic information may find what they want to know more easily in Kromayer and Veith.

time, scholarly progress in the course of a century is to be expected. The editors, however, show little respect for the pioneering work of Delbrück, essentially the founder of military history as an academic discipline. Current practitioners still employ his methods, although many avoid Delbrück's own shortcomings in their radical application.[15] Certainly Delbrück and Kromayer knew the Greek and Latin sources (in the original tongues) better than many current ancient military historians, reliant on translations, and often deficient in philological analysis of technical passages. The current trend toward studying war as culture in some ways returns to Delbrück's comprehensive approach. References to "progress" always require a reality check.

Hanson's assessment of the current historiography on ancient warfare rightly contrasts concrete solutions and expanding general knowledge or raising questions for discussion through theoretical social science, although like others in the *CHGRW* his own preference in the Hatters-Hares debate is clear.[16] Indeed Hanson has been on the "cutting edge" of a major trend in ancient military history, even if that "edge" is not quite as sharp as often imaged. Questions remain: which way should Alice go? Do we have the sources to produce "concrete solutions" rather than stimulants for discussion? In 2007 the present writer (by no means free of opinions) produced an evaluation of the current state of ancient military history for an edited volume on Greek military history (Homer to 362). The following survey of past and current scholarly trends in the study of Greek warfare draws (in part) on that discussion and extends it through the Hellenistic period.[17]

3. The "War and Society" School

Two approaches have dominated Anglophone ancient military history in the last two decades, the war-and-society school and the face-of-battle phenomenon. Both belong with the Hares and both share

---

15   The present writer confesses being an historical advisor and translator of the Greek and Latin quotations in vols. II-IV of Walter Renfroe's English version of Delbruck's *Geschichte* (1975-85).

16   Hanson 2007, 3-21. Hanson's attempt to marginalize philological discussion of ancient military concepts (2007, 15 with n.7) is misguided, misrepresents published work, and is self-serving, as the Graeco-Roman tradition of stratagems has always been an embarrassment to Hanson's view of a "Western way of war": see below and the remarks at Wheeler 2008, 58 n.8.

17   Wheeler 2007b.

descent from a common intellectual and historiographical milieu.[18] The former, termed (among Anglophones) the "new military history," began to appear in the 1970s. It stressed social and economic issues, military policies, and generally anything concerning the use and existence of armed forces except actual fighting. The novelty of this type of work was can be debated, as military history had never been exclusively study of technical aspects of the conduct of war, but it permitted military history to enter the flow of the tidal wave of interest in social history, which by that point had flooded history departments in American universities as the preferred academic type of history.[19]

The "new military history," hardly homegrown, was transplanted from the "hot bed" of intellectual trends and *haute couture*—Paris. During the twentieth century French historians had developed a particular socioeconomic approach to history stressing long-term historical trends (*la longue durée*) and incorporating the influence of geography (space), demography, anthropology, psychology (*mentalité*), and the perspective of the non-ruling elite ("history from the bottom up"). Eventually termed the *Annales* school, this perspective rejected the emphasis on "great" individuals and events (trivialities, i.e., epiphenomena), common to traditional political history, for study of sweeping historical change over time and the everyday lives of non-elites, although even the non-elite were essentially to be studied collectively as reflections of prevailing social structures.[20] Although the *Annales* school was not by definition Marxist, its preference for socioeconomic interpretations could lend itself to Marxist views. All depended on the individual historian's predilections. By no means hostile to studying war and armies, the *Annales* school, fostered a "war and society" approach, which subsequently inspired much of the Anglophone "new military history."[21] For ancient military history,

---

18 Hanson's distinction (2007, 10 with n.12, 12, 17) of "Continental influence" and the "French school" from face-of-battle studies is misleading. A brief survey of the role of military history in Western education and the academy before c.1970 must be sacrificed in the interest of space.

19 Chambers 1991; Black 2004a and 2004b; Wheeler 2007b, xiv; cf. above, Introduction.

20 The views of some in the war-and-society school that war is an "epiphenomenon" (triviality) of no consequence in the larger scheme of things, and that the individual is a mere prisoner of impersonal social structures constitute old wine in a new bottle: see already the complaints of Oman 1939: 159-75.

21 At least fourteen Greek "war and society" volumes were published in France 1999-2000 to prepare students for the announced theme of the next *agrégation* (some with useful papers; others quite pedestrian); listed at Wheeler 2007b: xi n.2.

André Aymard applied the *Annaliste* view to Greek affairs and his students Yvon Garlan, Raoul Lonis, and Pierre Ducrey have continued this tradition in many distinguished works.[22] The type of interdisciplinary conference, which the French do so well and Anglophones only imitate, occurred at the Centre de Recherches Comparées sur les Sociétes Anciennes at the Sorbonne in 1965. Here the *Annales* school met the circle of structural anthropologists, featuring Jean-Pierre Vernant, Marcel Detienne, and Pierre Vidat-Naquet—all inspired by the work of Claude Lévi-Strauss, Louis Gernet, Henri Jeanmaire, and Georges Dumézil.[23] The acta of this conference became a seminal work in the study of Greek warfare through the 1980s and its influence has resurfaced in the recent cultural approach to ancient warfare.[24] After all, this was a "new approach" and "cutting edge." This temporary union of the *Annalistes* and the structural anthropologists produced further fruit in Yvon Garlan's structuralist (and Marxist influenced) survey of Graeco-Roman warfare in 1972, and Detienne and Vernant's 1974 venture into the genre of *histoire des mentalités* (a relatively brief fad among *Annalistes*) with a study of *metis* in Greek society—a concept significant for the cultural context of stratagems in Greek warfare.[25]

But the *Annalistes* and the Vernant school were not exactly the same type of rabbit. In the 1990s the fad for structural anthropology waned, as Classical scholars grew weary of initiation rites, and ritualization ceased to be fashionable among anthropologists. The immediate Vernant circle, moving on to other topics, ceased to pursue military-

---

22 For the forerunners of the *Annales* school, see Dewald 2006; surveys, brief by Knapp (1992) and lengthier by Burgière (2009); an assessment of the *Annales* school's influence on military history at Paret (2009), although he omits the influence of the *Annaliste* perspective on ancient military history; Aymard's numerous valuable papers were posthumously published as *Études d'histoire ancienne* (1967). Limited space in the Wonderland of ancient military history precludes discussing *Annaliste* influence in the Anglophone "new archaeology," less significant for Greek military affairs than Roman, particularly frontier studies; a brief discussion at Wheeler 2007b: xviii-xix.

23 The major works of Gernet, Jeanmaire, and Dumézil are cited at Wheeler 2007b: xv nn.10-11. Application of anthropological work to Graeco-Roman rituals and religion also had British exponents: e.g., Frazer 1890 and the Cambridge "ritualists" of the 1920s: see (e.g.) Beard 2000. An emphasis on rituals and initiation rites in Greek society led to a curious work on border wars in Archaic Greece: Brelich 1961.

24 Vernant 1968; on the influence of this work, see Ducrey 1997, 123-38.

25 Garlan 1972, English trans., 1975; Detienne and Vernant 1974, English trans. 1978.

themes.[26] Nevertheless, *Annaliste* attitudes and concepts received a new impetus from an English translation of the second edition of Fernand Braudel's study of the age of the Hapsburg Philip II.[27] Endorsement and imitation of Braudel's version of *Annaliste* doctrine became not a fad but a mania among Anglophone ancient historians. The very vocabulary of history changed: analysis of "social structures" and history "from the bottom up" became preferred perspectives; aristocrats and nobles became the "ruling elite"; "ideology" replaced "propaganda" in historical parlance, even if more recently the fascination for transhumance has (mercifully) faded and an emphasis on la longue durée is also now being questioned.[28]

A series of seminars at the Universities of Leicester and Nottingham 1988-90 drew inspiration from Moses Finley, a participant in Vernant's 1965 Paris conference. In a 1985 essay on war and imperialism and a polemic against traditional historicism, Finley urged replacing historicism with social science theory and modeling; he further outlined a model for understanding ancient warfare as a structural factor.[29] He discounted the unreliability of numbers in ancient literary sources and encouraged generating "new evidence" through *comparanda* and modern methods of demography and statistical tables, despite those tools' creation through theory and assumptions (not always unproblematic). Predictably, from Finley's well-known Marxist proclivities, the study of ancient war should address profits from war and financing conflicts, as military aspects were unrecoverable from the poor state of the sources. The seminars yielded two 1993 war-and-society anthologies (one Greek, one Roman), mostly in keeping with Finley's manifesto for an economic approach to ancient warfare, although no papers were groundbreaking. Notable, too, no contributors to the Greek volume had a reputation for doing military history (of any kind) except

---

26 Influences of the Vernant school and even the work of Dumézil remain alive and well in France: see Sauzeau and Van Compernolle 2007, reviewed at Wheeler 2009.

27 Braudel 1966 (translated into English, 1972). I forego in the interest of space more recent efforts in "Mediterranean studies" only tangential to Greek and Hellenistic military history.

28 See, e.g., Malkin 2008; cf. Knauf 2009: "Credulists believe in the 'historicity' of narratives; social historians look for data that they can count and then calculate long-term trends."

29 Finley 1985, 47-66 and 67-87.

for Alastar Jackson, who (ironically) refuted Finley's view of the profit motive in raiding and warfare in Homer and the Greek Dark Age. [30]

Shipley's "Introduction" to the Greek volume *inter alia* rehearsed the basic tenets of Braudel's version of *Annaliste* doctrine as a definitive approach to history, as if he were saying something original, and added his own advocacy of presentism in historical interpretation.[31] Further, this Greek volume, along with its Roman companion, redefined "war": no longer a conflict between states, but any organized societal violence, including piracy, banditry, and even colonization. Definition of "war" has often been problematic not least from a legal perspective (terrorism, cold vs. hot wars) or from the word's metaphorical use. Although aware of the difficulties of his redefinition of war, Shipley declined to deal with them.[32] This anthropological view that any kind of violence is a form of war reappeared in the titles of a French work of 1999 and anthologies of 2000, 2005, and 2006.[33]

No subsequent war-and-society anthology has been quite so doctrinaire in its aims as the Rich and Shipley tomes, although by the end of the 1990s the perspective of *Annaliste* structuralism had become conventional. The acta of a 1996 war-and-society colloquium at the Center for Hellenic Studies offered a greater comparative emphasis, with coverage extended to the Near East, East Asia, and Mesoamerica.[34] As usual with anthologies, some individual papers stirred interest, but none represented a major breakthrough. Many were of the "rise

---

30 Jackson 1993; cf. Zimmermann (2007), who seems to accept all views in the Rich and Shipley tomes (1993a-b) as gospel.

31 Shipley 1993, 1-24; cf. his complaints (2006, 318, 319) about the lack of theorizing of the Hellenistic period, as if sociological theories should be the aim of historical research; the absence of *polemos* in the titles of Herodotus and Thucydides is one of Shipley's (unconvincing and Braudelian-inspired) arguments in attempting to minimize the role of war in Classical Greek civilization and to deny war as a concept of periodization; followed by Hornblower 2007, 22 n.4, 27 n.18; cf. my remarks at Wheeler 2007b: xliv n.95. Xenophanes' poignant inquiry (fr. 18 Diehl=Ath. 2.54e: "How old were you when the Mede arrived?") certainly suggests war as a basis of periodization in his mind; see also Darbo-Peschanski 1994, 177-79 on war and periodization in the context of the Greek view of war as a manifestation of divine justice.

32 Shipley 1993, 7-8.

33 Bernard 1999, with particular attention to psychological elements; cf. the earlier (and peculiar) Sagan 1979; also see van Wees (2000a), Bertrand (2005), and Styka (2006) on violence in Greek literature. Note also Zimmermann 2007, an hors d'oeuvre to a meaty project on "Formen extremer Gewalt in Bild und Text des Altertums" at Universität München. Zimmermann's claim (2007, 52-53) that no one has discussed the names of Greek wars and their typology overlooks Wheeler 1999.

34 Raaflaub and Rosenstein 1999.

and fall" variety from a structuralist perspective; some emphasized economic factors and structures, others not. Unlike the Rich and Shipley tomes, "society" in this volume denoted essentially "power" with no attention to religion, art, and literature. A specialist in pre-state warfare, Brian Ferguson, attempted to pull all the threads together from the perspective of anthropological theory. He both dared to suggest the role of powerful individual rulers in promoting expansion—heresy to the *Annalistes*—and took the extreme reductionist position of denying a difference between state and pre-state warfare.[35]

The most recent anthology in the ancient war-and-society genre derived from a 2003 conference on *vergleichende Kriegsgeschichte*.[36] Coverage, limited to Antiquity, included the Near East (Assyria, Israel, Achaemenid Persia, and the Parthians), but omitted Early Rome and the Middle Republic. Like the Raaflaub and Rosenstein tome, few individual papers (if adequately surveying their theme) actually contained any comparative work, leaving relevant comparisons to diligent readers. The editors genuflected before the model of French and Anglophone volumes on war and society without reference to *Annaliste* "structures" and (predictably) rejected study of strategy and tactics, although one paper on sixth-century Byzantine operations in northern Mesopotamia represented the "old military history."

Significantly, the German editors framed their task as inserting military history into a broader framework of *Kulturgeschichte*. Some ancient military historians, just as military historians working on other eras, have turned to a cultural approach, attempting to view war within the "big picture" of a civilization as a whole and without privileging socioeconomic interpretations in the mode of the Finleyites and some *Annalistes*.[37] This trend is refreshing. It is unfortunate that in Anglophone ancient military history the important theme of war and society has become a code word for one particular methodological-ideological view of historiography. Social, economic, and cultural aspects of war were discussed before the Braudelian invasion and merit treatment in a variety of ways.

Despite the pervasive influence of the various forms of the *Annales* school, the results of three anthologies on Greek and Hellenistic affairs,

---

35 Ferguson 1999, esp. 403-404, 426.
36 Meißner et al., 2005, reviewed at Wheeler 2006b.
37 On the cultural approach to war see, e.g., French 2003; Lynn 2003 (summarized in idem 2005); Eckstein 2005; discussion in Wheeler 2007b, xxv-xxvi.

even if (*faute de mieux*) useful for non-specialists, have not produced dramatic scholarly results. In fact, the more interesting papers in these works have not been on the Greeks (or the Romans). More topics concerning war are being discussed, as Hanson noted, and scholars who might not have otherwise ventured into military history are now doing so, although with varying levels of competence in studying war. But "where's the beef?" On the basis of three anthologies, the expected results from so modish an approach are not living up to the "hype." Anthologies, of course, do not represent the totality of scholarly production and *Annaliste* contributions must be broached again later. Interesting, however, is the cultural turn and looking at war within the totality of a civilization—a new version of what Delbrück was trying to do a century ago.[38] Nevertheless, another type of Hare, sometimes disguised as a Hatter, awaits discussion.

4. The Face of Greek Battle

The war-and-society school's disdain for the "blood and guts" of combat led to a rather abstract treatment of war. John Keegan's 1976 *Face of Battle*, based on the battles of Agincourt, Waterloo, and the Somme, incited a return to a more "up-close and personal" view of battle as an individual's experience. Keegan rejected traditional historiography's concern for battles from a general's perspective, in which military units seemed to be moved about like pawns on a chessboard. Human beings in battle were not faceless "automata." Keegan wanted to know what it was really like to be in a battle, not the strategic or tactical causes of victory or defeat.[39] Hence his discussion focused on the individual soldier's preparation for battle, his weapons and equipment, the individual as part of a military unit, his morale, fighting techniques, what happened in the combat of the front ranks, the effects of wounds, and treatment of the slain. Keegan drew inspiration from the *Études sur le combat* of Colonel Charles-Jean-Jacques-Joseph Ardant du Picq, killed in the opening stages of the Franco-Prussian War. Ardant

---

38 Delbrück (1975-85, 4, x-xi) conceived his work in terms of world history and cultural history. The current emphasis on "world history" in the contemporary age of globalization revives earlier concerns. Delbrück was a Berlin *ordinarius* in *allgemeine Geschichte und Weltgeschichte*, not *Kriegsgeschichte*.

39 Thus Kagan's concern (2006) for winners and losers in battle-narrative technique attempts to correct Keegan on something he explicitly stated (1976, 74-77) that he was not trying to do; her claim (3) that no one has questioned the face-of-battle approach exposes bibliographical ignorance; see below.

du Picq, who (like Keegan and Hanson) had never been in a major pitched battle, was a regimental officer concerned (apart from political motives) with the role of morale and improving combat efficiency at the command level of smaller units.[40]

Keegan's eloquent prose and the supposed novelty of the approach produced an adulatory response among Anglophone military historians essentially simultaneous with the tidal wave of enthusiasm for Braudel's work. Keegan's analysis of the earlier historiography of battle went unquestioned.[41] Numerous studies on the "daily life" of soldiers of particular eras anticipated Keegan's concerns, as did some historians' inclusion of soldiers' personal experiences from diaries and memoirs in traditional accounts of major battles, although without an overarching theoretical principle that Keegan imposed. Thucydides (7.44.1) had already realized the difficulty of understanding precisely what went on in a battle, as did Leo Tolstoy, whose efforts to reconstruct the Battle of Borodino for *War and Peace* led him to compare the tasks of battle historians and novelists.[42] Tolstoy's essay somehow escaped Keegan, who also did not observe that a concern for *ésprit* and *élan* (seen in Ardant du Picq) had flourished in French military theorists since the early eighteenth century and that *Annaliste* military historians in France were publishing on the psychology of soldiers in combat.[43]

Paradoxically, Keegan's book, in refuting the "automaton" view of battle, spawned a generation of automata uncritically copying his approach for their own "battle experience" books and articles in nearly all periods of history. More significantly from a curricular standpoint, *The Face of Battle* represented the "new military history": it was a form of social history "from the bottom up," coincided with an *Annaliste* concern for the trivia of daily life, and corresponded to the postmodernist obsession with an individual's identity.[44] Even

---

40 Ardant du Picq's work is available in both French and English: *Études sur le combat* (1880) and *Roots of Strategy, Book 2* (1987), 9-299.

41 No one really noticed the work's Anglocentrism: an Englishman's book about the British army written for a British audience (e.g., Waterloo and the Somme from a British perspective).

42 Tolstoy 1966, 1368-71; the essay's date is 1868.

43 Wheeler 2007b, xix-xx with n.29.

44 The appearance of *The Face of Battle* in the mid-1970s also coincided with a new enthusiasm for playing war games (board, not yet computer). Theodore Ropp, former professor of military history and the history of technology at Duke University (1938-89), attributed this fad in the midst of the Cold War's nuclear stalemate to romanticism about a type of war that would never be seen again.

more paradoxical, as the role of killing in war had been a key factor in marginalizing or excluding military history from the History curriculum, the face-of-battle school has generated more research on, and discussion of, the techniques and acts of killing than ever existed in traditional military history. In any case, the Anglophone face-of-battlers and the war-and-society enthusiasts share a common origin in the French *Annales* school.

No doubt it was inevitable that someone would apply Keegan's face-of-battle approach to Antiquity. The task fell to Victor Hanson, previously the author of an innovative study (1983) of agricultural destruction in Classical Greek warfare.[45] Hanson's *Western Way of War* adapted Keegan's approach to the hoplite warfare of Classical Greece and masterfully synthesized the literary and archaeological sources for what could be said about Greek battles between Homer and Epaminondas as of 1989.[46] Problematic "improvements" to Keegan's approach, however, were added. First, Hanson applied post-World War II "buddy theory" to the hoplite phalanx: an emphasis on the importance of the cohesion of the "primary group" in combat motivation, i.e., soldiers primarily fought for self-preservation and to avoid shame before their everyday companions rather than for patriotism or hatred of the enemy. Second, as insufficient details survive to describe all aspects of any single fifth- or fourth-century hoplite battle, Hanson reconstructed a "typical" battle from scattered literary and historical sources dating from Homer through the Hellenistic period. Imaginative conjectures filled gaps in the evidence. Third, Hanson saw hoplite battle as a central feature of Greek culture, a symbol of democracy in action, as middle-class Greek farmers defended their farms and freedom (civic militarism).[47] Finally, hoplite battle became in Hanson's view a doctrine of "decisive battle," which the Greeks invented and bequeathed to Western Civilization: a belief in resolving war by a

---

45 Hanson 1983 (1998).

46 Hanson 1989; a second edition (2000) includes a response to critics in which Hanson asserts that no one has proved him wrong in any respect—hardly credible in view of the work's intense scrutiny by other ancient historians; a recent reprint (2009) includes a new preface but otherwise reproduces the second edition unchanged.

47 Hanson (1995) combined his agrarian and military interests and hypothesized that the rules of hoplite warfare originated in Greek border wars of the Archaic period; on Western civic militarism, see also Hanson and Strauss 1999, where an idealized view of American Minutemen in 1775 seems tacitly to underlie the picture of Greek hoplites.

single bloody face-to-face clash annihilating the opponent—hence Hanson's "Western way of war."

Hanson subsequently assembled a group of scholars to further explore the fruits of his labors. The ensuing anthology with many useful papers investigated various aspects of hoplite battle without the other contributors explicitly endorsing Hanson's views and one paper (embarrassingly) argued against the expected "party line."[48] Enthusiasm for an ancient face-of-battle prompted a "day school" at the University of Wales, Swansea in 1993. Coverage was expanded beyond Classical Greece to New Kingdom Egypt, Homer, Alexander the Great, and the Romans with varying results. The Keegan-Hanson model was adaptable to other periods, if its assumptions were accepted. Culling the sources for evidence to produce the desired picture could become a bit formulaic.[49]

A further development in the face-of-battle school came in the Oxford D.Phil. thesis of Adrian Goldsworthy, whose analysis of the tactics of the cohortal legion attempted to convert the Keegan-Hanson model into a method. Blindly accepting the views of Ardant du Picq and "buddy theory," he further endorsed the controversial assessment of American combat participation in World War II of S. L. A. Marshall, which Keegan had wisely shunned. Marshall's arguments that only 25% of American soldiers in combat actually fired their weapons became a key component in Goldsworthy's reconstruction of Roman battle. Further, philological analysis of technical passages was ignored and his own assumptions of what Roman battle tactics had to be based on face-of-battle theory led to playing fast and loose with the ancient evidence—rejecting what did not fit the model and inventing imaginative scenarios.[50] The face-of-battle school gained additional exposure when Keegan selected his two ancient disciples to author Greek and Roman volumes in his *History of Warfare* series for Cassell.[51]

The face-of-battle school has recently advanced but in diverging directions: one toward war-gaming and another toward the campaign, as opposed to the battle, experience. Philip Sabin, a modern military

---

48 Hanson 1991a; Wheeler 1991.
49 Lloyd 1996a; note particularly Lloyd's paper (1996b).
50 Goldsworthy 1996; Marshall 1947; see Wheeler 1998a for criticisms of Goldsworthy's method.
51 Hanson 1999a; Goldsworthy 2000.

historian, has attempted to expand the "generic" ancient battles of Hanson and Goldsworthy into the ultimate ancient war-game. From a database drawn from all ancient battles but ignoring topographical issues of specific battle sites, he proposes to overcome discrepancies in the sources to arrive at a "best fit" model for resolving problems and gaps in the evidence. His result is a more radical use of *Sachkritik* than even Delbrück's and a disregard of historical methodology. "Source exegesis" is shunned in favor of his own assumptions of assigning numerical values to units represented by game counters, not to mention by-passing the basic philological problems of what technical terms in Greek or Latin actually mean and interpretation at a basic grammatical level of what passages of ancient texts really say.[52] Translations in Loeb and Penguin editions of the sources are inadequate for answers to many technical tactical questions.

In contrast stands a meticulous reconstruction of daily life among the Ten Thousand of Xenophon's *Anabasis*, which could represent (depending upon one's viewpoint) the ultimate study of the Greek (non-battle) military experience, or tedious speculations about the trivia of daily life.[53] Here "buddy theory" is accepted to create Xenophon's mercenaries as a conglomerate of *syskenai* (small groups of messmates), the existence of which is often a matter of theorizing from an assumed model (as the author concedes), rather than explicit and frequent attestation of such groupings in Xenophon's text. The real target, however, is Donald Engels' mechanical model (bordering on mono-causality) of Alexander the Great's logistics, which took no account of small groups.[54]

The salutary effect of the face-of-battle school has been to legitimize the study of warfare in History and Classics Departments and to make students and instructors think about the realities of combat and the role of war in ancient societies at the level of the individual. Whither the

---

52   See Sabin 2000 (unconvincing in my view); idem 2007a, 399-433; idem 2007b. Sabin (2007a and his polemics in idem 2007b) responded to criticisms of the face-of-battle school at Wheeler 2001, where Goldsworthy's 1996 views of missile weapons are demolished. The absurdity of some arguments, less temperate in Sabin 2007b than in the *CHGRW* piece, call for a detailed rebuttal elsewhere.

53   J.W.I. Lee 2007; cf. Brennan 2008 for some possible corrections to Lee.

54   Engels 1978; for criticisms of Engels, whose book enjoys more reverence among Anglophones than non-Anglophones, see J.W.I. Lee 2007, 7, 8 n.33; Sabin 2007b, xiv; Badian 1979, 54, 56; Hammond 1983, 27-31; and Seibert 1986; note also Lazenby 1994.

face-of-battle school in the future is anyone's guess, except for further imitations of the model.[55] Hanson applied this method to a study of the Peloponnesian War as a whole, even adding a face of naval battle, with all sorts of interesting statistics.[56] If investigation of the individual's experience in battle is undoubtedly a legitimate research topic, the basic assumptions underlying the Keegan-Hanson-Goldsworthy approach, not to mention some of their excesses, merit comment (however brief), if only to clarify problems for *tirones* to military studies. Some age-old issues in military history detract from the purported novelty of this approach.

5. MORALE AND DISCIPLINE

In the tradition of Ardant du Picq, the face-of-battle school stresses the importance of the individual soldier's morale in unit cohesion and combat motivation, in contrast to a supposed "automaton" view of battle in which soldiers perform like robots. Yet Ardant du Picq was neither terribly original in his views nor a writer *sine ira et studio*. He belonged to a clique of French officers opposing reforms (1867) to convert a relatively small professional army into a massive force of conscripts on the Prussian model. He hoped to demonstrate how a small army, properly trained and motivated, could defeat a large army. His stress on efficiency and morale at the regimental level reflected the smaller combat units, with which he was personally familiar. Ardant du Picq's morale (the will to win) as the key to victory was derived from earlier theorists and ultimately Xenophon.[57] He assembled a useful collection of material on morale in battle (largely derived from earlier French writers) as a tract of contemporary propaganda. His work must be consulted with caution and awareness of his political purpose as well as his historical context. What he wrote should not be taken as gospel.[58]

---

55 See, e.g., Daly 2002; but cf. Lenski 2007, who avoids many of the pitfalls of blind imitation of the face-of-battle school.

56 Hanson 2005; for evaluations see Flory 2006; Holoka 2006; and Wheeler 2006; in the naval genre also see Strauss 2000.

57 Xen. *Anab.* 3.1.42, *Cyr.* 3.3.14; I summarize here, as at Wheeler 2001, 172-73, from research for a monograph on the historiography of the ancient face of battle; Ardant du Picq's predecessors on morale included Marshal Marmont, *D'ésprit des institutions militaires* (1845), Maurice de Saxe, *Mes rêveries* (1732), and Henry Lloyd, *Mémoires militaires* (1781), Roger Spiller has in progress a new study of Ardant du Picq.

58 In teaching my own "face of battle" course, I always have students read Ardant du Picq before exposing them to Keegan, Hanson, or Goldsworthy.

Indeed the larger issue was the superiority of willing obedience to compulsory obedience, not morale vs. discipline, complementary principles. Morale and discipline in face-of-battle studies often emerge (falsely) as an either-or dichotomy, but neither of these principles can succeed without some degree of the other. After all, theoretically, discipline and drill function to so routinize military tasks that their performance in battle overcomes the innate elements of human fear and desire for self-preservation. Again, the debate is ancient, attested in Xenophon and Aristotle.[59]

As the face-of-battlers' colossus, Ardant du Picq, turns out to have feet of clay, Keegan's contrast of Caesar's legionary automata with Thucydides' supposed more realistic depiction of individuals in battle may also be queried.[60] Caesar's legionary automata would, given face-of-battle assumptions, suggest no role for morale in Caesar's accounts of battle. Similarly, face-of-battlers disdain the ancient military theorists, especially the drillbooks, as irrelevant to actual practice. Besides, such writers' depictions of "automata" represent heresy to face-of-battle doctrine.[61] Yet Caesar and Vegetius both stressed morale and combat motivation—Caesar in fact perhaps more than any other ancient writer.[62] A supposed conflict between morale and alleged automata on the battlefield is a chimera. As noted, the real issue is willing vs. compulsory obedience, although a distinction between a Greek stress on tactics and stratagems and a Roman emphasis on *virtus* and discipline may also be too sharp.[63] Caesar, after all, had read

---

59   References in Xenophon collected at Wheeler 1991, 155 n.15; cf. Arist. *Eth.Nic.* 3.8; on Greek views of military discipline, much laxer than the modern concept of "discipline" suggests, see Bettalli 2002, 107-21; Couvenhes 2005, 431-54; Lendon 2005, 72-77; Christ 2006, 45-124.

60   Keegan 1976, 65-67; cf. Kagan's critique: 2006, 182-89. Keegan later abandoned his critique of Caesar (1993, 269), as noted by Campbell 2002, 47 with n.6.

61   Hanson 1989, 11-12, 47-48; Goldsworthy 1996, 10-11; cf. Pritchett 1971-91, 1, 150 n.35, 153-54; on the validity of the theorists (e.g., Asclepiodotus, Aelianus Tacticus, Arrian, Vegetius), see Wheeler 1991, 167 n.135; idem 2004b, 129-30; cf. Sekunda 2001a.

62   References in Wheeler 2001, 170 n.6; Lendon 1999, 296, 303.

63   Lendon 1999, 273-79; idem 2005, 163-260; rejected by McDonnell (2006b, 308) whose own dichotomy of *virtus* for *gregarii milites* and stratagems for generals may also be too rigid, as acts of military trickery need not be the sole prerogative of commanders; note also Kagan (2006, 217 n.139, 112, 223 n.55, 113) on Lendon's *literary* analysis of Roman battle.

Xenophon, who preached that morale (men's souls) wins battles.[64] Greeks were hardly unaware of the significance of morale. Further, modern face-of-battle historians ignore the fashion for "tragic history" in Hellenistic and subsequently Roman historians with their emphasis on anecdotes of dramatic events and personal suffering or heroism. "Tragic history" certainly must color extant accounts of individuals in ancient battles.

Like willing vs. compulsory obedience, combat motivation and unit cohesion are eternal problems for armies. Hanson's innovative application of post-World-War II "buddy theory" to the hoplite phalanx assumes a "universal soldier," dealing with fear and death regardless of the technological character of his weapons and the conditions of combat. The view has its problems.[65] Infantry combat in small groups (a nineteenth-century development), as opposed to lengthy continuous lines of troops or deep columns, reacted to the increased lethality of firepower and defenders' more sophisticated field fortifications. The cohesion of modern small groups thus became vital to performance.

A theoretical debate about "shock" anticipated this development: does the collision of attackers with defenders actually occur? Alternatively, did either the attackers give up the assault and retreat, or the defenders flee their positions before contact? Was battle really a game of 'chicken'? From eighteenth-century theoretical debates on these issues Ardant du Picq favored the view that shock was a myth: the side with the greater morale or will to victory would win. Ancient examples illustrate the phenomenon, particularly Sparta's "tearless battle" against the Arcadians and Argives (368), when Sparta's opponents fled the field before contact.[66]

---

64 Xen. *Anab.* 3.1.42, *Cyr.* 3.3.14; cf. Polyb. fr. 58 Buethner-Wobst; Lendon 1999, 290-95; for Roman tactics and theory as a continuation (not a contradiction) of the Greek, see Wheeler 2004a, 323-58.

65 Goldsworthy's (1996) application to the Roman cohortal legion of Marshall's view (1947) that 75% of American soldiers in World War II combat were too scared to fire their weapons can be dismissed immediately: see Spiller's rebuttal (1988), followed by Wheeler 2001, 173; cf. Sidebottom 2004, 90-91 (unaware of Spiller and Wheeler 2001); cf. Engen 2009.

66 Xen. *Hell.* 7.1.28-32; Plut. *Ages.* 33.3. Panic, the sudden loss of confidence and disinte-gration of an army or an individual unit from a surprise attack or for totally irrational reasons, is related to, but not identical with, the issue of shock, in which the element of surprise is lacking; Hanson (1989, 160-61) questionably lumps these phenomena together; the only study of panic in ancient armies (by no means a comprehensive treatment) remains Wheeler 1988b.

Yet ancient battles between armies of states involved organized mass formations in close combat; hand-to-hand fighting was a reality. Indeed the face-of-battlers' excessive emphasis on the *individual* in combat seems to forget that battle is a *group* activity. Does the unit cohesion and psychology of the modern small combat group really apply to the mass formation of a phalanx? If the small groups were important for the phalanx's overall morale and cohesion—and phalanges were composites of smaller tactical units, as known at Sparta and Athens—identification of these small groups as components of the phalanx's cohesion ("the buddy group") are problematic.[67] Hanson does not argue this cohesive function for attested smaller units (e.g., tribe, *taxis*, *enomotia,* etc.), but relying on anecdotal examples suggests that friends, neighbors, and kinsmen surrounded the hoplite in a phalanx.[68] But the phalanx's building block was the file, not the rank. A friend or relative would more likely be in front or behind a hoplite rather than beside him. Hanson's scenario best fits Sparta, where the messmates of multiple *syssitia* combined to form an *enomotia* deployable in three to six files.[69] Less clear is the Athenian phalanx, as the Cleisthenic tribes, the basis of army organization, combined demes from different geographical areas of Attica. The aim of Cleisthenes' reform in breaking up the regionalism and clan connections in political organization would have had the same effect on the regionalism of tribal units for the army. Recent debate on the character of Athens as a face-to-face society—whether Athenians generally knew each other on the model of a village community—would also apply to the army, and the naysayers in this debate may have the stronger case.[70]

Of course the face-of-battlers can always evoke the argument from human nature for the universal soldier—explicit in Hanson and Sabin,

---

67   The same problem of whether the *gregarius miles'* chief identity lay with the *contu-bernium*, the *centurio*, or the *legio* confronts Romanists of the "legion as society" persuasion. The evidence is not clear, but see Lendon 2004, 443-46, and chapter three below; cf. J.W.I. Lee's conjectures (2007) about *syskenai* in Xenophon's *Anabasis*.

68   Hanson 1989, 89-95, 121-24.

69   On the organization of the phalanx and assigned places for individuals, see Wheeler 2007a, 206-207; cf. Christ 2006, 98; only Lazenby (1985, 13) doubts a connection between the *syssitia* and an *enomotia*.

70   Naysayers: E. Cohen 2000, 104-29, followed by Christ 2006, 99 with n.26; pro: D. Cohen 2002, vii-viii; the Theban Sacred Band was not quite the unit of lovers usually conceived, if Leitao (2002) is correct (but he probably is not).

and harkening back to Ardant du Picq and Thucydides.[71] An unchanging human nature would justify application of not only "buddy theory" to the hoplite phalanx, but also *comparanda* from any era to fill gaps in ancient evidence.[72] Hanson's mosaic of hoplite battle from scattered *tesserae* of evidence dating from the eighth century to the Hellenistic period, elaborated with imaginative reconstructions, corresponds to no known hoplite battle. Tolstoy's comparison of the novelist with the battle historian is apropos. Assembling scattered evidence from different epochs to form a composite of practice recalls a common method of social history, but (from one perspective) every battle is a unique event. However universal the human animal may be in his/her instinct for self-preservation and experiencing fear, circumstances, motivation, and other factors were not identical and constant.

The anthropological underpinnings of the face-of-battle's universal soldier with Hanson's presentation of hoplite battle as a distinct facet of Greek culture and his doctrine of decisive battle as a Greek contribution to Western Civilization spurred Keegan's adventurous anthropological analysis of warfare, *A History of Warfare* (1993). Here culture served as a foil to Clausewitz's dictum of war as a continuation of politics. Hanson's *Carnage and Culture* (2001) followed—a world-historical exposition of his 1989 doctrine of Greek decisive battle in Western Civilization. An appeal to culture, however, opened a Pandora's box of interpretative possibilities. The universal soldier was not an unalterable monolith. Culture denotes change and specificity. John Lynn produced in 2003 a thoughtful exposition of change and the universal soldier, as well as an attack on the idea of any single Western way of war: continuity and transmission of Hanson's doctrine of decisive battle in Western practice was a fantasy. Indeed the fallacy of the uniqueness of a Western concept of decisive battle had been asserted in 1990.[73]

---

71 Hanson 2010, 2-4; Sabin 2007a, 401; Ardant du Picq 1987, 65-66; Thuc. 1.22.4, 3.82.2; Sartre (2007, 625) attributes the "human nature" argument to Eckstein (2006a); cf. Quillen 2009.

72 E.g., Couvenhes' rejection (2005, 431) of Tritle's *From Melos to Mylai* (2000). Cf. Jonathan Shay's (1994) use of ancient warfare to highlight the issue of Post-Traumatic Stress Disorder among modern veterans. On PTSD see Young 1995. *Editor's note*: cf. chapter one n. 201 and the *DSM*-IV of the American Psychiatric Association.

73 Lynn 2003, esp. xiii-xxv, 1-27; cf. Lynn 2009; and Wheeler 1990. On the non-existence of a Western way of war see now Heuser (2010).

Nevertheless, an emphasis on a single pitched battle as a Greek phenomenon bequeathed to Western Civilization is also questionable.[74] The chief tactical and strategic doctrine of Greek and Roman military thought was not battle, but avoidance of battle, if possible; Greek and Roman theorists stressed trickery and the superiority of brains to brawn in generalship—the doctrine of stratagem. The face-of-battlers' rejection or marginalization of the stratagem collections of Frontinus and Polyaenus and even Vegetius, who incorporated stratagemic doctrine in his compendium of ancient military theory, is studied.

The Western-way-of-war perspective also misrepresents the Classical military heritage in another way. A dichotomy of Western battle and blood bravely shed vs. an Eastern reliance on avoiding battle and trickery will not withstand scrutiny.[75] The Chinese military treatise attributed to Sun Tzu (fourth century BC?) may represent a theoretical preference for trickery and deception, but such does not negate large Chinese armies and bloody battles in the so-called Warring States period (403-221). A tension exists—universally—in military ethics between open face-to-face confrontation in battle and obtaining one's goals without battle or at minimal risk or loss through trickery, deceit, and surprise (subsets of stratagem). These alternatives have been characterized as the Achilles ethos and the Odysseus ethos.[76] Use of one method or the other cannot be simplistically reduced to a zero-sum game for any single epoch, war, ethnicity, or individual commander, although some periods, peoples, and generals are more noted for stratagems than others.[77] If the Achilles ethos may often appear the Western preference in practice before Clausewitz, Western military theory essentially remained grounded in the Graeco-Roman tradition of military thought. A strong Western literary and theoretical tradition

---

74 The charge that a Western way of war has become an ideology was raised in an atmosphere of public discourse portraying a preemptive American war in Iraq as a defense of Western values and civilization: Sidebottom 2004, x, xiii, 7, 115-24, 126-28; Hanson 2010, esp. 107-112.

75 The Western-way-of-war perspective ignores or marginalizes evidence from the Near East; see chapter one.

76 Wheeler 1988a and, for a world-historical perspective, idem 1993; the genre of the stratagem collection is discussed at Wheeler 1994, views now updated at Wheeler 2010a, 19-36; note also the Lyon acta, H. Olivier et al. 2006, although the contributors, unaware of much bibliography, often forego active engagement with the published work they do cite.

77 Sabin's position (2007b, 29, 262 n.3) is self-contradictory: endorsing the Western-way-war perspective and simultaneously conceding the Achilles-Odysseus tension.

of trickery and the superiority of brains over brawn undercuts the Western-way-of-war's emphasis on battle and bloodshed.[78] An apparently widespread perception among some Anglophone ancient historians that the face-of-battlers have received no criticism and that everyone is riding the Keegan-Hanson bandwagon is certainly false.[79] Military history is a field in ferment and flux, as a scholarly discipline should be, with critical examination of trends.[80]

6. HISTORY AND MEMORY

A new trend, now gaining attention in Continental Europe but little known among Anglophones, merits note as an addendum to the face-of-battle perspective. In some ways it straddles both the war-and-society and the face-of-battle schools and likewise has its roots in not only *Annaliste* thought but also (to some extent) in critical analysis of battle narratives. As noted earlier, Thucydides and Tolstoy realized the difficulty of recounting precisely what happens in battle—also Keegan's query at the beginning of his *Face of Battle*.[81] Detailed historical knowledge of battles depends on physical aspects (e.g., site of the battle, including any relevant topographical landmarks, remnants of equipment and weapons, burials of the slain, etc.) and the memories of the participants, often known only through later documentary sources or historians' narratives, sometimes—but for Antiquity not always—contemporary. Hence any attempt to reconstruct battles must confront the history vs. memory quandary at a cognitive step earlier than issues

---

78 Note Lendon's assertion (2005, 169) that a modern Western perception of Roman discipline dates to Machiavelli's *Arte della Guerra* (1521), a plank in his view of Roman *virtus* (in some ways his version of the Achilles ethos), but Machiavelli extensively borrowed stratagems from Frontinus in the same treatise.

79 E.g., Sidebottom 2004; J.W.I. Lee 2005; Kagan 2006.

80 See Wilson's criticisms (2008) of the face-of-battle approach, the Western-way-of-war advocates, and the war-and-society school among others, although as an Early Modernist his views are less directly relevant to Antiquity; note also the penetrating criticisms of Black (2004a and b), who is particularly skeptical of the technological determinists. Most recently on the problems with technological determism in ancient history see Rey 2010. Gat's recent lengthy universal history of war (2006) displays a very limited scholarly gaze of Graeco-Roman material, a flaw corresponding to his gross underestimation of the influence of Greek and Roman military texts in his survey (1989) of eighteenth- and early-nineteenth-century military thinkers.

81 Tolstoy 1966, 1368-71. The issue is also raised by Whatley (1964, 120-21=Wheeler 2007b, 302-303), originally a post-World War I (1920) Oxonian response to Delbrück, which in the end agreed with him in many ways: see Wheeler 2007b, 1.

of narrative technique in an historian's use of rhetoric or principles of military theory.[82]

The history-memory problem for military studies may be better known for modern history: the accuracy of Paul Fussell's study of memory and World War I provoked a response from more traditional historians of that conflict.[83] A recent experimental anthology attempts to study the effects of "distortion from hindsight" (*Rückschauverzerrung*), the projection into the past of present (i.e., later) knowledge, a principle relevant to psychology and law (e.g., definition of negligence: should an act have been foreseen?).[84] Did survivors of battles or even the commanders really remember accurately what they later thought happened, issues of self-justification or defense of their own acts notwithstanding? In view of the paucity of detailed contemporary sources for ancient battles, one wonders if it is really possible to "fine tune" what survives to the extent this approach requires without innumerable conjectures.

More significantly, the *Annaliste* Georges Duby's 1973 study of the Battle of Bouvines in the French perception of their history[85] has prompted a new genre studying "battle myths" (*Schlachtenmythen*). Here stress is placed upon post-eventum interpretations of battle: the defeat of greater numbers to heroize the victors, stimulation of national feelings through perception of the enemy as outsiders, memory of the slain as a paradigm for later generations, war memorials as a visual means to aid identification with the battle, and the charisma of the winning general(s). Marathon, the first Greek battle offering the possibility of reconstruction—largely from Herodotus' detailed, if problematic account—has become a prime target of this approach.[86] In the current academic climate, in which heroes are out of fashion, this approach eagerly tends to find "myths" and later political

---

82   Cf. Lendon 1999, 279-81; Whitby 2007b, 61-62.
83   Fussell 1975; Prior and Wilson 1994.
84   Brodersen 2008.
85   Duby 1973.
86   See Krumeich and Brandt 2003; Krieger 2005; on Marathon most useful are Flasher 1996 and Jung 2006. Marathon in the Western military tradition is studied at Wheeler, forthcoming, where Marathon and the genre of *Schlachtenmythen* are discussed in more detail with additional bibliography. Two anniversary volumes (2500 years since Marathon), Billows (2010) and Krentz (2010), either rehearse traditional views of the battle for a general audience (Billows) in the tradition of Creasy's "decisive battles" (1851), or make a valiant attempt to salvage Herodotus' account (Krentz, aware of Jung but not addressing his arguments).

manipulations of the tradition at every turn—not always convincingly. From the perspective of the *Schlachtenmythen* school, essentially no ancient battle can be accurately reconstructed; all accounts are "myths" in one way or another.[87] The techniques of battle narrative also raise doubts about the value of literary sources for reconstructing battles. Gerlinger's dissertation, although focused on Sallust, Caesar, and Tacitus, posits the influence of Homer and epic poetry on battle narratives—hence Greek historiography potentially could also be contaminated—in producing conventions of *Schlachtenrhetorik*, e.g., exaggerated enemy casualties and the heroic speed of the commander/hero of the narrative. Writing in the tradition of Rambaud and others on Caesar's distortion of his generalship and his campaigns for his own self-promotion, Gerlinger sees not falsifications but exaggerations that an ancient reader expected and would understand as such. Unfortunately, Gerlinger's own bibliographical myopia and superficial knowledge of ancient military history undercut his work, which offers as many misses as hits at the target.[88]

Bichler's exercise in *histoire éventuelle*, part of a larger project on the narrative structure of battle reports and the limits on reconstruction of factual events, raises all the methodological issues that war-gamers do not want to hear: justification in cases of conflicting sources for preferring one source over another; the rational method to be employed in reducing grossly exaggerated numbers of participants, thus affecting the perception of where a king or commander actually stood on the battle-line or the length of battle-lines; the limited perspectives of sources (e.g., Thucydides on Mantinea, Caesar on Pharsalus) that focus on one sector of the battle and ignore what happened elsewhere, not to mention the opponent's view of the battle at various stages and in different parts of the field.[89] Despite valid criticisms of method, the desired goal remains unclear. The desideratum is not expressly the face-of-battle approach but a sort of combination of facts and experience, a totality of minutiae impossible to achieve in the paucity of the sources

---

87 See Richardson's observation (chapter one, above) on similar issues in the military history of the ANE.
88 Gerlinger 2008; Rambaud 1953. The supposed credulity of Lendon (1999 and 2005) and Goldsworthy in use of Caesar marks Gerlinger's point of departure, although he naively (and in self-contradiction?) takes Goldsworthy 1996 as the benchmark of the truth about Roman practice.
89 Bichler 2009.

for ancient battles and beyond management in the vast volume of data available for modern battles. In some ways this exercise in *histoire éventuelle* reopens old arguments about what history (of any event, military or otherwise) can be, since everything from every perspective at a single moment of time for even a single event cannot be known.

In any case, the new issues of battle myths, battle rhetoric, and criticisms of method in recounting complex events like battles, even if somewhat flawed, cast further doubt on the accuracy of attempts to reconstruct ancient battles. Yet new interpretations need not be based on novel approaches or methodologies. Old-fashioned reading and analysis of texts can also produce intriguing results, as in a recent paper questioning the so-called "defensive strategy" of Pericles, which (as argued) is really Thucydides' post-war invention.[90]

Hatters? Hares? Which way should Alice go? Greek military affairs must now be approached from a different direction.

7. WAR, PEACE, AND REVISIONISM

Hares feast on revisionism, although Hatters also partake of its delights. Neither monopolizes new interpretations. For Archaic and Classical Greece a recent trend takes a rather cynical view of Greek warfare, finding chiefly destruction and profits (honor as a pretext for gain) in conflicts without rules and restraints. A new universal Greek warrior emerges, whose mentality remained unchanged between Homer and Xenophon in one view or as late as Aristotle in another.[91] Accordingly, combat in Homer is taken literally and historically; the introduction of hoplite armor had no repercussions tactically or politically, as Greeks fought in a phalanx lacking any real organization before the fifth century and even then preserved a loose, open order rather than the closed mass usually perceived as a phalanx. Hence increased military participation by citizens lacks any political ramifications; rather, state formation (c.550-c.450) becomes more significant in spawning military and naval changes than either the Persian Wars or the Peloponnesian War. In fact, war itself ceases to be an agent of change. Yet almost in contradiction to the general tenor of these views, peace, not war, is conceived as the norm of Greek civilization.

---

90   Schubert and Laspe 2009.
91   Xenophon: Krentz 2000, 177; Aristotle: van Wees 2004, 2; a brief review of van Wees 2004 at Wheeler 2005.

This interpretation of Greek warfare seeks to overthrow many traditional interpretations and reacts to Hanson's various contentions about middle-class hoplites and agriculture; it owes much to the social-structures orientation of the war-and-society school.[92] Such views, if convincing, would mark a major reversal of the conventional wisdom, but much is problematic methodologically as well as conceptually. The implications of these views—not considered in detail by their advocates—not only render the Macedonian phalanx a much greater tactical change from an alleged "open" phalanx than previously realized, but also create a greater chasm between the Classical and Hellenistic period than seems credible.

Hans van Wees' *Greek Warfare: Myths and Realities*, although not a comprehensive study of Greek warfare, synthesizes this revisionism, summarizing numerous scattered papers and following the lead of Peter Krentz, long an advocate of the "open" hoplite phalanx.[93] Van Wees continues the discussion of his Homeric *Status Warriors* and draws inspiration from the Marxist flavored structural-anthropological approach of Garlan, although rejecting any elements of ritualization.[94] A *status quaestionis* on Homeric warfare, the development of the hoplite phalanx, and the arguments for an "open" phalanx have been offered recently elsewhere and need not be rehearsed here.[95] Discussion will be

---

92 According to Sidebottom (2004, 52) revision of the traditional view of the "hoplite revolution" belonged to a rejection in the 1970s and 1980s of a social-determinist and especially Marxist theories of historical change. He seems not to grasp that the war-and-society school often perpetuates the influence of these approaches.

93 Van Wees 2004; Krentz 1985a; idem 2002; idem 2007; cf. Rawlings 2007; idem 2009, where little new can be found; Rawlings essentially never disagrees with van Wees.

94 Van Wees 1992; Garlan 1972; idem 1975; rebuttals of van Wees' views of Homeric warfare can be found in Udwin 1999; Hellmann 2000; collected at Wheeler 2007a, 193-95. Van Wees' identification of his view of the style of Homeric combat with the pre-state combat of a New Guinea tribe (2004, 154-58), rejected by Schwartz (2009, 15, 113-15), even finds some supporters: Sidebottom 2004, 40; Lonsdale 2007, 31 with n.45; Wenger's (2008a-b) bibliographical gaze appears quite limited. Curiously, no advocates of this anthropological *comparandum* claim that the Homeric heroes and the New Guinea warriors share the same or a comparable level of societal development; the comparison is strictly tactical. LeBlanc (2003) finds (personal communication 26 February 2010) comparison of New Guinea and Homeric warfare ludicrous.

95 For an extended recent discussion of work on the emergence of the phalanx, Wheeler 2007a, 192-202, 206-12; idem 2007b, xxx-xxxiv. To those discussions should now be added Schwartz (2002, 2009) and Matthew 2009. Schwartz (esp. 2009), accepting Hanson's arguments (1991b) of technological determinism for the significance of the hoplite shield, and drawing on the phalangical tactics of contemporary Danish riot police, offers a point-by-point rebuttal of van Wees' view of an "open" phalanx, although

limited to rules of warfare, peace, international law, domestic military affairs, and war and the economy, before turning to the Hellenistic period.

RULES OF WARFARE

The cynical (if not presentist) views that a doctrine of "all's fair" governed Greek warfare and that concepts of limited warfare have never existed are methodologically flawed and betray an historical myopia.[96] Not all wars aim at total defeat and destruction of the enemy. The homogenization of warfare between Homer and some point in the fourth century, besides positing a universal Greek soldier for more than three centuries, leads to indiscriminate citation of evidence: Homer, for example, is cited as illustrative of fifth- or fourth-century events to demonstrate a supposed continuity of practices and attitudes. The method reflects anthropological universals, not historical specificity or proper consideration of the context of events. On the traditional interpretation, rules of warfare and inter-state conduct existed, but began to be bent, broken, or ignored in the fifth century, especially during the Peloponnesian War.[97] For the revisionists, however, violations of the traditionalists' "rules" in the fifth and fourth centuries indicate the absence of rules or a sudden imposition *ex nihilo* of a scheme of generally acknowledged but unwritten rules in the fifth century at some point before 431, but then broken repeatedly. Ober's rather superficial paper of 1994 is somehow taken as the definitive study of Greek rules

---

he also advocates a fully developed phalanx in Homer and no changes in Greek tactics c.750-338. Schwartz overlooks the *CHGRW* and much other Anglophone scholarship. Matthew, unware of Schwartz 2002 and sharing Schwartz's bibliographical myopia, endeavors (unconvincingly) to resolve the controversy of "the push" (*othismos*) in hoplite battles. His mix of Homer and Tyrtaeus with the Hellenistic tactical manuals on the Macedonian phalanx and a firm belief in the validity of re-enactments raise innumerable methodological and conceptual objections that would require a separate paper to correct. Note also the recent discussion of hoplite battle by Bettalli 2009.

96   The recent (unconvincing) study of Dayton 2006 (abbreviated and recycled with the same title at 2003) rejects the Greek concept of war as *agon* as a modern scholarly myth. His captious assault on the Vernant school and a constant mixing of apples and oranges in a muddled and perverse discussion of fruit cannot be taken seriously. A detailed refutation must be pursued elsewhere (cf. an initial salvo at Wheeler 2009, 418). Greek love of competition and the "element of play" in Western Civilization are not so easily discarded; on "play" see Huizinga 1950.

97   De Romilly 1968; cf. Raaflaub 2004, 67-73: a survey of archaic Greece warfare showing its limited character with only occasional destruction of cities.

of war, although both Ober and his critics ignore earlier bibliography.[98] As Ober posited several "rules" not explicitly attested as such in the sources, some of the revisionists' attacks represent "fair play."[99] On the other hand, as the contending parties agree that the rules were repeatedly broken in the fifth and fourth centuries, the revisionists' citation of such "violations" as proving their case is meaningless.

Less forgivable, however, are indiscriminate citations irrelevant to the case being argued, such as the revisionists' claim of no rules (except possibly for Spartans) prohibiting pursuit of a defeated enemy after a pitched battle beyond the battlefield, and the assertion that such pursuit could extend to the defended party's city. The rule applies to formal pitched battles between large forces, but the revisionists, ignoring the specific context, obfuscate the issue through citation of *any* military action. Sieges, surprise attacks, minor skirmishes are regarded the same as major battles.[100] Nor do the revisionists distinguish military behavior in civil war (*stasis*), by definition a legal anomaly, in which rules may or may not be applied, from inter-state conflict (*polemos*). This homogenization of all military action echoes the recent trend (noted earlier) to regard all violence as war.

Yet larger issues lurk. Before the creation of written international law, of which rules of warfare are a subset, customary practices determined conventions and norms of conduct. Much so-called international law initially only codified in writing customary practices. Historically, war has been a normative phenomenon, which circumscribed its violence

---

98   Ober 1994, recycled at 1996 and 1999 (in French); earlier bibliography collected at Wheeler 2007b, xlii n.90, 42 n.100; cf. the criticism of Ober by Ducrey (1999a, 19-21), who prefers Lonis 1969, even if not systematic and quantified; Gabrielsen (2007, 249) waffles on the existence of rules.

99   E.g., Krentz (2002, 27) justly rebuts Ober's contention (1994, 13) on the immunity of civilians from attack; cf. Kulesza 1999.

100 E.g., Dayton 2006, 74-75 (following Krentz 2002) on pursuit beyond the battlefield: Xen. *Hell.* 4.3.19 and *Ages.* 2.12 do not prove Spartan pursuit beyond the battlefield of Coronea, nor does Xen. *Hiero* 2.15.16 explicitly indicate ultra-battlefield pursuit; all other examples refer to fifth- or fourth century events, except Tyrt. fr. 23a.20-23 and Diod. 12.10.1. The Tyrtaus passage, too vague and fragmentary to permit an argument, involves pre-agonal battle in any case; for Diodorus on Sybaris vs. Croton *in southern Italy*, it is only assumed that agonal rules of the Greek mainland applied; van Wees (2004, 287 n.18) for pursuit after a pitched battle to the defeated city cites Hdt. 3.55 (Spartan siege of Samos—no field battle involved) and Xen. *Hell.* 4.7.6: neither—and certainly not a siege—is a formal pitched field battle; cf. 2004, 124-25, where the examples from wars between Greeks and wars with barbarians are not distinguished; intra-cultural and inter-cultural conflicts are not the same.

with rules particularly in intra-cultural conflicts, although restraints on violence could be ignored in inter-cultural conflicts, civil wars, and wars motivated by religion, race, or against supposed "inferiors." Even pre-state societies did not wage war without limits on conduct.[101] The unwritten *nomoi* of the Greeks noted in Thucydides must surely reflect practices developed over centuries rather than a fifth-century innovation, about which the sources are silent. From this perspective a distinction between "protocols" and tactics evaporates, as repeated practices become customary usage.[102] Indeed, employment of the Greek distinction of wars with heralds (and rules) from those without heralds or truces (i.e., without restraints and rules) could resolve the debate about rules.[103]

PEACE

De Romilly's 1968 discussion of Greek international relations (representative of some traditional views) has aroused revisionist reaction in other ways. The literary and epigraphical record clearly shows that Greek treaties often limited peace between poleis to a specific number of years, although other treaties could proclaim peace "forever." In the mutable climate of inter-state relations (whether ancient or modern), unlimited treaty commitments can become inconvenient or even embarrassing under subsequent changed circumstances. Greek treaties limiting the duration of peace may have been simply realistic, but they assume a different hue, if paired with Plato's apparent endorsement (*Leg.* 1.625e-26a) of war as the natural state of humans. The implications of warmongering Greeks interrupted by intervals of peace strike some as too extreme and unsavory: peace, they assert, was

---

101 E.g., Wayne Lee on Amerindians: 2004 and 2007; cf. Reid 2007.
102 Krentz (2002, 27, 31) justly rejects (cf. above) Ober's view that the withdrawal of civilians to a safe haven in the face of invasion was a convention; but such withdrawals would preferably be termed a strategic measure or commonsense rather than a "tactic," technically a term reserved for a battlefield situation. Emphasis (Krentz 2002) on the fifth-century date of the first attested case of a particular practice in extant sources essentially represents an argument from silence in the dearth of literary sources for the seventh and sixth centuries, especially as the sources do not identify fifth-century occurrences as "the first," as if they were new. The problem, for example, of the burial of Athenian war-dead associated with the creation of the *epitaphios* as a *patrios nomos* in 464 is more complex than Krentz believes: see Jung 2006, 61-65.
103 Wheeler 2007a, 189-90; idem 2007b, xliii-xlv; note also for later Greek historians, Stouder 2006. The stratagems, for example, notable in the Athenian-Aeginetan war of the early fifth century occur in a war "without herald"; cf. Krentz 2000.

the norm of Greek civilization. Yet positing the normality of peace sets the Classical era at odds with the Hellenistic world, for which many believe in the prevalence of war.[104] The traditional view permits more continuity between the Classical and Hellenistic eras. Did Greeks of the fourth century fight fewer wars than in the third century? As Garlan noted, Athens was at war on average two of every three years 490-338 and never experienced peace for ten consecutive years.[105] Not all Greek states shared Athenian ambitions and bellicosity. Generalizations about Athens or Greek states collectively may find exceptions in individual poleis. Further, we should ask what ancients meant by "peace." The modern vision of international peace is a relatively recent concept.[106]

If Shipley's Braudelian and Finleyite assertions (not arguments) that Greek warfare can be reduced to social structures, ideology, and profits may be discarded as doctrinaire, van Wees' case for peace as the norm offers more substance. As he correctly demonstrates, Plato's contention of war as the natural state of humankind is an exaggeration posited for later rebuttal. But Plato's pessimism about Greek proclivities to conflict re-emerges in a more thorough and philosophical study, which argues that Plato thought war inevitable and only to be thwarted in his ideal world of philosopher-kings.[107] Indeed the "might is right" and "right of the stronger" attitudes first seen in Hesiod and evident in some sophists, Platonic interlocutors of Socrates, and Thucydides may represent a more pervasive Greek attitude than many would like to concede.[108]

Van Wees' other pro-peace arguments are not so successful. Attributing to Homer's Panhellenes and Panachaeans a fifth- and fourth-century sense of Panhellenism is not credible. Nor can the idea of *koine eirene* in the fourth-century be taken as more than a splendid ideal never realized. Both the *koine eirene* of 387/386 and that of 338

---

104 Peace: Shipley 1993, 1-24, followed by Hornblower 2007, 22 n.4, 27 n.18, 50; van Wees 2004, 3-18; and idem 2007, 273 n.2, 299, followed by Rawlings 2007, 8-9; Hellenistic: Lévêque 1968, 282-87; Baker 2003, 385-86; Chaniotis 2005b, 71, 184; Serrati 2007, 461; cf. Ma 2000, 315-16. Timpe (2002), although bibliographically dated, surveys war's role in the city-state (both Greek and Roman).

105 Garlan 1975, 15; cf. Lévêque 1968, 279 n.108: only the years 299-297, 249-248, 205-204, and 159-149 were devoid of major conflicts in the Hellenistic period.

106 See Howard 2000; a recent comparativist anthology (Raaflaub 2007b) does not greatly enlighten for Graeco-Roman affairs and many papers are more literary than historical; no contributor seems aware of Howard 2000.

107 Van Wees 2004, 4 with nn.5-6; Hobbs 2007.

108 Green (1999) argues that Euripides' *Trojan Women* is not the anti-war drama usually supposed.

were imposed by outside powers: the King's Peace hardly inhibited Greek warfare after 386 and Philip of Macedon's "common peace" merely cloaked Macedonian hegemony. Similarly, an effort to counter the limited duration of peace treaties with details about *symbola*, kinship, alliances, and treaties of friendship (*philia*) obfuscates rather than refutes the literary and epigraphical evidence.[109] No one has ever argued that relations between Greek states were limited to peace treaties, but *only* peace treaties establish a legal condition of peace. Expiration of a peace treaty did not necessarily signal a renewal of active hostilities. The Platonic (or Hobbesian) natural state of war is only a metaphor or a philosophical construct.

INTERNATIONAL LAW

Since the end of the Cold War it hardly surprises to find a renewed interest in ancient inter-state relations, international law, and laws of war. In an age of globalization, human rights have become a recognized basis for international law—in some ways a return to the concept of natural law, increasingly discredited after the eighteenth century in favor of "voluntary" or treaty law. Further, issues of sovereignty and the future of the nation-state arise; the problems of defining terrorism as a war against non-state actors, terrorists as legitimate combatants (*iustus hostis*), and justification for pre-emptive war (*ius ad bellum*) stir public debate. The *Zeitgeist* is at work. Only an impression of this field's new richness can be offered.

General surveys, one for Antiquity as a whole (including the Near East) and another limited to the Greek world, have sprung from the pens of Bederman, a legal scholar, and the well-known Giovannini. In addition, Ilari's study of the concept of law(s) of war through the Hellenistic period assembles a vast array of information and bibliography, even if his interpretations do not always convince.[110] New studies of prisoners of war and their liberation may also (to some degree) reflect contemporary interests.[111]

Traditionally, the very existence of ancient international law has been subject to debate. Legal scholars, many trained in law schools and

---

109 Van Wees 2004, 3-18; idem 2007, 273 n.2, 299.
110 Bederman 2001; Giovannini 2007; Ilari 1980.
111 Ducrey 1999b: revision of the original 1968 edition; Bielman 1994; note also the equation of "private war" in Antiquity with terrorism and war with non-state actors: Zimmermann 2007.

no doubt better lawyers than ancient historians, have often privileged modern concepts and practices in assessing this issue—particularly for a period in which rules represent unwritten customary practices. Too often the views questioning ancient international law stress the problem of enforcement—in many ways a red herring, as enforcement of even contemporary international law is problematic: especially as major powers often observe only those tenets conducive to their own policies and self-interests without significant repercussions for infractions. A more valid criterion for ancient international law would stress a generally recognized (and practiced) common set of procedures and rules of conduct—even though unwritten—within a community of states. Thus inter-cultural conflict, e.g., Greeks vs. Persians, Carthaginians, or other barbarians, becomes intriguing, where in-group norms of one community may or may not be observed. As demonstrated, the unwritten Greek *koinoi nomoi* had validity as a source of law equal to that of treaties.[112]

Regardless of which side may be preferred in the debate about Greek rules of warfare (largely based on literary sources), the treaties preserved on stone readily demonstrate a consistency of vocabulary and concepts of inter-state practice. Greeks, for example, had definite ideas about the legality of territorial conquests and sophisticated means of avoiding a party's circumvention of agreements.[113] Concepts and a mechanism of arbitration for inter-state disputes existed, although in practice arbitration was generally limited to discord between minor powers.[114] A current fascination with orality has stimulated a new discussion of Greek diplomacy and the language of not only diplomacy but also international relations as a whole.[115]

Nevertheless, study of Greek inter-state relations has not escaped controversy and revisionist efforts. Thucydides' emphasis on power politics and Realism naturally upsets the peace advocates; others wonder whether the Thucydidean version of Greek international relations is really definitive. Revenge and *hybris* may play greater

112 Sheets 1994.
113 See Chaniotis 2004, abbreviated and recycled at 2005a; on avoiding circumvention of agreements see Wheeler 1984, now updated (2008) with responses to Gazzano 2005 and Bolmarcich 2007; also note on treaties Baltrusch 1994; Cozzo 2009.
114 Roebuck 2001; see also the corpora of texts: Piccirilli 1973-97; Ager 1996, reviewed from the perspective of international law at Wheeler 1998b.
115 Piccirilli 2002; Cresci et al. 2002; Santi Amantini 2005; Daverio Rocchi 2007.

roles than Thucydides' rational state-actors display.[116] In a highly nuanced study, to which justice cannot be done here, Polly Low also takes aim at Thucydides in rejecting modern theoretical frameworks of international relations, such as Realism, and seeking to understand the theoretical and ethical underpinnings of Greek inter-state relations.[117] Low offers much to ponder and debate. Certainly the exceptional power of the fifth-century Athenian Empire put Athens "above the law" and outside "the system"—a position of arrogance that Thucydides analyses. Nevertheless, Low's attempt to explain why the Greeks produced no treatise on international relations imposes the logical impossibility of proving a negative: why something did not happen, and her minimalizations of individual/state, private/public, and domestic/foreign actions and morality are not compelling.[118]

In contrast to Low, Eckstein affirms the application of such views to the second century.[119] His reassertion of a position long ago advocated by Theodor Mommsen finds the Mediterranean a "tough neighborhood," in which Rome had to play rough to survive in a cutthroat atmosphere of competition for power. Hence Rome's entry into the Eastern Mediterranean world after the Second Punic War did not upset the applecart of a balance of power between Antigonids, Seleucids, and Ptolemies. Certainly Eckstein's Thucydidean Polybius is on target, as is an assessment of Rome within a Mediterranean context, as opposed to a common view of Roman exceptionalism. A denial of international law, however, falls into the presentist trap emphasizing enforcement as the chief criterion for its existence. Polybius clearly indicates that recognized norms of international conduct were frequently ignored. The notion of a Hellenistic balance of power in the Eastern Mediterranean as a conscious policy and aim, a favorite idea of legal scholars, was refuted long ago.[120] Nevertheless, a situation of balance of power often results not from pursuit of a conscious policy,

---

116 See Lendon 2000, 2006, and esp. 2010; cf. Scheid 2005, although unaware of Lendon; peace advocates: above n.104.

117 Low 2007. For an assessment of some recent work on ancient international relations in terms of 'primitivists' versus 'realists', see Lendon 2002, although the characterizations can be curious (for example. Emst Badian as a ('primitivist').

118 Cf. Chaniotis 2005a, 197-201; Ager 2005; Wheeler 2008, 63; Darbo-Peschanski 1994.

119 Eckstein 2006a; cf. 2008; readers pressed for time may find the basic ideas summarized at his 2006b, 577-80; for critical assessments of Eckstein 2006a, see Sartre 2007; Quillen 2009.

120 Sartre (2007, 619-20, 624) chastises Eckstein for his denial of ancient international law; *pro* balance of power: e.g., Klose 1972; *contra*, Schmitt 1974.

but from circumstances, as power-seeking states exhaust their potential for expansion or clash with a state of equal or greater power, for whose overthrow or weakening an opportunity must be awaited. Middling and small powers can exploit conditions of a balance of power between larger states to pursue their own foreign policy objectives.[121]

DOMESTIC MILITARY AFFAIRS

Here Alice's choice between Hatters and Hares presents a true quandary from rampant revisionism on a myriad of topics, such as the role of armed forces in Greek society, the relationship of armed forces to a polis' constitution, the composition and organization of armies, the demographic effects of casualties, and gender issues. Again, much of the revisionism stems from the social-structures orientation of the war-and-society school. Just as Thucydides becomes a favorite target for correction in external affairs, Aristotle (whom scholars used to think was smart) is now argued to be sadly deficient. For these topics, which would merit lengthy detailed discussion in a separate paper, only limited suggestions can aid Alice's choice of paths.

The frequency of Greek wars raises the issue of how so many calls-to-arms affected Greek society. Homer, after all, (and not least the *Iliad*) was the staple of Greek education; an heroic death in battle defending one's city remained an ideal. Although Hanson would make the hoplite battle a central feature of Greek culture, his "Minuteman" hoplites—pragmatic, middle-class farmers—have little time for Homeric values, whereas the war-and-society perspective concedes an ideological role to war, but marginalizes it beside socioeconomic issues. Did Greek cities experience or have a concern for militarism, which the frequency of conflicts might suggest?

Like another problematic term, "imperialism," the word "militarism" is a heritage of the nineteenth century and generally refers to the undue influence of a military establishment on the policy of a state and its society.[122] "Militarism" assumes that the armed forces with a professional officer corps constitute a separate, permanent entity within a state. Greeks lacked professional officers before the changes initiated in the Peloponnesian War as well as standing armies.

---

121 See Koehn 2007, who applies the notion of *Mittelstaat*, current in the concerns of states like Canada and Australia in the founding of the United Nations, to Rhodes and other states in the second century.

122 Vagts 1959; for bibliography see Kohn 2009, 182-83 n.13-19.

No permanent officer corps existed in a Greek state of the Archaic or Classical period, although in the fifth century itinerant drill instructors, the *hoplomachoi*, sought employment and generals for hire made themselves available for offers after 404. Traditionally, Greeks could become professional soldiers in mercenary service outside their home polis and Greek states hired mercenaries as needed.[123] Indeed some argue for a split between the traditional military and political functions of generals during the Peloponnesian War, especially after 413, when commanders often became the focus of their men's loyalty rather than the state—a form of militarism.[124] Debate rages over whether a split of civil from military functions of both generals and citizens occurred in fourth-century Athens.[125] Nevertheless, Greek *poleis*—by necessity—had to be organized to defend themselves and to wage war in the typical hoplite field battle. For Greeks the issue must be not so much militarism from the top, but the extent to which the society as a whole was organized for war and appreciated martial ideals. From one perspective such would not be militarism but militarization, of which the on-set and development can be subtle rather than blatant.[126]

Sparta would seem to offer the best Greek example of a militarized society, for which Pericles' comparison of a liberal, open Athens with a closed militarized Sparta (Thuc. 2.37-39) finds confirmation in Xenophon's *Constitution of the Lacedaemonians.* Nothing is sacred, however, in the scholarly Wonderland of ancient history — Hodkinson now attacks this view of Sparta as a militarized society in a recent volume from the Sparta Seminar series.[127] Dispelling the "Spartan mirage" propagated in Hellenistic and Roman sources to discover

123 On mercenaries, see the recent studies of Bettalli 1995 and Trundle 2004; note also the important discussion of Luraghi 2006, demonstrating the significance of Greek mercenaries in Near Eastern employment already by c.700, although the siege scene on a bowl from Cyprian Amathus (710-675) will not prove a fully developed phalanx at that date (contra, Schwartz 2009, 129-34); on the *hoplomachoi*, see Wheeler 1983; for a case that the Macedonians developed the first officer corps, see Naiden 2007.

124 See Lengauer 1979, 74, 82-95; Boëldieu-Trevet, 2007, 218-66; on the political and civilian functions of Athenian generals see Hamel, 1998. Boëldieu-Trevet's study has the merit of treating both civil and military functions of generals at Athens and Sparta, although she does not actively engage with previous scholarship (e.g., Lengauer 1979; Hamel 1998; Wheeler 1991) despite awareness of it.

125 Civil-military split: e.g., Hansen 1983, 33-55, followed by Lendon, 2007; contra, Burckhardt 1996; Frölich 2008.

126 On the distinction of militarization from militarism see Wilson 2008, 39-41; cf. Kohn 2009.

127 Hodkinson 2006.

the "real Sparta" has long been a *desideratum* and the Sparta Seminar no longer seems (in this volume at least) so doctrinaire in privileging socioeconomic analyses. But has the effort to "normalize" Sparta swung the pendulum too far?

Hodkinson's attempt to de-militarize Sparta is highly problematic. Pericles' view of a militaristic Sparta in Thucydides is not refuted, nor does dancing around the implications of Thuc. 4.80 on the Helots as a cause of internal Spartan policy carry much conviction.[128] Interpretation of Xenophon's *Respublica Lacedaemoniorum* as an anti-Spartan tract rests on the curiously placed criticisms of chapter 14, which invite comparison to the sudden polemic against the Persians at *Cyropaedia* 8.8—spurious, as some think. Denial of a common Doric military organization (currently fashionable) mentions Crete but omits Cyrene, where the tradition of the equestrian *Triakatioi*, a parallel to the Spartan *Hippeis*, continued into the Hellenistic period.[129] Likewise, denials that Spartans drilled their army and subjected their youth to military training rest on rather perverse interpretations of Xenophon and run counter to other evidence. As recently shown from *stelai* at the Spartan sanctuary of Artemis Orthia, Spartan youth daily armed themselves with a small sickle, which they also employed in competitions.[130] No doubt exaggerations and philosophical musings cloud the image of Sparta in the sources, but Laconia should not yet be labeled a demilitarized zone.

As usual, Athens presents the opposite interpretative dilemma: ready acceptance of Pericles' idealized, gloriously liberal Athens in Thucydides' Funeral Oration and convenient amnesia that imperialism financed the marvels of Athens' "Golden Age." In modern eyes negative identification of Sparta with Stalinist Russia or Nazi Germany contrasts with a favorable disposition toward democratic Athens, as if democracies are never bellicose or aggrandizing.[131] The view can scarcely be reconciled with the jingoism and lust for loot when the

---

128 Incredibly, current scholarship tends to accept the historicity of the *krypteia* despite its absence in Herodotus, Thucydides, Xenophon, and Aristotle. A refreshing new view suggests the *krypteia* as a confused interpretation of Spartan guerilla activity after 369 against the newly independent Messenia and Laconian Helot refugees: see Christien 2006, 175-76.

129 Cordiano 2007; the parallel escaped notice in Figueira's otherwise thorough discussion (2006) of the Spartan *Hippeis*.

130 The denial of Spartan drill is also perversely argued (with even less credibility) at Humble 2006; Spartan sickle: Ducat 2007.

131 Hodkinson 2006, 111-13; cf. Robinson 2001.

Athenian expeditionary force departed for Sicily in 415.[132] Similarly, the *hoplomachoi* before the fourth century did a flourishing business at Athens in teaching tactical skills to eager students at the gymanasia—not a sign of Athenian disinterest in battle or the now often asserted non-military character of gymnastic exercises.[133] The real issue, however, concerns the culture within a polis, not its foreign policy. Ancient tradition has Spartans wearing their militarism "on their sleeves"; the supposedly un-militaristic Athenians, so frequently at war, may have a deceptive appearance.[134]

From a traditional perspective, a state's armed forces reflect its constitution: political participation and the right to fight are related.[135] In European pre-industrialized societies, military service, affording access to honor and personal glory, was an aristocratic privilege. Extension of the right to fight to non-nobles had political repercussions. Aristotle knew the principle even if his generalizations about Greek constitutional development in the Archaic period leave much to be desired.[136] A further qualification for political and military participation involved the means to provide one's own weapons, i.e., a qualification for full citizenship based on property or wealth. Development of the polis (from one perspective) came to be associated with a so-called "hoplite revolution," which equated the introduction of hoplite equipment with a closed phalanx formation of massed infantry, indicating a higher degree of political cohesion and incorporation of "middle-class" citizens (those capable of arming themselves but not members of the traditional aristocracy) into the army. It now seems clear, however, that the phalanx seen in Herodotus and Thucydides evolved over two centuries. In the *Iliad* masses of commoners (not just the heroes) participate in combat but not (unless sufficiently wealthy) in the organized massed formation of the later phalanx. Thus the problematic thesis that tyrants in the seventh- and sixth-centuries

---

132 Thuc. 6.24.3-4.
133 The effective functioning of a hoplite phalanx required at least some training and practice, although explicit references to unit drill first occur in the Hellenistic period: see Wheeler 2007a, 207-209; idem 2007b, xxxix-xl with nn.82-83; Matthew 2009, 408 nn.52; the connection between sport (agonistic games) and military training is defended at Rausch 1998; Jung 2006, 37 with n.43.
134 Garlan 1975, 15; cf. Lévêque 1968, 279 n.108.
135 Max Weber's notion of a monopoly on the use of violence as a criterion for a "state" no longer holds sway: Gabrielsen 2007, 248 (following Mogens Hansen); Wilson 2008, 23-24. Cf. Richardson in chapter one.
136 *Pol.* 4.13.7-11, 1297b.

rose to power on the shoulders of middle-class hoplites, flexing their military muscles from creation of the phalanx and seeking political and economic reforms, can no longer be maintained.

The poverty of sources for the Archaic period invites hypotheses. Commoners in combat in the *Iliad* provoke speculation about the political and social character of the polis in the eighth and seventh centuries, although some of these views also unduly historicize Homeric combat or posit a more developed form of the phalanx than the sources justify. Masses of non-nobles also participated in medieval battles without any advancement in rights or political clout.[137] Presence on the battlefield is not exclusively a contributor to social and political change.

A different spin comes from advocates of an open phalanx. According to this view, light infantry (slingers and archers) fought side-by-side with hoplites in an open formation until their exclusion in the fifth-century, although hoplites remained chiefly individual combatants with wide gaps between the files. The sources' aristocratic prejudice allegedly omits light infantry's subsequent role in hoplite battles. Further, any political consciousness of hoplites as a "middle class" at Athens is illusory. Hoplites cannot be identified with the *zeugitai* of Solon's classification of Athenian citizens, as *zeugitai* were wealthy, not middling in personal resources. Nor can the *thetes* class have derived any political consciousness from rowing in the Athenian fleet; many *thetes* actually served as volunteer hoplites, who (as argued) could amount to 50% of an Athenian army. Constitutional change at Athens, on this view, came for political and social reasons in a period of "state formation" c.550-c.450 without any input from war or military factors.[138]

Efforts to dilute with *thetes* the contingents of *zeugitai* and higher classes in the Athenian phalanx find a parallel in Spartan use of *perioikoi* as hoplites, although no joint brigading of Spartiates and *perioikoi* is demonstrable before the Peloponnesian War. Some would also add slaves as active combatants, conveniently justifying the silence of the sources as class prejudice.[139] As already noted, arguments from

137 The extensive bibliography on these issues is assembled at Wheeler 2007a, 192-202, 206-12; idem 2007b, xxviii-xxxii with notes.
138 Van Wees 2001, 45-71, views recycled frequently, e.g., idem 2007, 273-79, 294-97.
139 Hunt 1997 and 1998; but cf. Burckhardt 2001, 236-37; Sabin 2007b, 96; J.W.I. Lee 2007, 257-58, 261-62; Schwartz 2009, 139-40 with n.5; and the sharp criticisms of Ducrey 2000, 197-98, 204, 206; Hunt's arguments are credible to Hornblower 2007, 47

silence seem a favorite tool of revisionists. Identification of Solon's *zeugitai* with middle-class hoplites has always been problematic. Some authors deny any connection between the Solonian classes and Athenian military organization, but not the political consciousness of Athenian rowers.[140] Further, van Wees' case for wealthy *zeugitai*, based on his calculations about the size of Attic farms and their yields, is not compelling. Other such reconstructions yielded similar questionable results. Part of the problem is making sense of the details of Solon's economic criteria for his classes.[141] Nor does his view of the *thetes* escape objections.[142] The cost of hoplite equipment, generally assumed to be affordable (if not cheap), represents another factor. At least one scholar argues that the average Athenian wage earner could not afford it; another recent argument posits an Athenian state subsidy from about the mid-fourth century to facilitate citizens' purchase of hoplite arms and equipment, thus suggesting its expense and the need to expand the manpower base for conscription.[143]

Abandonment of the so-called "hoplite revolution" thesis creates a gap in interpretation of Archaic political development on the Greek mainland and how the nexus of who fights and who governs influenced the process. In the poverty of literary sources for the seventh and sixth centuries a new (and convincing) interpretation is awaited. Hypotheses are cheap; evidence is dear. In the case of Athens, too little is known about both the pre-Cleisthenic army and the details of domestic politics. Certainly the rate of change at Athens accelerated in the period c.550-c.450, but calling this period "state formation" (a current buzzword) implies the non-existence of an Athenian state before c.550. Solon might object. Further, labeling Athenian conflicts before the fifth century "primitive warfare" grossly distorts both pre-state battles and Archaic Athens.[144]

---

with n.63.

140 Gabrielson 2002a, esp. 214; idem 2002b, 95-98; cf. 86 with n.10 on arguments from silence; on the *zeugitai* note also Rosivach 2002.

141 Gabrielson 2002b, 88, 96 with n.34 (bibliography on earlier calculations).

142 Gabrielson 2002b, 86, 92-94; Christ 2006, 49 with n.15; cf. 52 n.21; cf. Strauss 1996, 313-25; Hale 2009: aimed at general readers.

143 Gröschel 1989; Couvenhes 2007; Schwartz 2009, 97 n.377; cf. Bertosa 2003.

144 Hunt 1998, 8-10 with n.35. Hunt's assertion that Athens engaged in pre-state warfare before the fifth century perversely applies Turney-High's concept of the "military horizon," the threshold separating pre-state and state warfare. The single battle of agonal warfare reflects the rules of limited warfare, not a lack of means to continue the conflict, a typical feature of pre-state conflicts. See Turney-High 1971, 30-31.

Who fights also determines who dies. Krentz's fundamental paper on casualties in hoplite battles has stimulated further discussions of casualties, mortality, and the demographics of hoplite warfare.[145] On this topic the face-of-battlers mingle fairly well with the war-and-society advocates, although Hanson's assessment of wounds and Krentz's statistics—like any set of numbers—invite criticism.[146] J.-N. Corvisier launched a project in 1994 at Université d'Artois to study the effects of warfare on Greek demography. A study of battle casualties in Plutarch's *Lives* led to the conclusion that a hoplite had a fifty-percent chance of surviving a battle.[147] A second paper, offering a summary of findings from major Greek historians as well as the Hippocratic corpus, seems less satisfying for military historians than for students of ancient medicine.[148] Corvisier, however, defends the accuracy of casualty figures in literary sources and has a firm belief in military lists despite work cautioning doubt.[149] For Corvisier the psychological effects of casualties exceeded war's demographic significance; manpower losses from frequent wars did not impede the Greeks' capacity to wage them. Such conclusions are of course relative: the city of Thespiae fought itself into oblivion.[150]

Hoplites died in battle to defend not only their polis in the abstract, but also home and hearth, family and kin. In the event of a siege, the threat intensified, as capture of a city left the fate of its inhabitants at the victor's discretion: often massacre of adult males and enslavement of women and children. Women, left behind in the city during a field battle, provided inspiration, but assumed a more active role in sieges or battles within a city. Among other activities, women disguised as males could man the walls to give the impression of a greater number of defenders, sacrifice their hair for the manufacture of twine for catapults, or during intramural combat hurl bulky roof tiles at the enemy, a potentially lethal

---

145 Krentz 1985b; cf. Majno 1975; Vaughn 1991; Geroulanos and Bridler 1994; Sternberg 1999; Salazar 2000.
146 Hanson 1989, 210-18; Brulé 1999.
147 Corvisier 1994.
148 Corvisier 1999, 57-79: tables at 71-78; cf. 57, 62-63: his captious criticism of earlier work (Krentz 1985b; Wheeler 1991) ignores these authors' self-imposed limits.
149 Corvisier 1999, 58, although unaware of Rubincam 1991; cf. Rubincam 2003; idem 2008; on lists see now Bakewell 2007.
150 Corvisier 1999, 69-71; Thespiae: Hanson 1999b; Dayton's discussion of battle casualties (2006, 99-100 with n.194) is premised on his misrepresentation of Hanson (1989, 224-25), who has always emphasized the intensity of hoplite battle; agonal rules did not attempt to limit the ferocity of fighting, as Dayton claims.

projectile.[151] Increased reliance on mercenaries in Hellenistic armies, particularly from the time of Alexander's Successors, actually brought women onto the battlefield. The baggage trains of armies included wives and children and often all the combatants' earthly possessions. As the loyalty of mercenaries stemmed from motives of personal gain rather than patriotism or devotion to a cause, capture of an opponent's baggage became a tactical objective in battle.[152] In the political chaos after Alexander the Great's death and throughout the period of the Successors, Macedonian women often assumed positions of rule and even field commands, setting a precedent for the political influence of Hellenistic queens. A Hellenistic genre, attested by Plutarch's *Mulierum Virtutes*, Book 8 of Polyaenus' *Strategika*, and an anonymous *Tractatus de mulieribus claris in bello*, eventually emerged combining Eastern examples of strong female rulers (e.g., Semiramis) with *exempla* of Greek women displaying bravery in battle and elsewhere.[153]

WAR AND THE ECONOMY

The blazing debate about the ancient economy, which Moses Finley's *The Ancient Economy* kindled among Anglophones in 1972, and his fiery 1985 model for studying war finances and profits as a structural element in ancient society might lead Alice to think that she should summon the fire department.[154] Despite intense discussions about the ancient economy, numerous treatments of Greek financing of wars and profits from war have elaborated on details without significant breakthroughs from a broader perspective—in other words, more smoke than fire.[155] Aristotle's frequently cited pronouncement on war as a natural form of acquisition—a boon for the Marxist-inspired—has

---

151 E.g. the death of Pyrrhus of Epirus at Argos (272). See Berry 1996; surveys of women and Greek warfare: Schaps 1982; Loman 2004; note also the speculations of Hornblower 2007, 43-47.

152 Holleaux (1926) remains the basic study of Hellenistic baggage trains; cf. J.W.I. Lee 2004; Loman 2005, partially recycled from Loman 2004. Lonsdale on Gaugamela (2007, 131) misses the point of the Persian attack on Alexander's baggage train.

153 Carney 2004; cf. Savalli-Lestrade 2003; Gera 1997: text, translation, and discussion of the *Tractatus de mulieribus*; cf. Wheeler (2010, 17-18) on stratagems of women and the element of paradoxography in Polyaenus.

154 Finley 1973; idem 1985; note also Chastagnol 1977: the acta of a French conference on economic aspects of ancient warfare.

155 For bibliography see Trundle 2010, and below n. 161.

been much abused.[156] Thucydides (2.13.2) had already stressed that war was a matter of "brains" and money, and money as the "sinews of war" became a motif of fourth-century sources. Few would dispute that war can be profitable, especially for the victors, although long-term expenses in controlling or administering territory could consume immediate gains; in contrast, even a costly war might eventually pay for itself through collection of tribute or taxes. Generalizations, however, are suspect, as political, social, and military factors, not simply economic gain or loss, determine the success or failure of a war from a broader perspective. Nor should causes of all wars be reduced to profitability.

For enthusiasts of ancient economic studies, fiscal data from literary sources combined with epigraphical texts and other sources suggest intriguing possibilities for re-creating state budgets for Greek cities and especially Athens, for which the most evidence of this type has survived. Numerous speculative attempts at reconstructing the annual military budget of the Roman Empire (none with definitive results) invite comparison. Although extant data can stimulate learned studies, dealing with fragmentary and lacunous financial evidence can also be deceptive. Athens' introduction of military pay in 463/462 remains only a conjecture, even if Athenian hoplites were certainly receiving pay after 431.[157] The occurrence of *misthos*, taken as state pay for Eretrian sailors in a fragmentary and obscure text from Eretria (*IG* XII.9 1274; sixth century), becomes the cornerstone for an elaborate reconstruction of late sixth and early fifth-century navies in the Aegean; hence Thucydides (1.13-14) must be wrong that Corinth was the first polis to finance a fleet. Unfortunately, this fragmentary text of uncertain meaning will not bear the weight of the interpretative edifice built upon it.[158] In fact, a leading scholar of Athenian finances denies that current evidence is sufficient to calculate budgets for Athenian fleets in the fifth and fourth centuries: too many unknowns and variables impede. The

---

156 Arist. *Pol.* 1.8-9.12, 1256a-b, esp. 1.8.12. Brun and Descat (2000, 216) cite Austin 1986 and Rihill 1993, but also conclude that wars were about profits, as does Migeotte (2000).

157 Couvenhes 2007, 535 with n.67.

158 Van Wees 2004, 203-206 (following Cairns 1991), elaborated at 2008 and recycled at 2010. Malitz (2008) rightly rejects van Wees' view and any notion of state pay for sailors or soldiers in the Archaic period. For a recent study of the influence of the intro-duction of coinage on warfare, see Trundle 2010.

same limitations apply to the war budgets of Hellenistic states.[159] Some Anglophone Hares might seek escape from this *aporia* in modeling and self-generated evidence, but they would not find applause from distinguished Francophone scholars, who lack interest in arguments by analogy, comparisons, and artificial creation of documentation.[160]

A *Tagung* in February 2007 at Universität Mannheim, "Kriegskosten und Kriegsfinanzierung von der Antike bis zur Neuzeit," inaugurated an ambitious project to assemble a digital data base of all available evidence on the economic issues associated with ancient warfare: e.g., amount of direct costs, social groups who bore the brunt of financing wars, means of financing wars, cost of successful wars in terms of post-war reconstruction, the defeated's payment of reparations, etc. The project, now based at Universität Erfurt, has produced an acta of the initial conference and preliminary findings.[161] Study of war and the ancient economy may be about to enter a new phase.

8. ALEXANDER THE GREAT

The studious Alice, ever indefatigable in pursuit of bibliography, is well aware of the flourishing Alexander-the-Great industry. She wonders, however, if (apart from updated details) general military evaluation of Alexander has really advanced much beyond the fundamental study of J. F. C. Fuller, who, despite writing under the influence of W. W. Tarn's now discredited thesis of Alexander's pursuit of creating a "brotherhood of humankind," understood war and the art of generalship better than many current military commentators.[162] Continued interest in Alexander has not yielded significant new work for the military historian. Non-specialists may find useful some fresh surveys, although ploughing familiar furrows. Even businessmen and re-enactors are now studying Alexander.[163] Lonsdale, influenced by the work of Colin S. Gray, a frequent commentator on contemporary strategy, approaches Alexander's campaigns from the viewpoint of modern strategic thought, even labeling the military reforms of Philip II a "RMA" ("revolution in military affairs"), like "state formation"

---

159 Gabrielsen 2008; Chaniotis 2005b, 121.
160 Andreau et al. 2000, 5.
161 Burrer and Müller 2008; cf. www.kriegskosten.de.
162 Fuller 1958.
163 Heckel 2008; Cartledge 2004; cf. Strauss 2003; businessmen: Bose 2003: a new sprout from the recent genre on "Sun Tzu for businessmen"; re-enactors: Matthews 2008.

a current buzzword.[164] Novices to the study of military history might benefit from exposure to Lonsdale's perspective. Cynicism and moral judgments can also appear in recent work. For some, Alexander becomes one of history's greatest butchers, a predatory raider devoid of higher aims, although others disagree.[165]

To highlight other work, Helmut Berve's magisterial prosopography of the age of Alexander has been updated (probably not replaced) through two volumes of Waldemar Heckel,[166] who has also probed the complex relationship between Alexander and his officers, the Macedonian nobility.[167] Alexander's use of intelligence and artillery have also received attention.[168] The most intriguing recent idea, however, suggests that the mutiny on the Hyphasis, ending Alexander's further advance into India, was contrived to shift the onus of turning back from Alexander to his army.[169] Caution about the number of ethnic Macedonians in the campaigns of Alexander and the Successors is also warranted. A Macedonia drained of its manpower in frequent wars may be inaccurate, as the sources often do not distinguish ethnic Macedonians from those trained for the Macedonian phalanx and thus called "Macedonians."[170]

For Alexander, Alice's choice between Hatters and Hares is less daunting than it was for the Archaic and Classical periods. Despite continued fascination with Alexander, saying something new from a military perspective is not easy, particularly given the well-known problems of the lack of detailed contemporary narrative sources.[171] The wheel is often re-invented in military studies of Alexander. Absent, however, is a genuine understanding of Philip II's reforms of the

---

164 Lonsdale 2007. RMA is not quite the same idea as the Early Modern "military revolution" debate spawned by Roberts (1956) and revised by Parker (1996a); examined and defined in Brice 2011b.

165 Bosworth 1996, a view carried further by Hanson 1999a, 183; idem 2001, 60-98; Worthington 1999a and b; idem 2000; contra, Holt 1999; idem 2000; Lonsdale 2007, 2; Heckel 2008, 188 n.31; idem 2009a, 76-77.

166 Berve 1926; Heckel 1992; idem 2006.

167 Heckel 2003; idem 2009a; idem 2009b; cf. Naiden 2007 on a Macedonian officer corps.

168 Intelligence: Engels 1980; cf. Russell 1999; artillery: Keyser 1994.

169 Spann 1999, 62-74, followed by Heckel 2003a, 224-25; idem 2003b; idem 2008, 121-25.

170 Bosworth 2002, 64-97.

171 Bosworth's preference (1980-95) for the Vulgate tradition over Arrian, is highly problematic and provoked defense of Arrian from N. G. L. Hammond in numerous works. See also Whitby (2007, 62-64) and Bichler (2009, 20-24) on the problems of conflicting sources.

Macedonian army and a full history of the Macedonian phalanx as a tactical formation from its origins under Philip II until its final hurrah as a formation under a Macedonian commander at Pydna (168). Philip, much discussed from a political perspective, merits more attention as a military reformer.[172] Hatzopoulos has already covered this terrain from an organizational and administrative perspective, but more needs to be done on the tactical aspects.[173] Conversion of the Classical hoplite phalanx armed with a *dory* into the Macedonian formation of phalangites with the *sarissa* involved more than superficial discussion reveals.[174] Macedonian terminology for infantry units changed over time under both Alexander and the Antigonids. Precisely who the hypaspists are, for example, and how their armament differed from the regular phalangites is assumed rather than really known. The multiple terms for different units of infantry and cavalry in the third and second centuries provokes much scratching of the head, if precision of armament and function is desired.[175]

9. Hellenistic Warfare

Alice now enters the final phase of her choice between Hatters and Hares in consideration of the Hellenistic period (323-31), an era with which she has already acquired some familiarity through Alexander and other topics previously encountered. A new survey of social aspects of Hellenistic warfare (more Hatter than Hare) covers the Aegean world and western Asia Minor well, although it betrays the author's Cretan orientation and the absence of much Trans-Euphrates material gives pause. Typical of the so-called "new military history," "social" in this title denotes "Hamlet without the Prince," i.e., omission of battles and

---

172 See most recently Worthington 2008, esp. 26-32 on military reforms, largely a derivative discussion without significant new insights; cf. Griffith, in Hammond and Griffith 1979, 405-49; Griffith 1980.

173 Hatzopoulos 1996; idem 2001.

174 See Wheeler 2004a, 328-31 on the terms *pyknosis* and *synaspismos* for file intervals with references to earlier work; see also Bar-Kochva 1989 with useful notes on the Hellenistic phalanx; the *sarissa* also is becoming better understood: Sekunda 2001b. Baker (2003, 379-80) on the Macedonian phalanx and tactics is unreliable.

175 For attempts to resolve some of these issues see Foulon 1996a and b (hardly definitive); a new anthology, Wheatley and Hannah 2009, includes insightful essays by Anson (*pezhetairoi*), and Heckel (*asthetairoi*).

technical *militaria*, for which other brief surveys may be consulted.[176] Treatments of the armed forces for the three major dynasties and even some smaller powers are already available.[177] A dearth of sources precludes saying much new about Parthian military capabilities, although many try, and an attempt at a comprehensive treatment of cataphracts in Antiquity has appeared.[178] The Getae and Dacians have also been studied.[179] In addition, a good bit can also be said about the army of the Nabataean Arabs.[180] The post-Pydna fad among Seleucids and Ptolemies for imitating Roman equipment and unit organization presents an intriguing opportunity to study cultural transfer of military ideas, although such imitation did not produce a total abandonment of Hellenistic practices. Nor can it be interpreted as proof of the legion's tactical superiority to the phalanx, despite Polybius' propagandistic excursus.[181]

Recent work on warfare in the Hellenistic period has generally not reflected the Hatter-Hare dichotomy to the extent seen for Archaic and Classical Greece. Some revisionism, however, not exclusively the monopoly of Hares, has occurred. Austin's much cited paper on war and the Hellenistic economy helped introduce the view of Alexander the predator, later echoed by Bosworth and Hanson, and extended the profit motive to the Successors and the later major dynasties, where a king's *philoi* (army officers, court officials, administrators, governors) expected to be properly compensated. Yet a detailed prosopographical and institutional study of Hellenistic *philoi* does not stress the motive

---

176 Chaniotis 2005b; cf. idem 1996; Bugh 2006b: a brief but useful introduction; note also Meißner 2007 with more concern for operations, especially siegecraft, than other military chapters in Hellenistic anthologies; the best military overview for the Hellenistic world as a whole is still Tarn 1930. Beston 2000 on Hellenistic generalship continues the discussion of the transition of the general's function from warrior to battle manager in Wheeler 1991.

177 Macedonians and Antigonids: see Hatzopoulos 1996; idem 2001; Seleucids: Bar-Kochva 1976; idem 1989; for prosopography see Grainger 1997; Ptolemies: Lesquier 1911; van't Dack 1988; for prosopography see Peremans and van't Dack 1950-81; Láda 2002; Hasmonaeans: Shatzman 1991; Bosporan Kingdom: Mielsczarek 1999: largely an illustration of how little is known.

178 Wiesehöfer 1998: essays of varying quality and usefulness; a military chapter is lacking, as is also the case in Yarshater 1983; Lerouge 2007; Gaibov and Koselenko 2008; in English the now dated Debevoise (1938) remains basic; cataphracts: Mielczarek 1993.

179 Stefan 2005, esp. 267-76, 505-26.

180 Graf 1994.

181 Polyb. 18.28-32. On the reforms see Sekunda 2001a; cf. *SEG* 52 (2002) nos. 1497, 1595, 1782 bis, 1786; Couvenhes 2009; legion vs. phalanx: Wheeler 2004a, 331-32, 337-40. A detailed study of Polyb. 18.28-32 is in preparation.

of personal gain.[182] Nor do Demetrius Poliorcetes and Lysimachus, both often in financial straits and the latter without major military achievements, fit the model.[183]

The re-assessment of the Seleucid Empire by Sherwin-White and Kuhrt boasted "new approach" in its title and combined *Annaliste* perspectives and the center-periphery model of the Neo-Marxist Immanuel Wallerstein (then "the rage" among many so-called "new" archaeologists) with a bold assault on the Hellenocentrism of previous work, which (they argued) ignored the true character of the Seleucids as Achaemenid heirs to a non-Greek empire centered in western Iran, Mesopotamia, and northern Syria. The work's approach was more cultural than political or military. Although the case presented was poorly documented (no footnotes or endnotes), ignored much epigraphical evidence, and did not treat Seleucids after 187 (and essentially only Seleucus I, Antiochus I, and Antiochus III before that date), the work hit enough of the right chords to be in tune with the multicultural chorus of contemporary Anglophone scholarship. French scholars, however, for whom Seleucid studies represent a special field—in part a heritage of French colonialism in Syria and elsewhere in the Near East—assembled a group to correct the work's numerous misrepresentations.[184] Despite numerous flaws and exaggerations, the book of Sherwin-White and Kuhrt has stimulated a greater concern for non-Graeco-Roman sources (e.g., Babylonian astronomical diaries).

A more recent "war and society" assessment of the Seleucids finds frequent wars an impediment to cultural development: the Seleucids paled in comparison to the cultural achievements fostered by the Ptolemies and the Attalids, although in all fairness the Seleucids had a more expansive territory with more ethnically diverse populations to govern.[185] Finally, a new study—only indirectly concerned with military affairs and a supposed replacement for Bickerman's fundamental study of institutions—focuses on Seleucid power, although its long-winded, abstract, and repetitive presentation of arguments deter its function as

---

182 Austin 1986; cf. Savalli-Lestrade 1998.
183 Bosworth 2002, 246-78; a new study on sale of booty has just appeared: Jacquemin 2009.
184 See articles in *Topoi* 4.2 (1994), 443-610, especially Bernard's paper (473-511).
185 Austin 2001; much the same ground is traversed in investigating ethnicities in the Seleucid administration and court at Istasse 2006; cf. the little known study of intellectuals in diplomacy: Sonnabend 1996.

more than an update. Curiously, Seleucid loss of territory is not seen as a diminution of power.[186] A more general trend, evident also in Capdetrey's examination of Seleucid power, reacts to an alleged over-emphasis on "great powers" and focuses on cities, as if scholars needed to be reminded that the polis as an institution did not disappear in the age of Philip II and Alexander. Mercenaries and the nature of the Hellenistic *ephebeia* thus attract attention. Cities as well as kings hired mercenaries. In Asia Minor, for which the relatively abundant epigraphical record permits study, distinguishing mercenaries from citizens is not always easy. At times cities could cut expenses and replenish their citizen bodies from grants of citizenship to mercenaries. Although local situations varied regarding the degree of intermarriage between natives and mercenaries, in religious practice mercenaries did not remain isolated from the locals. A supposed "professional cult" for mercenaries exclusively is difficult to prove. Hence the so-called "total institution" model (social and cultural isolation of military forces from the general population) may not be true for Hellenistic mercenaries. Application of this model to the Roman Imperial army has already been refuted.[187]

As mercenaries were expensive for cities to hire and maintain, cities retained their citizen armies. Accordingly, the gymnasium continued to be a locus of both military training and education, and the *ephebeia* prepared young males for their military duties. Far from being a dying institution of social significance only to the youth of wealthy families, a new appreciation of the *ephebeia* emphasizes its vitality both for military training and as a sign of a city's autonomy.[188] Citizens of Hellenistic cities, like those of their Classical predecessors, experienced military activities. Local disputes and antagonisms led to various degrees of conflict, even if those cities belonged to larger empires. Such micro-imperialisms, however, should not be exaggerated, as kings had to keep the "lid on the kettle" to prevent regional conflicts or potential threats to their own control. Politics

---

186 Capdetrey 2007, strongly influenced by a new study of the Seleucid economy: Aperghis 2005; for an assessment see Muccioli 2008; cf. Bickerman 1938.

187 Couvenhes 2004; "total institution": Pollard 2000, elaborating on the views of Shaw 1983, but soundly rebutted by Stoll 2001; on the inadequacies of the "total institution" model see also Wilson 2008, 29-31.

188 Ducrey 2000; gymnasia: Kah and Scholz 2004; Gauthier and Hatzopoulos 1993; Cordiano 2007; Perrin-Saminadayar 2007: a nearly exhaustive treatment of the Hellenistic Athenian *ephebeia*.

rather than socioeconomic concerns motivated wars and in the case of larger conflicts cities naturally wanted to be on the winning side.[189]

10. ALICE'S QUANDARY

A decision can no longer be delayed, although many aspects of Greek and Hellenistic warfare have not been discussed. Which way should Alice go? She seeks not to offend either party by her decision. She is aware that Hares tend to be notoriously thin-skinned, defensive, and quick to counterattack—perhaps a sign of insecurity; Hatters possess a thicker epidermis, hardened from the Hares' repeated assaults and their false sense of the superiority of novelty. The choice is methodological, as both Hatters and Hares seek innovative interpretations and both want to be revisionists or expand current knowledge. As Heckel notes, "'New approaches' are fine, indeed desirable, but they are at the same time little more than new ways of asking the old questions: for the most part, the answers continue to elude us."[190] Similarly, Hanson's contrast between "concrete solutions" and merely expanding knowledge or raising issues for discussion exaggerates the extent to which "concrete solutions" are possible for ancient history, a field for which it is often difficult to say much without qualifying it with "probably" or use of the subjunctive mood.[191] Some scholars are more honest about inserting these qualifications into their prose than others. The sources available are too limited to achieve the historicist's dream of re-creating "how it really was." Nevertheless, respecting the sources (despite their scarcity and foibles) *and their limits* permits having some control over probable interpretations and avoids flights of fancy and excessive conjectures. The problem is particularly acute for military history, a field in which "Monday morning quarterbacking" can be rampant. Anyone can have an opinion, whether qualified by real expertise or not. Sometimes in ancient history it would be better to say: "We just don't know."

Alice is aware that ancient military historians, like historians in general, should do more thinking and reflecting and less publishing. No one can read all or even the bulk of the current profusion of publications, nor (given the quality of much of it) should anyone have that desire. Authors deceive themselves, if they equate publishing with actually

---

189 Ma 2000; Sartre 2004, 250-54.
190 Heckel 1994.
191 Hanson, 2007, 3-21.

being read. Just keeping abreast of the sheer volume of publications in multiple languages is taxing. Despite supposed "globalization" and "internationalism," scholarly gaze can still be limited to the author's native tongue or work published within particular national borders.

Frustration with limited sources is understandable. Seeking a solution to an historical *aporia* in social science methodologies at first glance appears reasonable. Hatter historicism is far from perfect. Too often, however, little consideration is given to the differences in basic assumptions and doctrinal or theoretical disputes within those social sciences. Specific views of anthropologists or sociologists may not be unproblematic or favored by all within those respective disciplines. Primitive or pre-state warfare, for example, has been a branch of anthropology for decades, but (despite anthropologists' pursuit of universals) a single view of what it is and how it functions in multiple cultures is elusive.[192] Resort to social science methodology can also seem at times ideological or simply the opportunism of jumping on a bandwagon to attract attention and ride the wave of a fad. Ideological themes, which may "score points" in American academia, can become the butt of derision among European scholars.[193] Nevertheless, "talking points" books can be useful. After all, the essence of scholarship is debate and discussion, not one scholar's supposed definitive view of the proper methodology or what really happened.

But do the Hares suffer self-deception in their boastful assertions about "progress?" The applause of the moment is quite ephemeral. As this discussion has shown, many of the so-called "new approaches" to ancient military history may generate publications (and sexier marketing for presses), but tend to be rather problematic in their results or really not all that "new." Lasting effect determines progress, not flashes in the pan. The frequent equation of "new" with "better" is a common sleight of hand in academia. New approaches, always desirable in scholarship, must pass the test of being convincing in *la longue durée*.

The best advice for Alice, however, is that if she wants to do ancient military history, she needs to learn something about war in general

---

192 Besides the works of Turney-High (1971, 1981), Ferguson (1999), W. Lee (2004, 2007), and Reid (2007), see Ferguson and Farragher 1988; Haas 1990; LeBlanc 2003; and Otterbein 2004; note also Cioffi-Revilla 2000, a political scientist's world-historical approach to the origins of war, if somewhat repetitive and disappointing.

193 Ducrey (2000, 197-98, 204, 206) takes Hunt to task for "political correctness," whereas Sartre (2007, 619-20, 624) finds Neocon ideology underlying Eckstein 2006a.

(not just its ancient versions), including war's various manifestations and types in all cultures, and the historiography of military history and theory. If Alice just wants to be a revisionist, then (as the Cheshire-Cat rightly points out) it does not matter which path she takes: "they're both mad." Few purists of either the Hatter or Hare variety exist in actual practice. Alice ponders the Cheshire-Cat's enigmatic grin....

3

NEW APPROACHES TO THE ROMAN ARMY

SARA E. PHANG

1. INTRODUCTION

The Romans themselves idealized the traditions of their military, a mindset exemplified (and perhaps exaggerated) by the later Roman Latin author Vegetius, who constructed his composite picture of the ideal Roman army from past authors of the Republic and imperial age. Vegetius states that he has digested these authors "so that should anyone wish to be diligent in raising and training recruits, he may be able easily to strengthen an army in emulation of ancient military virtue."[1] It is easy to understand if readers have a superficial impression (abetted by Hollywood productions) that the Roman army did not change over the centuries, or that approaches to academic Roman military studies had not changed either. Both impressions are false, as current scholars well know and this chapter will show.

Roman army studies have traditionally focused on the material and institutional history of the military, such as campaigns and battles, the archaeology of forts and frontier works, the archaeology of arms and armor, order of battle, and internal organization and promotion patterns. New directions in the study of the Roman army emphasize the demographic, political, economic, and cultural characteristics of the societies that shaped it. Novel topics include the soldier's experience of combat, the demography of the military, gender and sexuality, and how the Romans perceived their enemies. New approaches emphasize warfare as cultural history, examining the social construction of *militia* (the Roman term for military service) from Roman concepts of status

---

1 Veg. *Epit.* 1.28. On Vegetius' problematic date, Milner (1996), xxv-xxix (late fourth century AD); Charles 2007; cf. chapter four.

or class, gender, ethnicity and tradition. Some recent narrative histories incorporate these new approaches.[2]

This chapter is not a general review of Roman army studies, for which a reader can now consult essays on future prospects as well as thematic and retrospective collections.[3] It is also weighted towards classical historical studies more than archaeology, except for archaeological studies focusing on social context.[4] I will focus on work published in the last 10-15 years and on themes and interpretive methods from Roman social and cultural history which shed new light on material familiar to Roman military historians.

To write about "The" Roman army is to over-generalize. At any one time, there were different divisions—*auxilia*, fleets, legions, Praetorians, guards, and ethnic units. The social and institutional culture may have differed regionally.[5] A unit may well have differed from one commander to another, even if we discount the ancient writers' discourse of praise and invective. Legionaries, auxiliaries and other personnel displayed varying levels of acculturation, as seen in documents, inscriptions, and archaeological finds, such as the spread of Arretine ware along the Rhine frontier.[6] Campaigns should, therefore, be studied intensively in provincial and local cultural contexts. Future

---

2   Ash 1999; Goldsworthy 2003; Potter 2004; Lendon 2005; Morgan 2006; Osgood 2006; Roth 2010.

3   On the future of ancient military history, Hanson 1999c; idem 2007 (Hellenocentric); James 2002; Kaegi 2009; Rosenstein 2009b. Recent "companion" volumes with predominantly military focus include *CRA*; *CHGRW*; Tritle and Campbell 2011. Of the works in English, Campbell (1984) and *CRA* provide fuller references to ancient sources and recent controversies. Besides the LIMES conference collections and the MAVORS reprints, important collections of specialist papers include Birley 1988; Breeze and Dobson 1993; Rich and Shipley 1993a and b; Le Bohec 1995; Lloyd 1996; Webster and Cooper 1996; Mattingly 1997; Raaflaub and Rosenstein 1999; Goldsworthy and Haynes 1999; Alföldy, Dobson, and Eck 2000; Le Bohec 2003; Wilkes 2003; Dillon and Welch 2006; Seitz 2006; Blois and Lo Cascio 2007; Bragg, Hau and Macaulay-Lewis 2008; Morris and Scheidel 2009; Fagan and Trundle 2010. More accessible textbooks include Le Bohec 1994; Campbell 1994 (sources in translation), and 2002; Campbell 2004 (literary sources); Champion 2004 (imperialism); Southern 2007; Webster 1998; Keppie 1998; Roth 2010. Watson (1969) is still useful. James (2002) provides a critical examination of Roman military studies and surveys new approaches.

4   For archaeological approaches with a social emphasis, Coulston 2004; Mattingly 2004; Pollard 2004; Whittaker 2004; Wilkes 2005; Bowman 2006; Downey 2006; James 2006; Blois and Lo Cascio 2007; Grane 2007; Revell 2007.

5   Wheeler 1996.

6   J. Adams (1999 and 2003, 550-3, 560-1, 754-5) discusses literacy and culture; on Arretine ware, Wallace-Hadrill 2008, 417, 439; on elite needs for interpreters on the frontier, Peretz 2006.

Roman army studies may adopt recent approaches to cultural identities in the Roman empire.[7] Nonetheless, the Roman army promoted a dominant, Latin culture, on which this chapter focuses.

In the interests of accessibility, this chapter avoids technical terms and titles that abound in many standard works on the Roman army. The "nobles" were the aristocrats of the mid- and late Republic, senators and future senators. Those elites of the Empire, when Augustus regularized their status, were the "upper orders" comprising senators and equestrians, groups defined by status as well as wealth. "Officers" refers to consuls, proconsuls and legates, military tribunes and prefects, all of whom came from the upper orders in the imperial period. "Subaltern officers" include centurions and, below the centurionate, specialists such as clerks and standard-bearers. Men in these posts were usually paid more than common soldiers, but came from the same social strata; centurions may have come from more literate and affluent backgrounds than men from the lower ranks.

2. Modern Perceptions

Nineteenth- and twentieth-century Anglo-German Roman army studies, long termed the "Durham School" after the academic affiliation of its leader, Eric Birley, emphasized the reconstruction of Roman military organization and careers from the study of Latin inscriptions.[8] Many nineteenth- and twentieth-century archaeologists and historians of the Roman army had themselves served as British, French, and German officers and imported certain assumptions about the rationality of the Roman military from their modern experience.[9]

Even when historians define Roman army studies more broadly, social historians of the military need to choose diachronic comparisons carefully to avoid anachronism. For example, MacMullen, working on social bonds in the Roman army, employed Shils and Janowitz's canonical study of "cohesion" in combat in World War II to suggest that Roman legionaries underwent similar bonding.[10] In contrast with World War II's unprecedentedly long and spatially extensive battles, Roman soldiers' experience of battle was much shorter and more

---

7   Noy 2000; Schäfer 2003; Isaac 2004; Dench 2005; see also works cited in n. 3.
8   James 2002, 2-26; E. Birley 1988; M. P. Speidel 1992.
9   James 2002, 19.
10 MacMullen 1984 = 1990, 230-1; Shils and Janowitz.

intermittent.[11] The evidence for social bonds among Roman soldiers is much less intimate; comrades were as likely to be rivals competing for distinction.[12]

Another peril is the imposition of British (or other modern European) regimental terminology and organizational models, a habit perhaps unconscious in older British Roman army studies.[13] J. E. Lendon, for example, draws on British regimental comparisons to fill out his depiction of the Roman army, though he also emphasizes differences between the ancient and modern worlds.[14] Anachronism persists in English translations of Latin and Greek authors in the Loeb Classical Library and Penguin Classics, the texts most accessible to students and non-classicists.[15] Comparative methods such as the study of world military history in periods with similar technology can provide an antidote to such modernization, unconscious or otherwise, of the Roman army.[16]

The modern concept of "grand strategy," while a popular topic of late, has also been challenged as anachronistic. In this modern thesis, the emperors—starting with Augustus' advice to Tiberius, but most commonly attributed to Hadrian—adopted a rationally conceived grand strategy in which troops defended linear frontiers chosen to maximize geostrategic advantage.[17] This view of grand strategy still dominates, but has been challenged by some scholars. Literary texts that seem to suggest a "linear" frontier strategy probably represent an idealized social order relegating soldiers to the social periphery, "stationed like a wall" around the edges of the empire.[18] According to Susan Mattern, elite officers' and emperors' concepts of strategy were conditioned by ancient geographical concepts and by moral discourse rather than by

---

11 Keegan 1976, 308-20; Sabin 2000.
12 Lendon 1999, 279-80, 286-7; idem 2004; idem 2005, 178-81; McDonnell 2006b, 310-11; Phang 2008, 47, 71-2; cf. chapter two, above.
13 James 2002, 10; for a full study of the effect Hingley 2000; persistent in Davies 1989.
14 Lendon 1997, 236, 240, 249-50, 264; avoided in Lendon 2005.
15 See also edited selections in Campbell 2004; Champion 2004.
16 Raaflaub and Rosenstein 1999; Rosenstein 2009a; Hopkins 2009.
17 Grand strategy was emphasized by Luttwak 1976; criticized by Isaac (1992), Mattern (1999) and Whittaker (2004, 28-49); defended by Wheeler (1993a, 2007c, 237-8, and 2010b); Goldsworthy (2007, 108-113) reviews the controversy; Champion (2004) provides an entry point to the debate.
18 Aelius Aristides, *To Rome* 10; 82; Oliver 1953, 904, 937-8; Carrié 1993, 103-4; Woolf 1993, 178-9.

the rationality projected upon the Romans by modern authors.[19] Grand
strategy also presupposes the modern "map mentality" (the world
as two-dimensional plane or as a globe) which Romans lacked; they
perceived space in "hodological" terms, as locations strung along
routes.[20]

Besides modern anachronisms, students and non-classicists should
beware of the antiquarianism that affects ancient, especially Latin,
literary sources on the Roman army. Because the ancient sources are
scattered, the temptation is to treat them all as pieces of the same puzzle
or ancient mosaic. The resulting reconstructions of the Roman army are
often idealized and artificial.[21] Mary Beard discusses the problem with
respect to reconstructing the Roman triumph, as does J. E. Lendon on
Vegetius' representation of the Roman army.[22] A full-scale treatment is
needed that analyzes Late Republican and early imperial commanders'
and authors' "invention" or at least idealization of military tradition
and how this affected contemporary practices, such as the revival of
ancient punishments by the emperors Augustus and Tiberius.[23]

3. SOURCES

For Roman warfare, Greek and Roman narrative histories, biography,
orations, letters, and anecdotal and topical works provide much
information. The authors of these belonged mainly to the upper social
strata: in the early second century AD, Tacitus and Pliny the Younger
were senators, Pliny a governor of Bithynia in Asia Minor; Martial
and many other literary authors were equestrians; many Greek authors
belonged to provincial elites. A few equestrians had risen to that status
through military service, but normally a social gulf divided senatorial
and equestrian officers from the soldiers. Many of the elite authors
regarded the soldiers (*milites, stratiôtai*) as a potentially threatening
mob of social inferiors. This perspective, long taken for granted,
contrasts with the documentary sources and the status of soldiers
relative to the masses of the Empire (discussed below). In fact, social

---

19 Mattern 1999, 81-122, and 162-202.
20 On the "hodological" model see most recently Talbert 2010.
21 Rüpke 1990; Barton 2001; to a lesser degree standard works such as Watson 1969.
22 Beard 2008, 80-106; Lendon 2005, 280-5; cf. Rawson 1971. On the Later Roman army
    also Lee (2007).
23 On "invention of tradition" in other genres, Wallace-Hadrill 2008, 231-7; emperors'
    punishments, Suet. *Aug.* 24; *Tib.* 19.

differentiation existed within the *milites*, between legionaries and auxiliaries, specialists and simple soldiers, soldiers and their servants, and soldiers and low-status civilians.[24] The elite authors' biases include a propensity for praise and blame, the tendency to see in moral terms, and impatience with technical detail. Even supposed military experts received an education that emphasized rhetoric, oratory, and literary tradition rather than specifically military preparation.[25] Roman jurists are often prescriptive, telling us not what was actually done but what should be done. Literary authors were often antiquarian. Finally, as in other eras, such literary authors are often triumphalist, celebrating the Roman victors and disparaging their enemies.[26] It follows that Roman military studies that use literary sources should examine their social and cultural assumptions. Scholars need to close the divide between military studies and classical studies at large, though many of the best classicists and ancient historians have united both areas. (Many Roman army scholars enter military studies from archaeology, discussed below.) Reconstructions of some of the most alien practices of Roman warfare—religious ritual surrounding the making of war, for example, and the human sacrifice of captives—illustrate problems of teasing out antiquarian from historical evidence.[27]

Documentary sources include stone inscriptions, bronze discharge diplomata given to auxiliary, fleet, and Praetorian veterans, papyri and wooden tablets, and ostraka (potsherds used as writing material).[28] Latin and Greek inscriptions attest to the geographical and temporal location of military units, the careers of aristocratic and subaltern officers, and the public culture of the army, including records of victories, commemorative lists of personnel, vows or dedications to gods or the emperor, and *collegia* or military clubs. The Durham school of Roman army studies has reconstructed the order of battle (distribution of units

---

24 Legionaries and auxiliaries, Revell 2007; for specialists, Dobson 1970, 1974; for servants, usually slaves, Phang 2005 and n. 35 below; Amiri 2007. Isaac (1992), Alston (1998), James (1999), and Garraffoni (2004) stress military conflict with civilians, or at least a sharp differentiation.

25 Mattern 1999, 1-23.

26 Morillo 2006, 45; for Romans' views of enemies, Champion 2004; Isaac 2004.

27 Rüpke (1990) attempted a systematic reconstruction, criticized by Beard 2008; for closer examinations, Drogula 2007; Várhelyi 2007.

28 Campbell (1994) collects and translates important and representative documents; see also Phang 2007; on diplomata, Eck and Woolf 1986; Roxan 1994; Wilkes 2003; Holder 2006; Speidel and Lieb 2007; Bingen 1992 on ostraka at the site of Mons Claudianus; on tablets, Bowman 2003 (discussed below).

over time) and organization of the army and the promotion patterns of officers from extensive study of such inscriptions.[29] Papyri and tablets represent surviving military bureaucratic documents: rosters, reports, and forms; they also include correspondence of varying degrees of formality.[30] Literary authors allude to this documentation, as in the exchange of letters between Pliny and Trajan that attests to some slaves who had been recruited but had not yet been entered on the rosters (*in numeros referri*), or when the jurists' discussion of desertion assumes the documentation of grants of furlough, for which instances survive.[31]

Soldiers' private letters survive from both Roman Egypt and from Vindolanda, an auxiliary fort on Hadrian's Wall in the early second century AD. These give vivid glimpses of the soldiers' daily lives and social connections, but rarely display soldiers' attitudes to their military service in the social or moral sense.[32] Nor do we have extensive "popular" sources for Roman military culture such as the songs, novels, and memoirs or personal narratives from early modern and modern Europe and North America. Scholars have attempted to reconstruct the popular culture of the Roman army from texts, but iconographic sources may also be useful.[33]

Latin funerary epitaphs represent a more formal type of communication by soldiers. They represent social roles that the deceased or their commemorators wanted to publicize and preserve for posterity. They may, for instance, depict soldiers' de facto marriages (the partners use "husband" and "wife" terms), but not more informal or transient sexual behavior.[34]

---

29 Domaszewski 1908; E. Birley 1988; Dobson 1970, 1974; Breeze 1969, 1971, 1974; M. P. Speidel 1992a and 1992b; the tradition continues with Le Bohec (1995, 2003, 2007) and Blois (2001). The question of the promotion of "amateur" versus experienced officers is discussed elsewhere in this chapter.
30 Fink 1971; Wilkes 2003; Stauner 2004; for a survey, Phang 2007; for translations and commentary, Campbell 1994.
31 Plin. *Ep.* 10.29-30; D. 49.16.14.pr. (not explicit); documentary examples, *T. Vindol.*2.166-177; *O. Florida* 1; *SB* 9272.
32 Bowman 2003 is most accessible; see also <http://vindolanda.csad.ox.ac.uk/>>, hosted by the Centre for the Study of Ancient Documents at Oxford University (accessed 2/19/2011). Davies (1974) 1989 uses earlier documents, mostly from Egypt and Bu Ngem, to assemble a picture of the daily life of Roman soldiers.
33 Texts: Davies (1974) 1989; MacMullen 1984; Carrié 1993, 126-30; James 1999; Roth 1999; Horsfall 2003, 103-115; iconographic, see "Enemies of Empire," below; use of funerary monuments, Carrié 1993, 131-2; Keppie 2003; Noelke and Kibilka 2005.
34 Phang 2001, 142-96.

The archaeology of the army is another important source of information. Besides providing material evidence for troop movements and occupation, arms and armor, and logistics and commerce, archaeological sources can correct information distorted by textual sources. Outside the elite discourse on the military budget and donatives (see "Patronage," below) archaeology furnishes more evidence on the local economies of the Roman army in the provinces.[35] Though elite ideas of propriety frowned on the presence of noncombatants (see "Gender, Marriage, and Sexuality," below), women's and children's shoes have been found at the Vindolanda auxiliary fort, suggesting the presence of soldiers' families (or *familia*, slaves).[36] On soldiers' diet, the literary evidence emphasizes campaign staples such as wheat, oil, cheese and vinegar; archaeological finds suggest a more varied diet, with a significant impact on local and regional trade.[37] Though regions differed, archaeological studies can also estimate the extent of interaction of soldiers and civilians, Romans, and 'barbarians'. Material evidence suggests that the boundaries of the Roman empire, at local level, were more diffuse than the linear geographical boundaries stereotypical of Roman "grand strategy," for the army regulated rather than prevented the passage of native peoples across the frontier to trade or pasture animals; cultural influences also diffused across frontiers.[38] The nature of Roman power, however, meant that its culture (represented in this case by the military) remained distinctive.[39]

Finally, the Romans also commemorated warfare in iconographic media: statues, historical reliefs such as those adorning the Columns of Trajan and Marcus Aurelius, and other triumphal art, including that set up in the provinces.[40] Since the Romans plundered the artistic treasures of Greek Sicily, Greece, and the East, much Roman art relates to warfare even when its overt iconography is not warlike (the ancient authors were highly conscious of this, linking the looted art to historical

---

35 Erdkamp 2002; Stallibrass and Thomas 2008.
36 Van Driel-Murray 1995; M. A. Speidel 1997; Allason-Jones 1999; Allison 2006. Recent work by Greene (2011) will expand on this topic. On slave servants and camp followers in the Roman army, Welwei 1988; Thorburn 2003; Phang 2005.
37 Junkelmann 1997; Roth 1999; Kehne 2007; C. Adams 2007, 226-30; Stallibrass and Thomas 2008.
38 Whittaker 1994; idem 2004; on the extent of trade and cross-cultural influence, Pollard 2004; Grane 2007; Mode and Tubach 2006; influencing Roman military armor and dress, Downey 2006; James 2006.
39 Bowman 2006; Mattingly 2004; Coulston 2004.
40 Pirson 1996; Ferris 2000.

triumphs). Such artistic evidence is now being studied to provide extensive "nonverbal" evidence for Roman views and representations of warfare.[41] Provincial art, such as the tombstones of soldiers, suggests how imperial iconography trickled down and was influenced by local cultures.[42]

4. The Army of the Early and Middle Republic

The compulsive war-making of the Republican Romans has been well remarked: "almost every year the legions went out and did massive violence to someone."[43] The last several decades' scholarship has examined how the Republic's political and social structure supported warfare.[44] In the last decade emphasis has shifted from material social structure and political culture to focus more on values and ideas and include gender: the Republican male ideal of *virtus* or "manliness," better translated as "martial aggression."[45]

The history of the early Republic, in the eighth through fourth centuries BC, is preserved only in later authors, often antiquarian or anachronistic. Attributed to Servius Tullius, the Servian constitution divided Roman society into socio-economically determined groups that were the basis for military recruitment. The middle Servian classes, the *assidui*, were small landowning farmers able to afford the expense of armor and equipment, and furnished the bulk of the legions. This model of military service resembled the near-contemporary Greek hoplite armies of citizen warriors who did not depend on military service for income, in contrast with Hellenistic mercenary armies (chapter two) or the late Republican and imperial professional army. The Servian recruitment model did not demand complex expenditures on the army. The Roman state did not begin to coin money to pay the troops until around 300 BC.[46]

---

41 Edwards 2003; Welch and Dillon 2006; Wallace-Hadrill 2008.
42 Revell 2009.
43 Harris 1979, 53.
44 Brunt 1971; Hopkins 1978; Harris 1979; Rich 1993; Keppie 1997; Rosenstein 1990; idem 1999; idem 2004; idem 2006; Alston 2007; Hopkins 2009, 179-80.
45 Barton 2001 (with caution); McDonnell 2006b; Dillon & Welch 2006, 7; Phang 2008, 17-18, 46. Recent work on values and ideas: Flower 1996; Barton 2001; Hölscher 2006; Rosenstein 2006; Bragg 2008; Lendon 1997 and 2005.
46 Harl 1996, 22-3; the constitution remains a matter of debate, see Erdkamp 2007; Armstrong 2008, 49-51.

The early Republic was marked by internal conflicts, such as the patrician-plebeian struggles of the fifth and fourth centuries BC. The creation of a new patrician-plebeian aristocracy resolved part of these conflicts while conquest, opportunities for plunder, and veteran settlement provided a safety valve for the lower census groups.[47] As the Romans expanded into Italy, they settled veterans in colonies (formally constituted towns) that provided garrisons, staging areas for campaigns, and future manpower. The Romans also recruited conquered Italian peoples, giving them the opportunity to fight for Rome as Latins or allies.[48] Rome required the Latins and allies to supply manpower in wartime. In return, they received a share of the booty; Latins were settled in Latin colonies, and both received a share of the booty; the Roman citizenship was not yet extended to them.

In the middle Republic Roman elites' political competition for office promoted military expansion.[49] Each man was required to serve ten campaigns before he could run for office, thus at least his youth from about age 17 to 27 would be spent on campaign. If an aristocrat displayed military valor, he was more likely to be voted into offices by the citizens, though his career might not be much affected by a defeat as long as he had shown personal valor.[50] At the top of the hierarchy of political offices was the consulship, the supreme military command during most of the Republic.

The extent to which this political culture emphasized military glory was displayed in the triumph ceremony and triumphal art. A commander whose military campaign was successful and yielded booty and captives could request a triumph, the formal procession of the victor, his troops, and representative captives and material spoils through the city of Rome to the Capitoline Temple.[51] Modern scholars have suggested a variety of interpretations of the ritual but a new study of the triumph stresses the artificiality of these reconstructions, the conflicting sources, and the ambivalence of victory.[52] Cicero's letters of 51 BC, in which he sought a triumph for his campaign in Cilicia, provide our only first-hand evidence of how a Roman victor actually

---

47 Develin 2005.
48 Hollander 2005; Ligt 2007; Hopkins 2009, 179-80.
49 Harris 1979, 14-5, 69; Rosenstein 1990; idem 2006; McDonnell 2006b, 181-2.
50 Rosenstein 1990, 176.
51 The amount of booty and captives necessary for a triumph was not set, but a matter of negotiation with peers, see Beard 2008, 187-99 (Cicero).
52 Beard 2008, 81-92, 225-38.

negotiated for a triumph; they display his desire to tread carefully with his peers.[53]

The fame of military victory lasted beyond the triumph. The descendants of a conquering general commemorated his *virtus* and *gloria* in "banquet songs" that have not survived; the Romans of the late third and early second century BC began to compose patriotic epics.[54] Elite families held elaborate funeral processions in which the living wore the death masks of their famous ancestors; *elogia* or praise orations were delivered at these funerals of leading men (such pomp was considered inappropriate for the funerals of women).[55] A recent collection examines the evidence for this martial public image and the impact of Hellenization from the second century BC onwards. The houses of distinguished families were decorated with the trophies of ancestors' battles, and then with the artistic treasures of conquered Greece. By the mid-second century BC, the architectural monuments of Roman victors were invading the public spaces of the city of Rome.[56]

5. THE ARMY OF THE LATE REPUBLIC

These traditions began to fall apart in the last two centuries BC as a consequence of socio-economic pressures. The immense wealth that Rome acquired from conquering Africa and the East was politically destabilizing, generating greater socio-economic inequality. Some nobles became extremely wealthy from conquests. Small farmers initially benefited from booty and the general influx of wealth, which may have enabled them to raise more children. The result was impoverishment in the next generation, since Roman partitive inheritance meant that if there were more children per family, each child received less land.[57] As the socio-economic status of the *assidui* declined, the Senate was forced to lower the property qualification for military service, even before Marius took the step of recruiting landless male citizens to the legions. Other reforms attributed to Marius (such as improvements in equipment) may also have been introduced earlier.[58]

---

53 Beard 2008, 187-97.
54 Goldberg 2005a; idem 2005b, 23-5.
55 Harris 1979, 24-5; Flower 1996.
56 Welch 2006; Wallace-Hadrill 2008, 218-20.
57 Rosenstein 2004, 141-54, 161-2.
58 Rankov 2007, 31-2.

The enrollment of landless citizens in the army meant that many soldiers and veterans were dependent on military service for their income in the form of money and land. Military service thus became decoupled from the city-state structure. The ancient authors depicted the soldiers of the late Republic as greedy mercenaries, switching allegiance to the generals who promised the most reward.[59] Lawrence Keppie, Jean-Michel Carrié and Lukas de Blois have downplayed this negative picture and stress the professionalism and rational motivations of post-Marian Roman soldiers. Most of the generals of the late Republic, from Marius to Octavian and Mark Antony, represented themselves as fighting for the defense of the Republic.[60] In this period an army of diverse peoples became an army of culturally Roman citizens.[61]

6. "Laws of War" and Making Peace

The striking thing about Roman warfare is not its tradition of "laws of war" that was developed anachronistically by modern scholars, but its governance by irrational factors. Expediency was a potential legitimate cause of war. The Romans of the Republic had made treaties with their enemies, but frequently found reasons to break them, claiming that their opponents had broken these agreements first.[62] Religious forms were adhered to; portents, such as the behavior of birds, might justify warfare or offensives in the field.[63] Prosecution of individual commanders for what we might term "war crimes" (massacre of captives, misappropriation of booty, or cruelty towards subjects) were part of the political competition of the middle and late Republican nobility, and did not reflect a consensus on the humanitarian conduct of war.[64] (See "Enemies of Empire," below.)

---

59 Phang 2008, 155-62.
60 Patterson 1993; Carrié 1993, 111; Goldsworthy 1996; Keppie 1997; Alston 1998, 209-11; idem 2007, 179-85; Blois 2000; idem 2007, 176; Cagniart 2007; Keaveney 2007; Brice 2011a. The standard works on the late Republican army remain R. E. Smith (1958) and Keppie (1998).
61 Creation of Roman *auxilia* from Sicilians, Prag 2007; soldiers' Roman identity in literary authors, Dewar 2003.
62 Harris 1979, 166-75; Rosenstein 2007.
63 Harris 1979, 122; Sidebottom 2007, 15-6.
64 Rosenstein 1990; Bauman 1996, 22-6.

Much of Roman war-making was governed by honor and shame.[65] Capitulation to the enemy, or even making a treaty that was favorable to the enemy, was shameful for elite Romans. For example, in the 130s BC, when the Roman commander Gaius Hostilius Mancinus surrendered to the Numantines, the Senate decided that he should be returned "naked" to them in order to humiliate him.[66] Conversely, the Romans might fight to avenge a defeat or an insult to their honor.[67] As such anecdotes suggest, peace (*pax*) was not a positive value during the Republic. Peace signified merely inaction, the absence of war, and brought the threats of *otium* (idleness) and *luxuria* (extravagance), the amusements of idleness.[68]

Only after the civil wars of the late Republic did *pax* become a positive value, emphasized by Augustus, who also emphasized that this peace was won by the sword. *Pax* displayed his mercy towards Rome's enemies, who had been (to employ the modern term) "pacified" by Roman force of arms.[69] In the Principate, though emperors might be depicted as peacemakers, imperialistic warfare remained a virtue; the literary authors criticize emperors who did not wage active wars or at least lead and train their armies.[70] Though major wars became less common, the Roman army was often engaged in some form of low-intensity conflict against external enemies or internal enemies, such as brigands and rebels.[71]

7. CULTURAL CHANGE AND PROMOTION OF *disciplina*

Warfare does not simply bring political changes, demographic growth or contraction, or economic profit or loss; it changes the cultures of the victors and vanquished. The Roman conquest of the East brought great wealth and a new culture to Rome; against this cultural destabilization, a conservative ideology of *disciplina militaris* arose. Little recent work has been done on the cultural history of *disciplina militaris*, though

---

65 Mattern 1999, 162-220; Sidebottom 2007, 25-7.
66 Rosenstein 1990, 136, 148; idem 2007, 227. On stripping as a Roman punishment for cowardly officers, Phang 2007, 141-2; also from this time period, Val. Max. 2.7.9.
67 Goldsworthy 2007, 197.
68 Raaflaub 2007, 7-8; Barton 2007, 247.
69 Raaflaub 2007, 7-8, 15; Barton 2007, 251.
70 Emperors as peacemakers, De Souza 2008b; Woolf 1993; as warriors, Campbell 1984, 32-69.
71 Bradley 2004, 299; on brigands and revolts, Shaw 1984; Riess 2000, 2001, 2007; Grünewald [1999] 2004; Brélaz 2008; Urbainczyk 2008.

advances in the cultural history of Roman conquest may make it possible.[72]

Horace's line, *Graecia capta ferum victorem cepit* ("Defeated Greece took captive her fierce victor") suggests the Roman elite's ambivalence towards their conquest of the Hellenistic East in the last two centuries BC.[73] The Roman Republican elite regarded Hellenic culture with ambivalence, as the culture of a conquered people and as a culture more sophisticated than their own. Of course, the elite of the late Republic and early Empire could not and did not reject Greek learning; some luxury was also necessary for hospitality and social competitiveness. Contributors to *Representations of War in Ancient Rome* (2006) explore the ways in which Roman victors and their descendants in fact adopted Hellenistic Greek models of victory.[74]

Perhaps in competition, some Roman commanders and authors in the last two centuries BC began to impose an idealized, archaic image on military service. Cato the Elder boasted that his Spanish campaign in 194 would be "self-supporting" and was known for his opposition to Greek luxury at home; Scipio Aemilianus imposed an austerity on the Roman army at Carthage in 146 and at Numantia in 134 BC, and Sallust's Marius emphasized his rugged military role and lack of Hellenic sophistication.[75] This anti-Hellenic ethos was a part of the political elite's competition for influence and legitimacy. The Roman elite's conflict over Hellenism was also conflict over the proper use and display of wealth, seen in controversies over the display of spoils in triumphs.[76]

This discomfort with wealth as the profit of victory and source of social and political power influenced elite views of the post-Marian army as greedy, contrasting the *miles improbus* with the ideal citizen-soldier of the earlier Republic.[77] The ideal citizen-soldier, Livy's Spurius Ligustinus was the son of a Sabine farmer, accustomed to hard-working poverty, who entered the army of the early second century BC and distinguished himself, attaining the rank of centurion; as an elderly

---

72 Lendon 2005, 177-231; Phang 2008; cultural history: Beard 2008; Wallace-Hadrill 2008.
73 Hor. *Epist.* 2.1.156.
74 Dillon & Welch 2006.
75 Livy 34.9.12; App. *Iber.* 85; Livy *Per.* 57; Sall. *Jug.* 85 and 100. On the "austerity" tradition Dench 1996, 1998; as competitive discourse, see also Gruen 1992, 170-4.
76 Beard 2008, 9-13, 143-86 and on prestige see her discussion, 31-6.
77 Nicolet 1980, 127-8; Carrié 1993, 105-6.

man in 171 BC he volunteered to serve again, displaying his patriotism in contrast with the young.[78]

In addition to the necessities of training and controlling their soldiers, second- and first-century BC Roman leaders probably promoted *disciplina militaris* as a legitimating ideology, reassuring the polity and their envious peers that they controlled their soldiers. Scipio Africanus, Scipio Aemilianus, and Marius stand out as enforcers of discipline. By enforcing discipline, they dissociated their (sometimes irregular) commands from luxury, "bad" Hellenism, and venality, promoting an antiquarian "Roman" (and morally superior) identity. The Senate's sumptuary legislation in this period offers a suggestive parallel.[79] However, through the late Republic, *disciplina militaris* and the "austere" model may also have been used to weld together troops from many different ethnic groups and levels of society.[80] In the last two centuries of the Republic, a "Roman" army was created from Roman citizens, Latins, and allies (the distinction ceased to apply after the Social War of 89 BC); the Oscan ethnic groups from mountainous central Italy, speaking a different dialect of Latin, underwent Romanization, as did recruits from more alien regions such as Sicily and Cisalpine Gaul (north Italy) and probably even the descendants of Greek slaves.[81]

8. THE FACE OF COMBAT

Traditional military history reconstructed battles in the abstract, reducing them to diagrams of block-like tactical units on maps. This approach to military history is ahistorical. Recent Roman military historians have returned to the ancient sources, emphasizing pre-modern mentalities and varying perspectives: the general's battle, the unit's battle, and the soldier's battle.[82] Ancient battle descriptions are often impressionistic and rhetorical, emphasizing heroic action and moral qualities.[83] Recent Roman military history emphasizes

---

78 Alston 1998, 210; Blois 2007, 166; Rathbone 2008, 308.
79 Wallace-Hadrill 2008, 329-33, 345-55.
80 Phang 2008, 276-9; cf. Dench 1996, 1998.
81 On this process Noy 2000; Dewar 2003; Dench 1995; Dench 2005; Prag 2007. Slaves and freedmen were not normally recruited, but the sons and descendants of freedmen were not excluded.
82 Lee 1996; Gilliver 1996; idem 2007a; Goldsworthy 1996; Lendon 1999; idem 2005; Sabin 2000; Thorne 2007.
83 Lendon 1999; Gilliver 2007a, 123; Gerlinger 2008.

the individual fighter's experience of combat and his motivations or psychological state, including fear, rage, and courage or competitive spirit.[84] Such an approach is closer to the focus of ancient elite authors on personalities and individuals. Roman approaches to tactics might focus on elevation (up- and downhill) rather than spatial extension.[85]

Reconstructing Roman combat deployment has been a long-running controversy.[86] Modern reconstructions (such as Hollywood films and television miniseries) stereotyped Roman combat deployment as observing machine-like discipline, rank and file standing in perfect order and moving in coordination.[87] Secondary works on the Roman military continue to emphasize order, but some recent studies have deemphasized order, stressing the individual soldier's initiative and aggression. The nature of ancient combat meant that a fighter needed space in which to move freely to parry his adversary; Roman infantry formations were considerably looser and wider than either ancient hoplite or early modern infantry formations.[88] Roman cavalry needed even more space to allow horses to gallop; when cavalry met infantry or other cavalry, any formation was lost as the horses and riders dispersed to avoid colliding with the enemy. Machine-like drill is an anachronism imported from seventeenth- to nineteenth-century Western European warfare when drilling and firing in unison enhanced the effectiveness of infantry in battle.[89] For Roman troops, dense or coordinated formation was merely an option. The account in Arrian's *Tactica* of highly coordinated cavalry drill appears to be a spectacle rather than intended for combat; the riders wear ornate clothing and armor unlikely to be used in the field.[90]

A new approach to Roman combat emphasizes emotional factors, in keeping with recent investigations of the history of emotion in the classical world. Ancient weapon combat required a high degree of individual initiative and confidence. Lengthy physical training in personal combat techniques instilled this confidence or spiritedness

---

84 Lee 1996; Lendon 1999; idem 2005, 177-212; Sabin 2000; James 2002; Morillo 2006, 41.
85 Lendon 1999, 316-22.
86 Reviewed by Goldsworthy 1996, 171-3; Gilliver 2007a, 128-30. A. Richardson (2001 and 2003) and Peretz (2005) employ new methods of reconstructing order of battle.
87 Brice 2008.
88 Goldsworthy 1996; Lendon 1999; idem 2005, 186-8, 252, 257.
89 James 2002, 8-9; Phang 2008, 49-51.
90 Dense formation, Wheeler 1979; on Arrian, Wheeler 1978; Lendon 2005, 270-4.

(*animus*), which Roman commanders encouraged.[91] *Animus* could get out of hand, as shown by the reputation of Roman soldiers for brutality both to their enemies and to civilians (see "Enemies of Empire," below). The relationship between soldiers' spiritedness and their anger vexed the Stoic philosopher Seneca, who wished to attribute anger to barbarians, not Roman soldiers.[92]

9. AUGUSTUS AND THE PRINCIPATE

As victor of the late Republic's civil wars, Augustus established the imperial order, which was dependent on the support of the army. After demobilizing many troops and reducing the number of legions, he ensured the stability of the army by regularizing the service of soldiers, now required to serve sixteen to twenty years (later extended to twenty-five years, twenty-eight in some types of units). The creation of the *aerarium militare*, a special fund filled by taxing inheritances, provided legionary pensions; other taxation funded soldiers' pay. Legionaries in the late Republic initially received land upon discharge, but after the reforms this land was commuted to cash; non-citizen troops received the Roman citizenship.[93]

Augustus also regularized the Praetorian Guard and the navy. Antecedents of the Praetorians had existed earlier, Pompey had been given an extraordinary command to suppress rampant piracy in the Mediterranean Sea, and Octavian had mobilized a navy to fight Cleopatra at Actium, but now the Praetorians and fleets were established as distinct units of the Roman military.[94] The Praetorians were recruited from a somewhat higher socio-economic stratum than legionaries or auxiliaries, or might be promoted from the legions; they served sixteen years. They were supplemented by the emperor's horse guards; the urban cohorts, tasked with keeping order in the city of Rome; and the *vigiles* or fire watch, recruited from freedmen.[95] The fleets were later based at Misenum (near Naples), Ravenna, and on the

---

91 Lendon 1999, 290, 296-305; on training, Horsmann 1991.
92 Sen. *De ira* 1.9.1-4, 1.13.5, 2.1.5.
93 On the Augustan reforms of the army, Raaflaub 1987; M. A. Speidel 2000a; Alston 2007, 185-9; Gilliver 2007c, 184-8; Rankov 2007, 35-7.
94 Praetorians: Durry 1935, 1938; Passerini 1939; Bingham 1997; navy, Starr 1993.
95 Horse guards: M. P. Speidel 1978a; idem 1994; urban cohorts, Ricci 1994; *vigiles,* Sablayrolles 1996; on the general dynamics of the various troops in Rome, Sablayrolles 2000 and Rivière 2004b.

Rhine and Danube rivers. Sailors had the longest service (28 years) and the lowest prestige of the major Roman forces.

To those familiar with early modern European military history, the Augustan regime's creation of a permanent, long-service army financed by the state might resemble Gustavus Adolphus's Sweden or Frederick the Great's Prussia, but such an interpretation misreads Augustus's institutions and political strategies. Augustus gave the appearance of ruling lightly; he did not develop a sophisticated civilian bureaucracy staffed with soldiers or formally trained civil servants but relied on the emperor's household, including slaves and freedmen. This relatively minimal government was illusory, intended to conciliate the senatorial elite.

In the provinces, the emperors also employed soldiers, especially low-ranking officers, in roles that a modern government might assign to civilians, including tax collection, assisting provincial governors, and customs duties.[96] Nonetheless, the Roman military was quite small in proportion to the empire's breadth, especially if one compares it to the armies of early modern and modern European nations.[97] A patronage model of power, furthermore, prevailed in the Roman military as in other aspects of the Roman state (see "Promotion and Patronage" below).

Another, contrasting stereotype is that Augustus "demilitarized" the Roman elite by making military service a profession of volunteer soldiers. Conscription continued to be employed in the Principate in shortages and emergencies. Though the political expectation that candidates would have served ten campaigns was already in desuetude in the late Republic, and though most senatorial aristocrats did not pursue military commands, some Roman senators and certainly equestrians continued to hold posts as military officers; the governors of certain provinces were nominally commanders.[98] Most males of the upper orders who did not adopt military career paths continued to participate vicariously through the celebration of imperial triumphs and of Roman historical victories (see "Imagining Warfare," below).

Furthermore, the emperor's public image remained that of a commander or warrior, as has been emphasized in recent years.[99] This

---

96   On these officers see the various works by Rankov (1990; 1994, 1999a, 1999b, 2002), as well as Petraccia Lucernoni 2001; Drogula 2005; Brélaz 2008.
97   Addington 1990, 140-1.
98   Hopkins and Burton 1998a.
99   Campbell 1984; idem 2002; Mattern 1999, 194-202; Hekster 2007.

is just as true of the emperors to whom historians have attributed a "defensive" grand strategy. In portrait statues and triumphal reliefs, the emperor often is shown wearing armor and a military cloak; on numerous coin types, he addresses his troops or even stands with one foot on the body or head of a defeated enemy. Imperial titles, such as Germanicus, Britannicus, Dacicus, or Parthicus, proclaimed his victories.[100] In imperial art, deities favored him and attended his victories.[101] In fact, in the early and middle Empire, not the emperor but his deputies (usually men of the imperial house) led campaigns in person. When the emperor was present, he was not expected to fight in the ranks in person; he generally risked only minor exposure.[102] In contrast, many Republican nobles, including consuls, had indeed died or been wounded in combat.[103] The emperor might also display his *virtus* through exertion, traveling on foot or riding with his soldiers and participating in their training exercises.[104]

The emphasis of scholarship has been on the close relationship of the emperor and the army, emphasizing imperial patronage of the army or (depending on perspective) the emperor at the mercy of his soldiers' demands.[105] Another perspective suggests that emperors needed to conciliate and win the support of the urban elite (the upper orders and provincial elites) as much as the soldiers.[106] Following this view, the emperor's treatment of the soldiers, especially imposing *disciplina militaris*, was intended to reassure the elite that he was not just a warlord supported by mercenary troops, but intended to govern in the (antiquarian) tradition of the Republic.[107] Our sources (especially Tacitus) attempt to strip away this illusion, but the illusion was necessary to the stability of the imperial order.

---

100 Mattern 1999, 190-7.
101 Koortbojian 2006; Kousser 2006.
102 Campbell 1984, 65-8; Gleason 2001; Levitham 2008.
103 Rosenstein 1990, 118-24 and 118 n. 7; Barton (2001, 141-3) stresses this "expend-ability"; Bragg 2008 explores elite rhetorical use of wounds and scars.
104 Phang 2008, 244.
105 Campbell 1984; idem 2002; M. P. Speidel 1993; Blois 2002; Keaveney 2007; Hekster 2007, 352-3; in documentary sources such as diplomata, Eck 2000; idem 2003; at the mercy of soldiers, Birley 2007.
106 Ando 2007, 369.
107 Phang 2008, 71-2; on punishment, 150-1; payments to army, 179-82, 199-200; Alston 2007, 191.

10. IMAGINING WARFARE: IMPERIAL ELITE PARTICIPATION

Mid-twentieth century military history has emphasized "military participation" as a demographic fact, but military history includes the civilian support of warfare.[108] In contrast with the Republic, in the imperial period many Roman elite males had little direct contact with the Roman army, contrasting with the minority of *viri militares* holding military commands.[109] The tendency to regard the Principate as a rupture, an absolute break, with the Republic is an accident of modern scholarship's periodization. Despite the new order, the Roman elites continued to manifest an imperialist mentality, regarding Roman conquest and domination of other peoples as praiseworthy, lauding the campaigns of the emperor or his deputies, and thus participating vicariously in imperialism.[110]

Elite authors invoked continuity between the Roman past and present, between their civilian education and the military sphere, when they employed heroic (mythological or historical) imagery to represent military activity. The aristocratic families of the Republic adapted Hellenistic heroic iconography.[111] Writing eulogies to friends in military service, or panegyrizing the emperor Domitian's conquests, the poets Martial and Statius employed heroic imagery. A generation later, Lucian's *How To Write History* parodies Greek and Roman civilian gentlemen's deployment of heroic models of warfare, whether Atticizing (Herodotus and Thucydides), or Republican Roman, to praise Lucius Verus' campaign against Parthia. Elite authors' accounts of mythological warfare may also reflect upon Roman imperialism; Virgil's *Aeneid* is the most well known instance. Heroic iconography was highly visual and understandable, bridging the gap between social strata. A heroic image could be adopted by soldiers as well, such as Soranus, the Batavian horseman whose epitaph records Homeric exploits.[112]

Late Republican and imperial authors also adopted military imagery for non-military pursuits, such as philosophy, employing the exemplars of Roman historiography to inspire contemporary elite readers to strive

---

108 As shown for World War I and interwar Europe by Bourke 1996; Mossé 1996.
109 Hopkins and Burton 1983a; Campbell 1984, 319-32; idem 2002, 40-1; Lendon 1997, 185-91; Mattern 1999, 16-17.
110 Mattern 1999, 162-71.
111 Dillon and Welch 2006.
112 M. P. Speidel 1991; Lendon 1997, 243-5.

for excellence or endure pain or grief, seen in Seneca the Younger's *De constantia*. This literary tradition was part of the acculturation of the Roman elite, an elite that was constantly renewed from below (from regional aristocracies, still well above the common soldiers). Ironically, it widened the gulf between the elites and the common soldiers, whom the literary authors represent as boorish and uncultured, lacking self-control. In the end, senators were excluded from military commands in the crisis of the third century; in practice, fewer and fewer held commands. Equestrians dominated military commands, and the separation of the educated elite from the military increased. The prestige of military activity in the late third and fourth centuries AD, however, did not wane (see chapter four, below).[113]

11. IMPERIAL MILITARY DISCIPLINE

The most famous stereotype of the ancient Roman army is perhaps its discipline, in Latin *disciplina militaris*.[114] Most recently, scholars have discussed *disciplina militaris* mainly in contrast to *virtus* in combat. In the view of Nathan Rosenstein, *disciplina* as combat discipline emphasized the maintenance of order in battle and provided a rationale for winning or losing battles that was less opprobrious than the general's personal *virtus* or cowardice.[115] Recently, J. E. Lendon has argued that *disciplina* was also a counterbalance to excessive *virtus*, such as Caesar's soldiers' fury for combat at Gergovia, contrary to orders.[116] This was so especially when the excessive *virtus* of individual generals began to destabilize the Republican political order.[117] Lendon argues that in the Empire, *disciplina* was appropriate to legionaries, depicted in their military engineering projects on the Column of Trajan; auxiliaries might display fierce *virtus* in combat.[118] During the Empire, emphasis on *disciplina* earned commanders prestige but minimized the risk of pursuing aggressive campaigns; the emperor might be jealous of the *virtus* of victorious senatorial commanders, potential usurpers.[119]

---

113 Lendon 2005, 280-5; Lee 2007.
114 Found in most older works and expressed best by Keegan (1976, 68). On decimation, also Pickford 2005; desertion, Cosme 2003.
115 Rosenstein 1990, 173-4.
116 Lendon 1999, 307-9; idem 2005, 220-223.
117 McDonnell 2006b, 71.
118 Lendon 2005, 242-3, 250-2.
119 Phang 2008, 243-6.

Authors also saw *disciplina* as differentiating Roman soldiers from barbarians' lack of self-control or military organization.[120]

Disciplina militaris, however, also promoted and maintained the *virtus* of soldiers, especially in peacetime.[121] The association of austerity with traditional Roman virtue has been mentioned above. Discipline included dietary austerity—the opposite of the feasting and revelry of the army at a triumph.[122] Civilian authors exaggerated the appetites of soldiers for food and wine, symbolizing the excessive military budget in the eyes of its critics.[123] Hard work and austerity promoted *virtus* in soldiers. Roman authors believed that *otium* (idleness or leisure) demoralized soldiers, making them prone to mutiny. Recent work on indiscipline suggests that in some cases the accusation of idleness was a means to criticize other troops and commanders. In these contexts mutiny and military unrest are topics receiving more attention; such studies will contribute much to a more complete understanding of *disciplina militaris.*[124] As will be seen, the disbursement of wealth to soldiers by commanders and emperors, a blatant form of patronage, was also regarded as promoting indiscipline. Of course, during the Principate's long-term service and relative peace, most of these values were probably honored in the breach. Austerity does not leave archaeological remains. Nonetheless *disciplina* themes furnished the Roman elite with a rhetoric of praise and blame. Displayed by low-ranking officers in inscriptions, this rhetoric was probably part of officers' acculturation.[125]

In its discouragement of patronage (discussed below), imperial *disciplina militaris* restrained both the army and the commanders who might indulge the army to promote their usurpation. The *Senatus Consultum de Cn. Pisone patre,* an edict condemning the provincial governor Cn. Calpurnius Piso (the alleged murderer of Germanicus, Tiberius' heir), displays this conceptualization of discipline. Piso was guilty of giving donatives to the army in his own name; Tacitus adds

---

120 Mattern 1999, 202-7.
121 Phang 2008, 241-6.
122 On triumphal feasts, Beard 2008, 257-63. Representations of dietary austerity in *militia* resemble the 2nd c. BC sumptuary legislation, Corbier 1989; in general on austerity, Wallace-Hadrill 2008, 315-55.
123 Carrié 1993, 118-20.
124 On idleness as an accusation see Wheeler 1996; on mutiny and indiscipline see Chris-santhos 2001; Brice 2011a; Phang 2008, 221-6.
125 J. Adams 1999; Phang 2008, 209-11, 224-5, 241-2.

that he gave unlimited furloughs and allowed himself to be called "father of the army."[126]

Disciplina militaris was thus deeply embedded in Roman political and cultural ideologies. In contrast with modern armies, the Roman army was lacking in formal discipline, including standardized and identical uniform, parade-ground drill, marching music, and elaborate etiquette.[127] Armor played the role of uniform for purposes of display and discipline. Soldiers "on parade" wore armor, different troops and officers were differentiated by their armor, and soldiers who did not wear armor or who sold or threw it away were punished.[128] In the age of spear and sword combat, Roman battlefield order lacked the rigid, mechanical drill of eighteenth-century infantry. Roman soldiers were notably outspoken to their commanders, and not only in mutinies. Caesar represents his soldiers as frequently urging him to attack, and it was his task to curb them.[129]

12. DEMOGRAPHY OF THE ROMAN MILITARY

Demography is a recent topic in Roman military studies. Key demographic factors shaping a population are mortality, marriage, and fertility. The ancient Roman world's low average life expectancy (as in other societies without modern medicine) does not mean that adults had much shorter lifespans than modern people. A low average life expectancy is connected with high infant and early childhood mortality; once past childhood, the Roman expectation of life was not particularly low. The Republic's levies conscripted men aged between 17 and 47; imperial veterans, recruited in their late teens or early twenties, would be discharged at latest in their middle fifties. It is notable that the Romans thought a man of 47 to 55 would still be vigorous enough to serve (cf. the even older Spurius Ligustinus).[130]

Due to normal age-related mortality, recruits in the same age cohort (no relation to the tactical cohort) would not all reach discharge. Walter Scheidel estimates that according to model 'life tables' at least a third of an age cohort of recruits would die from natural mortality

---

126 Eck, Caballos and Fernández 1996; Potter 1999; Robinson 2007, 56-77; on discipline, Phang 2008, 179-80.
127 Phang 2008, 81-92. On modern formal discipline Myerly 1996.
128 Gilliver 2007b, 3-4, 10-11, 14-17; see also Rankov 2007, 58-62.
129 Lendon 1999; Chrissanthos 2004.
130 Livy 42.34.1-11.

before they reached discharge.[131] Extant *laterculi* (inscriptions listing discharged soldiers) suggest that a larger number, nearly one-half, suffered attrition, not necessarily from natural death. Desertion, premature discharge (dishonorable or medical), and combat casualties could account for the additional missing veterans.[132] Though the Roman army provided medical care for its troops, even sending them to medical installations with hot springs, a soldier with physical disabilities that affected his ability to fight would be unable to serve.[133] In the Principate, however, there were probably fewer combat-related deaths versus deaths from infectious disease, due to increasingly dense settlements on the frontier; urbanized regions in antiquity were hotbeds of disease.[134]

Attrition from natural mortality reduced the number of veterans for whom the Roman government had to pay pensions. By extending the length of service, Augustus or his advisers may have estimated savings for the military budget, since fewer soldiers in an age cohort would reach discharge.[135] Whether Augustus or his advisors actually carried out any mathematical calculation or even estimate is unknown.

The marriage and fertility patterns of late Republican soldiers were probably distorted by long service abroad and by impoverishment. Though the wealth and land added by conquest resulted in economic and demographic growth in Italy, demographic growth impoverished the sons of the small farmers (*assidui*) from whom the legions were recruited. These sons, young men without prospects as farmers, entered the army, usually serving a decade and more before marrying and raising families, a marked delay in comparison with civilian men.[136]

Such patterns persisted in the imperial army, which denied soldiers legal marriages (see "Gender, Marriage, and Sexuality," below). The "marriage ban" affected the legal status of the unions, not *de facto* practices. Some soldiers formed stable *de facto* unions

---

131 Scheidel 2007a, 426.
132 Scheidel 2007a, 427.
133 Goldsworthy and Haynes 1999; Baker 2004.
134 On the extent to which imperial soldiers were a "wartime" or "peacetime" army, Dobson 1986. The smallpox epidemic of the period 165-180 AD is said to have devastated the army, which allegedly brought it back from Lucius Verus's Parthian campaign, Duncan-Jones 1996. On disease in the city of Rome, Scheidel 2003, 165-66, 173; generally, Scheidel 2007a, 427-8.
135 Scheidel 1996a; Gilliver 2007c; on the age of soldiers in tombstones also Hope 2007.
136 Rosenstein 2004, 83-8, 152-4.

with women. These unions were socially equivalent to marriage and were commemorated as such on tombstones, recorded also in papyri, ostraca, and tablets.[137] When they did 'marry,' soldiers still tended to do so in their late thirties, later than civilian Roman men; children of the unions were not numerous. Many soldiers did not form long-term relationships with women at all; their tombstones record comrades as commemorators. The reasons for these patterns are not known, but at least in the first century AD, the pay of imperial legionaries, though substantial for a single individual, was insufficient to support multiple dependents. Auxiliaries may have been paid less.[138] Soldiers had enough disposable income to attract women, but may have spent it on slave women or prostitutes.[139] In contrast with civilian men, the proportion of soldiers commemorated by wives does not exceed a third until soldiers are in their late forties.[140] At any rate, too few soldiers raised children to lend much support to the old idea that the later Roman army became "hereditary," recruited from soldiers' sons.

Roman soldiers' social attitudes to youth and middle age may have influenced these patterns. Prowess in combat was a young man's attribute, and by their mid-thirties Republican cavalry were no longer expected to skirmish ahead of the lines. By their late thirties, imperial soldiers may have been ready to settle down.[141]

13. Ethnic and Religious Identities

Demographic shifts in recruitment also occurred: the imperial army became more and more representative of the provincials as opposed to Italians, continuing a process of assimilation that had begun in the late Republic. Recruitment from Italy waned in the late first century BC and the early first century AD.[142] Attracted by the higher pay and privileges, Italian men continued to join the Praetorian Guard (to which provincial legionaries might be promoted); many died young in the

---

137 Phang 2001, 22-52, 142-96; see now Noelke and Kibilka 2005; (tombstones); Ahmed Gouda 2006 (ostraka); Scheidel 2007b questions the basis of age at first marriage estimates from epitaphs.
138 Phang 2001, 176-90.
139 Phang 2001, 231-40; idem 2004 (slave women); Scheidel 2007a, 423-4; idem 2009b, 302.
140 Scheidel 2007a, 421.
141 McDonnell 2005.
142 Forni 1953; Keppie 1997.

population sink of the city of Rome.[143] Septimius Severus disbanded the Italian Praetorians to punish them for overthrowing Pertinax in 193, and recruited the Guard from provincial legionaries.[144]

By the later first and second centuries AD, legionaries were increasingly recruited from frontier provinces; their nomenclature suggests that their families had received Roman citizenship a few generations earlier. By the late second and third centuries, legionaries were recruited from the frontier zones of the provinces, and most auxiliaries were now Roman citizens even before Caracalla conferred the citizenship on all free inhabitants of the Empire in 212.[145] These shifts also affected the political history of the army, for Hellenic urban aristocrats such as the historian Dio Cassius (a senator and provincial governor in the late second and early third centuries AD) judged the provincial Praetorians, recruited from Latin-speaking provinces, as "barbarous" and uncouth in manners and speech.[146] Additional work on demography might further set the Praetorians in the context of the demography and health conditions of the imperial megalopolis.

However, ethnic identity is a complex phenomenon that may manifest differently in different roles and registers, as J. N. Adams has shown for language use in the Roman army.[147] Latin was the "language of power," employed for official functions and oaths of obedience; many recruits in the Greek East took Latin nomenclature on enlistment; soldiers attempting to assert authority over Greek-speaking civilians might address them in Latin. But Eastern military personnel also used Greek for some administrative documents; they are likely to have spoken Greek in daily usage and friendly interaction with civilians. The complexities of soldiers' ethnic identity are also attested in archaeological evidence such as pottery.[148]

Ethnic identity blurred further in the practice of religion. On the one hand, the army had its own religious cult practices, holidays, and rituals, that honored traditional Roman deities (as well as the deified emperors and their family members) and was probably intended to reinforce loyalty to the emperor and promote an imperial and military

---

143 Scheidel 1996, 128-9; Phang 2001, 163.
144 Potter 2004, 125-33.
145 Forni 1953; Mann 1983.
146 Dio 49.36.2-4; 75.2.5; 80.1.3.
147 Adams 2003.
148 Pottery: Pollard 2004; archaeology and epigraphy, Ligt, Hemelrijk, and Singor 2004; Pollard 2000; Roman influence penetrated beyond the frontier as well, Grane 2007.

identity.[149] On the other hand, soldiers and even elite officers honored local cults of non-Roman deities and did not regard this behavior as inappropriate.[150] Over time, Roman cults took on a local coloring and vice versa, seen in the military deities that the Roman army at Dura-Europos venerated in the mid-third century AD.[151] The exception was the monotheistic religions, Judaism and Christianity, which denied the divinity of the emperors and the validity of other cults. According to Josephus, imperial soldiers' disrespect for Jewish religious practices helped to spark the Jewish War of AD 68-70. In Christian martyrdom accounts, soldiers usually appear as guards or torturers, though a few miraculously converted.[152]

14. GENDER AND SEXUALITY

A new area in Roman army studies concerns the role of gender and sexuality, now an accepted aspect of modern military studies.[153] It has not caught up with studies of Roman civilian gender and sexuality, and we still know relatively little about sexual behavior as such on the frontiers.[154] In a slave-owning society, soldiers' sexual partners included slaves of both genders, prostitutes, and long-term de facto wives. Roman soldiers customarily captured and enslaved defeated enemies; they were also presumed to rape captive enemy women and youths (see "Enemies of Empire," below). The Romans accepted homosexual practices involving civilian slave or prostitute partners, and same-sex relationships between men of equal rank may have been tolerated, but homosexual relationships between Roman officers and soldiers evoked both brutal punishment and cultural anxiety.[155] Heterosexual adultery across the ranks was also a source of anxiety; Tacitus relates that in the early first century AD, a young officer committed adultery with his commander's wife; Pliny reports that Trajan tried a case in which

149 On the *Feriale Duranum* (P. *Dura* 54), Fink, Hoey, and Snyder 1940; Campbell 1994, no. 207; Irby-Massie 1999; Southern 2007, 160-1.
150 Accounts of Roman military religion thus tend to be regional; Britain, Irby-Massie 1999; Dacia, Popescu 2004; some cults crossed geographic boundaries, M. P. Speidel 1978b.
151 Pollard 2000; idem 2004.
152 Shaw 2003.
153 Mossé 1996; Bourke 1996; Goldstein 2001.
154 Phang 2001, 229-95; Whittaker 2004, 115-43; Ahmed Gouda 2006; Scheidel 2009b, 301-3.
155 Phang 2001, 262-95; punishment, Fantham 1991; anxiety, Walters 1997; Gunderson 2003, 153-90.

a commander's wife committed adultery with a centurion. Plancina, wife of the aforementioned Cn. Calpurnius Piso, was also charged with having watched soldiers at exercises.[156] Roman officers, concerned for their authority and *virtus*, feared its subversion by sexual impropriety.

Another approach to gender focuses on cultural constructions. *Militia* was a zone of masculinity; *virtus* meant both courage in battle and manliness.[157] This ideology shapes Caesar's disapproval of Roman soldiers marrying local women at Alexandria during the Civil Wars as losing their Roman identity—including *virtus*.[158] In Roman conceptions of masculinity, Roman *virtus* maintained imperial domination over less masculine peoples (Greeks and Easterners; Gauls and Germans were fierce but lacked self-control) but was itself in constant danger of decline through luxury or effeminacy.[159] The *topos* recurs that legionaries were made effeminate by station in the East, legionaries stationed in Syria allegedly even engaged in self-depilating (considered a highly effeminate trait in Roman culture).[160] Besides practical concerns about military readiness, concerns about maintaining *virtus* thus may have shaped Augustus' decision, not directly attested, to deny serving soldiers' legitimate marriage to women.[161]

As the anecdotes of sexual impropriety suggest, *militia* as a zone of masculinity also applied to elite officers. The Augustan marriage legislation required men of the senatorial and equestrian orders to marry or to face financial penalties, and made adultery criminal.[162] Senatorial and equestrian officers thus probably had wives, but whether their wives should accompany them to their military postings was a credible topic of debate in the Senate.[163] These representations bore little resemblance to actual practice; certainly by the late first century AD, officers' and commanders' wives usually accompanied them to their posts (see below). Such representations belong to an elite discourse fashioning appropriate masculine gender roles for Roman

---

156 Tac. *Hist.* 1.48; Plin. *Ep.* 6.31; Tac. *Ann.* 2.55. Marshall 1975; Kuijper 1973; Phang 2001, 368-71.

157 Lendon 1999, 304; Williams 2010, 145-8; McDonnell 2006b; a broader collection on *virtus* is Partoens, Roskam, and van Houdt 2004.

158 Caes. *B. Civ.* 3.110; Caesar's view of *virtus* in Lendon 1999, 304-10.

159 Williams 2010, 145-8.

160 Fronto *ad Verum* 2.14; on the ethnographic discourse, avoiding gender, Wheeler 1996.

161 Phang 2001, 345-50; Scheidel 2007a.

162 McGinn 1998.

163 Tac. *Ann.* 3.33-4; D. 1.16.4.2; Phang 2001, 361-72.

males in military service. Whether there were separate masculinities for Roman officers and soldiers, or whether *virtus* could be a unifying ideology, and how it changed with the late Republic and new imperial order, are questions that still need answering.[164]

15. Promotion and Patronage

German military historians as well as the so-called "Durham school" of Roman army studies reconstructed promotion patterns, diagramming cycles of promotion for subaltern officers (of centurion rank and below, recruited from the lower orders) and for elite officers.[165] These scholars tended to impose a rationalist model, assuming that the most effective or qualified personnel were promoted.[166] More recent researchers stress that commanders were amateurs; there is no evidence of a formal training school like that of modern Western armies.[167] The surviving sources suggest that promotion was based on combat valor or on moral criteria, seen in recommendation letters and in terms of praise in the epitaphs of officers that recorded their careers.[168] Seniority was another criterion for promotion; chief centurions were men in late middle age who had held a series of centurion posts in a complex hierarchy.[169]

As in many traditional social and political hierarchies, Roman promotion was also based on personal patronage.[170] Letters survive in which soldiers beseeched their commander, as patron, for favors such as furlough.[171] Other forms of patronage involved blatant bribery; soldiers paid bribes to their centurions in return for furlough, a practice repressed by the emperors.[172] Imperial patronage to the army, especially in the form of pay increases, donatives and other benefits, has been emphasized.[173] Patronage, however, coexisted with greater bureaucratic

---

164 Alston 1998 is a bold but not entirely satisfactory attempt.
165 Dobson 1970; 1974; Breeze 1969; idem 1971; idem 1974; Blois 2001; James 2002.
166 Still argued by A. Birley 1992, 2001, 2003; Eck 2001. On rationalism, Morillo 2006, 30-31, 48-50.
167 Campbell 1984, 319-32; idem 2002, 40-1; Lendon 1997, 185-9; Mattern 1999, 16-17; reviewed, Gilliver 2007c, 188-200; Phang 2008, 17.
168 A. Birley 2003.
169 Gilliver 2007c, 191-92 reviews the controversy over reconstructing this hierarchy.
170 Campbell 1984, 325-47; Lendon 1997, 238-43, 252-65; James 2002, 40-41.
171 *Tab. Vindol.* II 225, 250.
172 Tac. *Ann.* 1.17; *Hist.* 1.46; 1.58; HA *Hadr.* 10.3.
173 Campbell 1984, 181-98; M. A. Speidel 2000a; idem 2000b; Stäcker 2003; A. Birley 2007; discussed, Phang 2008, 179-97. The evidence for pay scales requires partial extrapolation; see M. A. Speidel 1992; idem 2000b.

impersonality: though a soldier or veteran might still appeal to the emperor for personal assistance, he might receive personal favor or he might be treated more impersonally.[174] *Disciplina militaris* restrained patronage of the army. Later emperors acted as patrons in other respects, providing soldiers with access to legal advice, though not guaranteeing a favorable judgment or ruling ("Military Law," below).

There were political motives for downplaying patronage, as a usurper could seek military support through gifts to the army. The exchange of gifts between social equals in a political context was hazardous, as the recipients owed *gratia* (support, collusion). The exchange of gifts across social strata, as when generals gave pay, land, or donatives to soldiers, was more dangerous, leveling the Late Republican generals and soldiers, as both Appian and Plutarch perceived in hindsight. In this literary tradition, the distribution of wealth to soldiers risked their debilitation by luxury or the increase of their desires, causing them to support civil war leaders who promised them rewards. This attitude is unchanged in Herodian's condemnation of the increase in army pay made by the emperor Septimius Severus in 197.[175] A preventative of undue patronage was the routinization and rationalization of pay, donatives, and other benefits, made regular and thus more impersonal; even donatives were given routinely at certain occasions.

Soldiers negotiated their privileges with the Roman elite and the emperors; that the emperors always favored soldiers over civilians and granted excessive privileges is an over-simplification. Emperors shared social attitudes with the elite and needed to retain legitimacy in elite eyes. Part of the art of command, by emperors or local commanders, included motivating soldiers to accept disciplinary practices—at least physical training, campaign rations, and *labor*. Roman success in combat required the emotional motivation of soldiers. For this reason, commanders and even emperors made a show of participation in the toil and hardships of training exercises and campaigns.

16. THE ROMAN ARMY AND THE ECONOMY

The initial economic impact of Roman conquests on the frontiers was probably deleterious, harming the local economies due to casualties and the plundering and enslavement of the defeated, routine

---

174 Phang 2008, 188.
175 Hdn. 3.8.5; Phang 2001, 17-8, 381-2.

practices of ancient warfare. Nonetheless, longer-term archaeological and epigraphic studies stress the Roman military's promotion of "development" (a somewhat anachronistic term) for its own logistic needs. The military's supply needs promoted the building of roads, local trade, long-distance trade, and monetization. Private traders (sometimes veterans) followed the army and settled in the civilian settlements near forts.[176] Both military supply and soldiers' petty cash purchases injected coinage into the local economy. Latin inscriptions themselves, both military and civilian, attest the economic development of the frontier provinces, since inscribed tombstones and monuments were relatively expensive; their numbers increase in the late first through early third centuries AD (depending on region), long after the initial conquests.

As the presence of traders implies, soldiers had an additional economic role as consumers, introducing Roman consumption patterns to northern regions with different material cultures and eating habits.[177] Such consumption posed a problem for military discipline, most obviously in drunken soldiers and the presence of traders and prostitutes, but also as elite fears that extravagant soldiers would overspend their pay and support usurpers who promised them donatives.[178]

Soldiers also contributed to "civilian" aspects of the economy, administering taxation, mines and quarries, and customs duties. The imperial government lacked sufficient civilian personnel for low-level administration and transport, and caravans might need a military presence to defend themselves and their cargo from bandits.[179] In these "civilian" roles, soldiers were sometimes guilty of corruption, extortion, and brutality.[180] Soldiers were known for extortion of transport animals and lodgings from provincials and also had a

---

176 MacMullen (1963) remains a classic. Recent collections include Erdkamp 2002; Blois and Rich 2002.
177 Roth (1999) focuses on the needs of the army at war; on soldiers as consumers, Carrié 1993, 124-5; Woolf 1998, 243-5.
178 Phang 2008, 160-2, 175-7, 256-7; on donatives and imperial finances, Chastagnol 1977; Stäcker 2003; on consumerism in antiquity, Wallace-Hadrill (2008) provides perspective.
179 On soldiers as low-level administrators, see above n. 96 above; on bandits and brigands in the Roman Empire, Shaw 1984; Grunewald 1999; Reiss 2000-01; idem 2001; idem 2007.
180 MacMullen 1963; idem 1988, 129-32; Campbell 1984, 246-54; Alston 1995, 81-96; Whittaker 2004, 129-32.

reputation for violence when thwarted by civilians. It was difficult to police the army in a society with poorly developed local civilian police forces and slow communications and transportation.[181] But soldiers were also a symbolic target for provincial resentment of the imperial power or for invectives on particular rulers.

17. SOCIAL STATUS OF SOLDIERS

In the early and middle (down to c. 300 BC) Republic, the hoplite model of warfare, borrowed from Greeks, required infantry soldiers to be recruited from a relatively prosperous smallholder class, able to bear the costs of armor and arms and absence from the farm. The Servian constitution required legionaries to meet a property qualification in order to serve. Poorer citizens were relegated to supporting roles as more lightly armed troops.

In contrast with this "middle class" vision of military service, traditional scholarship has emphasized that during the second and first centuries BC the aristocracy (now both patrician and plebeian) became much wealthier and the small landowners became impoverished, creating a manpower crisis. Marius took the step of recruiting landless citizens; later Republican and imperial authors regarded these men as desperate mercenaries exploited in the civil wars.[182] More recent studies, based on archaeology and demography, suggest that the economic situation of small farmers in the late Republic was more complex. Some at least prospered, leaving behind more children who, because in Roman law all children received a share of inheritance, created a second-generation shortage of land.[183]

The social status of imperial Roman soldiers is another controversy in Roman military studies. Whether soldiers were a privileged group remains a point of debate.[184] It is difficult to separate hard data (often lacking) from rhetoric; the soldiers beseeching Drusus and Germanicus in the mutinies of AD 14 emphasized their poverty and degradation, whereas provincials abused by soldiers, and the elite authors, stress

---

181 Extortion: e.g., Mitchell 1976. On civilian police in the Roman Empire, Nippel 1995; Brélaz 2008; Fuhrmann 2011; on customs duties, Duncan-Jones 2006.

182 Carrié 1993, 104-5.

183 Rosenstein 2004; de Ligt and Northwood 2008.

184 Campbell (1984, 177-81, 207-99) stresses soldiers' privileges; their lack of privilege at least in Roman Egypt by Alston 1995, 105-8; idem 1998, 216-19; Phang 2001, 65-80. Generally, Southern 2007, 165-8; Wesch-Klein 2007, 435-60.

soldiers' privileges and arrogance.[185] Military law as it developed by the early third century AD conferred various legal privileges on serving soldiers that were intended to expedite their readiness for action (see "Military Law" below). Roman civilians probably did not differentiate well between soldiers and subaltern officers or veterans. Subaltern officers such as centurions held obvious authority and received higher pay; legionary and Praetorian veterans received large pensions and all veterans had additional legal privileges, including immunity from corporal punishment.[186] The sub-equestrian officers, of course, provided a trickle of ascendants into the equestrian order: chief centurions were promoted to equestrian status upon their discharge.

Roman imperial soldiers can be described as a "sub-elite" respective to the masses—the baseline inhabitants—of the Roman Empire. These baseline inhabitants, peasants and urban dwellers, were probably illiterate and lived at subsistence level; the urban dwellers were overcrowded and suffered high mortality in population sinks such as ancient Rome or Alexandria.[187] Soldiers, in contrast, were at least somewhat literate; they sent and received letters, though others may have read and written for them.[188] Their erection of inscriptions presumes a minimum of wealth and identification with imperial public culture; their use of Greek (in the Eastern Empire) and Latin claimed membership in the empire's dominant cultures.[189] Though soldiers risked the spread of disease in camps and urban settlements, they were better nourished and healthier than the baseline inhabitants. Estimates of the Roman military diet combine literary sources for campaign rations (heavy on wheat) with archaeological findings of a more diverse diet.[190]

Soldiers received regular pay, though there is controversy over how much of it was disposable income and how much auxiliaries were paid

---

185 On abuse of civilians, Campbell 1984, 246-54; C. Adams (2007, 195-6) points out that elite authors employ the theme; Ando (2007, 374-5) emphasizes petitioners' expectations that emperors would punish the abusive soldiers; on policing, Fuhrmann 2011.

186 On veterans, Wesch-Klein 2007, 443-9.

187 On these social and demographic conditions, Morley 2006; Scheidel 2006; idem 2009; idem 2010. Scheidel (2010) suggests that in Roman socio-economic conditions a stark "rich/poor" dichotomy is overstated.

188 Phang 2007, 299-300 (on literacy in general, Harris 1989).

189 J. Adams 2003, 383, 560-1, 614-18; Phang 2007, 300-01.

190 Groenman-van Waateringe 1997; Roth 1999; Stallibrass and Thomas 2008.

(less than legionaries, but estimates vary).[191] Disposable income was reduced by compulsory deductions from pay for equipment, fodder, and clothing. Domitian and later Septimius Severus and Caracalla raised soldiers' pay, and the compulsory deductions seem to have been abandoned in the second century AD, so that a legionary soldier in the early third century AD received more pay in cash; its value, however, was reduced by inflation due to debasement of the Roman Empire's silver coinage. Nonetheless soldiers and their families had money for letter-writing services, funerary inscriptions, and the luxuries they could afford, especially ornamented armor, food items, and pottery.[192]

Soldiers also sought to own one or two slaves to cook food, carry baggage, and tend equipment and horses (and provide sexual services); a poor man, in the Roman empire, was one who owned no slaves. In the name of discipline, commanders such as Scipio Aemilianus and Marius expelled soldiers' slaves and made soldiers carry their own gear. Nonetheless, legal and documentary sources confirm that imperial soldiers often owned slaves.[193]

18. MILITARY LAW

In the period of Republican expansion, Roman law in military affairs focused on the making and breaking of treaties with other state entities; these acts were infused with religious ritual. Roman law, *ius civile*, terminated at the boundary of Roman territory. There was no "military law" as such. The Republic's oldest legal texts, the Twelve Tables, did not cover military discipline, which commanders were empowered by their office to administer in a summary fashion, as they thought best.[194] Literary authors such as Livy emphasized the harshness of individual mid-Republican commanders in a number of exemplary anecdotes. By the late Republic, however, decimation (collective punishment)

---

191 On pay (both literary and documentary sources) there is a large bibliography: most recently, M.A. Speidel 1992; idem 2000b; Mattern 1999, 123-42; Rathbone 2007, 158-65; Herz 2007, 308-13; Phang 2008, 166-71.
192 Carrie 1993, 120, 123-4; Wallace-Hadrill 2008, 415-16, 439; see also Veen 2003.
193 M. P. Speidel 1989; Phang 2005, 205-8.
194 Phang 2008, 115-16. The legal aspects of Greek, Hellenistic and Roman warfare are surveyed by Brizzi (2002). Giuffrè's work (1974, 1983, 1996) collects and synthesizes the sources on Roman military law (from a legalistic standpoint). Gabba (2002) and Drogula (2007) examine the legal status of Roman commanders (in the Republic, consuls with *imperium*); on the secularization of Roman warfare see also Sordi 2002a.

might be a punishment for cowardice or mutiny.[195] The instances of decimation were not numerous; certainly after Tiberius' reign it was regarded as excessive.[196] Corporal punishment and forms of public shaming were also used as military punishment during the Republic.[197]

Imperial military law affected not so much Rome's relations with other states and peoples, but the property rights, legal privileges, and discipline of Roman soldiers.[198] Since imperial soldiers served for at least twenty years, their legal status could not go undefined, but required differentiation from that of civilian citizen males. Soldiers faced obvious practical impediments to legal process, such as serving far from where they were born, restrictions on furlough, and ignorance of Roman law. Civilian advocates might be unavailable on the frontiers. For these reasons the emperors Nerva, Trajan, and Hadrian created the *testamentum militare* or military will, which exempted soldiers from most of the formalities of civil testation.[199] Though the legitimate sons of Roman citizen fathers were in their power (*in patria potestate*) and could not legally own property, the *peculium castrense* was created to allow citizen soldiers with surviving fathers to manage their property (their pay, donatives, and any other wealth) independently.[200] Soldiers were exempted from serving personal *munera*, the corvée labor imposed on lower-status civilians in their hometowns. The emperors also allowed soldiers legal access, judging and ruling upon legal difficulties presented by soldiers.[201] Historians usually construe these institutions as privileges granted soldiers by their imperial patrons, affirming the special relationship between the emperors and their soldiers.

Viewing Roman military law as providing only privileges for soldiers is incorrect; the emperors and their legal experts did not always show favoritism to soldiers, and soldiers were liable to harsh corporal

---

195 Phang 2008, 123-7; on punishment, Taubenschlag 1932; Sander 1960; Campbell 1984, 303-14.
196 Phang 2008, 127-8.
197 Phang 2008, 129, 140-42.
198 Sander 1958; Jung 1982; Phang (2001, 197-228) reviews these legal issues with respect to soldiers' families.
199 Campbell 1984, 210-229; Champlin 1987 discusses the *Testamentum Porcelli*, a possible parody of a soldier's will.
200 Lehmann 1982; Campbell 1984, 229-36.
201 Exemption, Campbell 1984, 236-42; legal access, 264-75. Disciplinary practices in the jurists or in surviving military documents (at Vindolanda, Peachin 1999) might be less sensational than in the literary sources.

and capital punishment. The emperors and their deputies might rule against soldiers, reproving them, not least concerning the marriage ban for serving soldiers between 13 BC and AD 197 (see "Gender, Marriage, and Sexuality" above). In their legal treatises *de re militari*, the senatorial and equestrian jurists interpreted military law rather harshly, adding prescriptive statements that might invoke Republican traditions.[202] Nearly every serious military offence in *Digest* 49.16, including flight in battle, desertion to the enemy, creating a disturbance, mutiny, or insubordination towards a superior officer, results in capital punishment. Flight from battle due to cowardice was also shameful and could result in capital punishment.[203] In practice, commanders adopted a range of punishments, including corporal punishment, fines, exclusion from camps, and public shaming.[204] Work that remains to be done—an intractable subject—includes the explanation of the practical and cultural significance of the death penalty in Roman military punishment, including archaic penalties and decimation.[205]

Beyond military law that emphasized punishments, the Roman army is also an important source for local administrative practices, such as the collection of customs duties at the frontier or (attested in Egypt and in Asia Minor) policing, in which centurions as low-ranking officers responded to petitions submitted by civilians.[206] Soldiers thus provided civilians with an access point to the Roman legal system.

19. ENEMIES OF EMPIRE

Another new direction in Roman military studies focuses not just on the victors but also on how the Romans portrayed their victims, the conquered enemies of Rome.[207] The paradigm of Roman conquest was the enslavement of the defeated enemy. Romans assumed that their enemies would enslave them if they were captured, and developed law

---

202 Phang 2008, 135-6.
203 Phang 2008, 122, 125-6, 139-43.
204 Phang 2008, 135-9.
205 On decimation, Pickford 2005; Phang 2008, 123-9; on military punishment as a whole, Phang 2008, 111-151. French authors have taken recent interest in Roman capital punishment: Thomas 1984 (with caution); Rivière 1994; idem 2004a; on martyrs, Shaw 2003. On desertion, also Cosme 2003.
206 Petitions, discussed by Alston 1995, are reviewed by Whitehorne 2004; Peachin 2007; in Asia Minor, Shibano 2002; for the relationship of the army to mining and other "civilian" public works in the Egyptian desert, Cuvigny 2006.
207 James 2002, 27; Lange 2008; see also Morillo 2006, 66.

to handle Roman citizen captives' "social death" and the reinstatement of their legal personality upon return.[208] Capture might entail sexual humiliation.[209] Ancient authors assumed that victors would rape female and adolescent male captives, though rape was never a deliberate directive.[210] Another *topos* was the mass suicide of a non-Roman community in order to escape capture and enslavement by the Romans.[211] Though the jurist Ulpian states that enslavement was not usual in civil warfare, the shame of defeat was part of civil warfare.[212]

In imperial art, iconography of barbarian captives emphasized these harsh attitudes towards the conquered.[213] On a relief from the Sebasteion at Aphrodisias, commemorating the Roman conquest of Britain, the emperor Claudius in heroic form subdues a female personification of Britain (Britannia). Britannia displays the iconography of a rape victim in classical myth, her dress slipping off and her hair disarrayed. Captive figures or personifications of defeated peoples are chained or sit in postures of dejection on Roman imperial reliefs and coins.[214] These images of abject captives were widely diffused, also found on pottery tableware and lamps.[215] The Column of Marcus Aurelius depicts Roman soldiers seizing captive women and pulling them by the hair; soldiers drag away a captive woman from the child she tries to protect. The brutality of conquest as sexual assault was part of the Romans' self-concept, advertising the aggressive nature of their collective *virtus*.[216]

In practice, after initial conquest, Roman soldiers attained a more amicable relationship with provincials, less dictated by the discourses of Roman imperialism. The families of soldiers attest this development, as does the development of the areas adjacent to military camps into urban or town-like communities, termed *canabae* and *vici* respectively. In interaction with civilians, soldiers may have been able to juggle

208 D. 49.15; Bradley 2004; Phang 2004, 212-13; Barton 2007, 248-9.
209 Phang 2001, 266-7; idem 2004; Whittaker 2004, 128-30; Beard 2008, 147; Williams 2010, 112-114; implied in Barton 2007, 249; Joshel 2010, 40-1, 87-9, 151-2.
210 Ziolkowski 1993; Phang 2004, 212-13.
211 Phang 2004, 214, e.g., Liv. 21.14.1-4 (Saguntum); 28.22.1-23.5 (Astapa); Jos. *BJ* 7.369-401 (Masada).
212 Gaughan 2009, 49-50.
213 Pirson 1996; Ferris 2000; Edwards 2003, 60-8; Bradley 2004, 299-306; Phang 2004; attitudes towards conquered peoples in literary texts, Sidebottom 2007.
214 On these *simulacra gentium* (not all of which are shown as humiliated), Ando 2000, 281-5, 316-17.
215 Bradley 2004, 301.
216 Dillon & Welch 2006, 19-20; for the Column of Marcus Aurelius, Dillon 2006, 262-3.

different official and social roles and registers (as seen in the section on "Ethnic and Religious Identities," above), intermarrying and sharing religious practices with local civilians.

20. Conclusion

The study of any one period of military history can occupy a scholarly career, and modern historians often specialize in a particular theater of warfare or even campaign. It is easy to lose sight of the forest for the trees, especially in classical studies with its traditionally exhaustive citation-collection and in classical archaeology with its focus on sites and regions. Roman military historians may benefit from a broader perspective, that of world history, comparing and contrasting societies and their modes of warfare at a comparable technological level.[217] Such a perspective may suggest the reexamination of classical Roman history. A world perspective also frees scholars somewhat from the Anglo- and certainly Eurocentric bias of traditional classical studies and much military history.

The other radical perspective is that of time. Today's writers necessarily view the Roman army through modern eyes. A recent surge of work in classical studies focuses on the reception of the classical tradition by modern sources. In such studies the modern sources are usually older scholarly or popular works; as in the detection of art forgeries, modern preconceptions may be more obvious a century later when such assumptions have changed. Such studies may examine artistic, fictional and cinematic representations of Roman warfare and imperialism. Recent instances are James' survey of Roman army studies, two collections on the reception of Roman imperialism, a study of modern representations of Roman imperialism in Britain, and a collection on the reception of Caesar.[218] Reception studies of Roman warfare and its modern representations are probably the newest area of Roman military studies; future developments are awaited.

Another new desirable direction is cyberspace: the development of Internet resources for Roman military scholars and fans. This is particularly desirable for attracting younger scholars and enthusiasts. The following review features the best-known resources:

---

217 James 2002, 36; Morillo 2006; examples, Raaflaub and Rosenstein 1999; Morris and Scheidel 2009; Scheidel 2009.
218 Mattingly 1997; Webster and Cooper 1996; Hingley 2000; Wyke 2006.

A good all-around website on the Roman army in Britain, combining primary documents, archaeological information, and historical and social context, is Vindolanda Tablets Online, a production of the Centre for the Study of Ancient Documents at Oxford University.[219] There are several important bibliographic sites on Roman army studies.[220] Databases of Roman inscriptions and Greek papyri contain much evidence on the army, but the searcher must know the citations and abbreviations used.[221]

The digitization of secondary scholarship on the Roman army is also desirable.[222] Roman army studies (as with classical studies as a whole) rests on a mountain of prior scholarship, much of which edits, collects, or synthesizes primary sources and thus still provides valuable data. It is likely that the audience for a digital archive of Roman army resources (primary texts and secondary scholarship) would be much wider than the inner circle of professional scholars, especially if the archive includes archaeology and artistic evidence and is engagingly written, well indexed, and usably designed.

Scholarly education and publishing conventions have tended to separate Roman army studies from Roman historical and cultural studies. Archaeology, history, and classical literature are often separate academic departments. Publishers assign discrete categories to monographs and articles, and the impact of this indexing grows as scholars increasingly rely on electronic searching to retrieve publications.

Such a "civil–military" separation has not been possible for historians of the Roman Republic, where military affairs are inescapable. In many of the works cited in this chapter, Roman military studies return from the frontiers, as it were, and engage with larger aspects of Roman economy, society, culture, and law. This engagement is not a destructive conflict but fruitful for both sides, and hopefully it will continue and grow. In the author's view, many aspects of the Roman military are not part of the

---

219 http://vindolanda.csad.ox.ac.uk/ (accessed 2/19/11).

220 For example, http://www.csun.edu/~hcfll004/armybibl.html, accessed 2/19/11.

221 The *Corpus Inscriptionum Latinarum* is now available as an online database, http://cil.bbaw.de/cil_en/index_en.html. It has links to other databases of inscriptions, not all of which are easy to use. A general portal to Greek, Latin and other papyri is Advanced Papyrological Information System (APIS), http://www.columbia.edu/cu/lweb/projects/digital/apis/index.html, which permits browsing for index terms in English (all accessed 2/19/11).

222 On the digital future of classical scholarship, Crane and Terras, 2009 (various articles).

(conventional) grand trajectory of military history, but are embedded in ancient institutions, society and culture. As our understanding of ancient Roman institutions, society and culture grows and changes, so will our understanding of the Roman army.

4

MILITARY HISTORY
IN LATE ANTIQUITY:
CHANGING PERSPECTIVES AND PARADIGMS

Doug Lee
University of Nottingham, UK

1. Introduction

Late antiquity is a period full of interest for the student of military history. Generally defined as the four hundred years or so from the early third to the early seventh century, it was a time of great turbulence for the Roman empire, with much of that turbulence generated by war. The chronological parameters of the period themselves reflect major military developments. The earlier limit is linked to the advent of the Sasanian dynasty in Persia in the 220s, which for the first time in many centuries presented the empire with the challenge of a neighboring power with comparable capabilities; warfare with Persia in the mid-sixth century, together with new threats from Germanic tribes to the north, tested the empire to the limit and, by the beginning of the fourth century, had contributed to major reshaping of the empire's political, administrative and military infrastructure.[1] The later time limit coincides with the impact of the Islamic invasions of the 630s, which deprived the empire of many of its most valuable eastern provinces, thereby fundamentally reconfiguring the geopolitical balance of the empire while also toppling the Sasanian regime. The intervening centuries also witnessed many major events with military dimensions, including the Gothic victory at Adrianople in 378—reputedly the heaviest Roman defeat since Cannae; the fragmentation and disappearance of the western half of the empire over the course of the fifth century, to be replaced by a mosaic of Germanic kingdoms; and the reconquest of parts of the west by the

---

1 All dates in this chapter are AD unless otherwise indicated.

eastern half of the empire during the reign of the emperor Justinian in the mid-sixth century.

Given that so many of these momentous events represented setbacks for the empire, it remains tempting to approach the period via Gibbon's influential paradigm of "Decline and Fall" and assume that the historian's primary task is to explain defeat. After all, Gibbon's blunt diagnosis of the empire's woes—"the triumph of barbarism and religion"—is surely apposite to a period noted for barbarian invasions, an influx of Germans into the Roman army, and the empire's adoption of Christianity with its pacifist tendencies. It is therefore noteworthy that much recent scholarship on the military history of late antiquity has challenged preconceptions about an inevitable decline in the empire's military capability and suggested more positive perspectives on a period traditionally associated with doom and despair.

In what follows, the focus is on work about warfare and the Roman army in late antiquity, particularly in their broader social and cultural context, which has appeared in the last twenty years or so. The emphasis is on work published in English, since Anglo-American scholarship has been responsible for many of the most important studies in this period, but occasional reference is also made to work in other languages where that work is particularly important. The emphasis is also on historical studies, rather than archaeological work, although the latter has necessarily contributed important insights to some topics; in particular, there is no attempt here to summarize recent work on the archaeology of late Roman frontiers. After opening sections concerning general works about the army and warfare in late antiquity and concerning recent scholarship on the most important ancient sources, attention shifts to a range of more discrete topics— the army's organization and effectiveness, tactical and technological change, demographics, recruitment and identity, the military and politics, the economics of war, the military and society, and religion and ideology.[2] In approaching these topics, it is worth bearing in mind that although late antiquity is increasingly acknowledged as a historical period in its own right, portions of the period it encompasses also form part of other recognized scholarly subject areas, whether it be the late

---

2   In presenting this survey, attention should also be drawn to the valuable series of overviews of recent work on the late Roman army by the French scholars Carrié and Janniard in the journal *Antiquité tardive*: Carrié and Janniard 2000; Janniard 2001; Carrié 2002.

Roman empire, the early Middle Ages, or the early Byzantine empire. As a result it is not uncommon to find treatments of relevant subjects which focus on more restricted periods within late antiquity, or on the eastern or western half of the empire.

2. GENERAL WORKS

The benchmark for the study of many aspects of the late Roman army was set by A.H.M. Jones in the relevant chapter of his 1964 *magnum opus* on the Later Roman Empire, and much of what he wrote then has stood the test of time.[3] Nevertheless, in keeping with the overall concern of his study, Jones' focus was on the organizational and administrative aspects of the army, leaving scope for further work in a variety of other directions, particularly, on the one hand, the more obviously military aspects of war and the army in action—strategy and tactics, battles and sieges—and on the other, warfare and the army in their wider social and cultural contexts. A number of monographs in recent decades have given particular attention to the former, as well as organizational aspects, notably Elton, Nicasie, and Le Bohec, although all three largely restrict themselves to the fourth century, while Lee is concerned with the latter across the whole of late antiquity. Haldon gives balanced consideration to all aspects, but since his focus is Byzantium, he only begins in the mid-sixth century.[4] The recent *Cambridge History of Greek and Roman Warfare* (*CHGRW*) includes six chapters on the Late Empire which aim to give even coverage of all major elements (international relations, military forces, war, battle, warfare and the state, and war and society), and has benefited from the authors of the individual chapters having the opportunity to view and discuss drafts of one another's contributions well in advance of publication. The final volumes of the new edition of the *Cambridge Ancient History* have also included a useful sequence of chapters on the late Roman army.[5] For all the merits of these different endeavors, however, there remains room for a single-author study which deals with all the different aspects of the army and warfare across the whole of late antiquity.

---

3   Jones 1964, 607-86. For a recent assessment of his legacy in this respect, see Tomlin 2008.
4   Elton 1996; Nicasie; 1998; Le Bohec 2006; Lee 2007; Haldon 1999.
5   Campbell 2005; Lee 1998; Whitby 2000; and see also Zuckerman 2004.

Since the study of warfare in late antiquity inevitably involves engagement with the vast literature concerning the demise of the Roman empire in the west in the fifth century, it is worth mentioning a number of recent broader studies of this subject which particularly emphasize the military dimension, notably Heather's *The Fall of the Roman Empire*, which stresses the pivotal role of the Huns, and Halsall's *Barbarian Migrations and the Roman West* and Goldsworthy's *How Rome Fell*, both of which highlight the impact of civil war.[6] In this context, Drinkwater's recent study of Roman relations with the Alamanni is noteworthy, since it argues, provocatively, that the Alamanni never posed any real threat to the empire; rather, emperors exaggerated the danger they presented in order to justify the resources channeled into the army and frontier installations.[7]

3. SOURCES

Because war was such a pervasive feature of the empire's affairs during late antiquity, there are few sources which do not have something to contribute to some aspect of the subject.[8] There are, however, a number of sources which are particularly important and on which there has been valuable recent work. The first group of these is the so-called classicizing narrative histories, inspired by and seeking to emulate the canonical works of earlier centuries—Herodotus, Thucydides, Tacitus and the like, who took it for granted that the historian's primary focus should be politics and war. In the study of fourth-century military history, Ammianus Marcellinus holds the pre-eminent place. Although the surviving portion of his history covers no more than twenty-five years (354-78), those years included particularly important military events—the Roman victory over the Alamanni at Strasbourg (357), Julian's abortive Persian campaign (363), and the Gothic victory over the Romans at Adrianople (378)—and Ammianus usually covers these, and many other episodes, in very full detail, intelligently informed by his experience as an army officer and his personal participation in some of them. His personal loyalties to his commander Ursicinus and to the

---

6   Heather 2005, expanding on Heather 1995, defended in idem 2009a, and further developed in idem 2009b; Halsall 2007; Goldsworthy 2009.

7   Drinkwater 2007; reviewed in Heather 2008.

8   For discussions of the contribution of literary, papyrological, epigraphic and numismatic evidence to understanding of the army in the fourth century, see the contributions by, respectively, Sabbah, Palme, Absil and Reddé in Le Bohec and Wolff 2004.

emperor Julian need to be taken into account when reading his history, but its overall value remains undeniable.[9]

The other major classicizing historian of late antiquity is Procopius, with his detailed narrative of Justinian's wars in the sixth century against the Persians, Vandals and Goths. Although Procopius has tended to attract more attention for another of his works—the salacious invective popularly known as the *Secret History*—there is no doubting the value of his *Wars* as a source for military history. While not a soldier himself, Procopius' role as secretary to Justinian's leading general Belisarius gave him a privileged vantage point for many of the events he describes and a network of contacts to draw on for others.[10] Procopius inspired a succession of continuators, one of whom—Theophylact Simocatta— wrote a detailed history of the wars of the emperor Maurice in the final decades of the sixth century, although it does not display the same quality and control as Procopius.[11]

Ammianus wrote in Latin and Procopius and Theophylact in Greek, but Syriac—a dialect of the Semitic language Aramaic—also became prominent as a literary medium in the eastern provinces of the empire during late antiquity, with a particularly important text for military history being written in this language in the early sixth century. This is the *Chronicle* traditionally, but wrongly, attributed to Joshua the Stylite, which recounts events in northern Mesopotamia during the late fifth and early sixth century from a provincial perspective and without the same concern for literary embellishment evident in Ammianus and Procopius. Since the bulk of the narrative concerns the war between

---

9   Matthews (1989), in the most important recent study, has a high regard for Ammianus and in general, is keen to defend his reliability as a historian, particularly in relation to military matters. The first half of Matthews' monograph includes important chapters on Julian's military campaigns in Gaul and Persia, while the second half has valuable chapters on warfare and on half a dozen of the peoples who posed major military problems for the empire; see also Drijvers and Hunt 1999, 17-50. More recent studies of Ammianus have shown a greater willingness to emphasize his limitations and biases: Barnes (1998) has less to say directly about military affairs, but that of Kelly (2008) sounds a note of caution through its emphasis on the literary qualities and construction of Ammianus' battle descriptions. Note also Kelso 2003.

10 For Procopius as a military historian, see Greatrex 1998 and Rance 2005. Kaldellis (2004) emphasizes the literary qualities in Procopius' writing, though with little direct comment on military matters. A recent slew of doctoral theses on military aspects of Procopius' history is likely to result in further relevant publications in the near future: see Kouroumali 2005; Sarantis 2005; Whately 2009.

11 For Theophylact, see Whitby 1988, while Treadgold (2007) offers an excellent intro- duction to Ammianus, Procopius and other historical writers in late antiquity.

the empire and Persia in the first decade of the sixth century, including sieges of Amida and Edessa, it is an invaluable resource for military historians, especially for the impact of warfare and the army on provincial communities.[12]

Armies tend to generate bureaucratic paraphernalia, and the Roman army in late antiquity was no exception. In addition to the mass of low-level documentation preserved on papyri, there are two particularly important high-level documents of relevance. The first is the text known as the *Notitia Dignitatum*—the register of honors. Although it comprises lists, rather than continuous text, it includes data which sheds light on the structure and distribution of the army in the late fourth and early fifth century, and its value and limitations are increasingly better understood.[13] The second is the legal compilation known as the *Theodosian Code*. Commissioned by the emperor Theodosius II and published in 438, the *Code* comprises extracts from imperial laws of the previous one and a half centuries, organized by subject. Although Book VII, on military matters, is of most immediately obvious relevance for the military historian, the way in which the army impinged on so many aspects of society means that pertinent material can be found throughout this important text.[14]

An additional category of source which warrants special comment is that of military treatises, a number of which were written during late antiquity. The best known of these in Latin is that by Vegetius, from the late fourth or early fifth century, which advocated a return to past practices in the selection, training and use of infantry. While it is not always easy to differentiate comments based on contemporary experience from those based on his reading of earlier sources, the second half contains much material of relevance to his own day. The best known late Roman treatise in Greek is the *Strategikon* ("Book of the General") attributed to the emperor Maurice, which offers much insight into the army and warfare in the late sixth century and, unusually, includes an excursus on the military capabilities of the

---

12   Trombley and Watt 2000 provides a helpful new translation and commentary; Greatrex 1998 also includes much reference to this text.

13   See the articles by Brennan (1996, 1998), who is also completing an edition, translation and commentary; also Kulikowski 2000.

14   Although its specifically military elements have not been the subject of focused attention in recent scholarship, more general understanding of the *Code* as a historical source has been greatly advanced in Matthews 2000.

empire's major enemies.[15] Another shorter treatise, traditionally known as the "anonymous work on strategy," has also generated a number of publications in recent times, although its sixth-century date has increasingly been called into question.[16] Finally, mention should be made of a number of useful collections of sources in translation relevant to the military history of late antiquity. Campbell's sourcebook on the Roman army includes a final chapter on the later empire which does not, however, extend beyond the end of Constantine's reign. The twin volumes by, on the one hand, Dodgeon and Lieu and, on the other, Greatrex and Lieu, provide detailed and comprehensive coverage of sources relating to Roman warfare and relations with Sasanian Persia. Heather and Matthews have produced a useful compendium of diverse sources relating to the fourth-century Goths, some of which are relevant to military matters.[17]

4. THE ARMY: ORGANIZATION AND EFFECTIVENESS

The Roman army of the fourth century and beyond was organized differently from that of the Principate—the result of adaptations to the pressures of the third century and the need for emperors to be more mobile. The most significant change was the emergence of the distinction between units based in frontier provinces, known initially by a variety of names (e.g., *ripenses, burgarii*) but eventually referred to as *limitanei*, and the higher-status units which accompanied the emperor as a mobile field army—the so-called *comitatenses*. Though the origins of this distinction can be traced back into the third century,

---

15   There is an excellent overview of these and other treatises by Rance (2007b, 343-8), who is also completing a new translation and commentary on the *Strategikon*; Milner (1996) provides a good translation of Vegetius, while the much-discussed question of its date has recently been the subject of a monograph (Charles 2007) which also eluci- dates broader aspects of the work. There has also been important work on less familiar examples of this genre. Greatrex, Elton, and Burgess (2005) have produced a new edition and translation, with commentary, of the early sixth century treatise by Urbicius,
16   Re-published with a translation by Dennis 1985. Zuckerman (1990) has demonstrated that this treatise was part of a compendium by Syrianus; although this Syrianus is otherwise unknown, it means that the authorship of the work should no longer be referred to as anonymous. A later, possibly ninth-century, date is increasingly favored for the treatise: see Rance 2007a, with references to earlier literature.
17   Campbell 1994; Dodgeon and Lieu 1991 (for the period 226-363); Greatrex and Lieu 2002 (for the period 363-630). The latter volume is more user-friendly by virtue of its valuable editorial comment and Greatrex maintaining a website with regular updates on recent relevant research; Heather and Matthews 1991.

Constantine is usually regarded as having played a major role in the formalization of this structure; it is important, however, to emphasize that the evidence for this is more fragile than often assumed.[18] Moreover, a strong element of flexibility persisted in the operation of this dual structure, beginning with the succession of Constantine's three sons, each of whom required his own field army in a different part of the empire, and continuing through the major upheavals in the empire's fortunes in the fifth and sixth centuries.[19] That flexibility was aided by the fact that the size of individual units in late antiquity was much smaller than during the Principate. By the fourth century, legions which had once contained 5,000 or so men became bodies of one thousand or fewer—hence the much larger number of units recorded in the *Notitia Dignitatum*. This important shift was in part the making permanent of the earlier practice of temporarily detaching cohorts from legions for particular missions, but there was also often an element of specialization involved.[20]

How effective was this dual structure? The separation out of the *limitanei* has often been seen as a weakness, on the assumption that their inferior status to the *comitatenses* implied inferior quality and must have had an adverse impact on their morale. Moreover, their association with landholding in the frontier provinces has led to their sometimes being portrayed as a part-time peasant militia, with all the pejorative overtones which that description carries. This characterization of the *limitanei* has been firmly rejected in recent scholarship. It has been noted that, even in the sixth century, units of *limitanei* were sometimes used for offensive operations and are, therefore, unlikely to have been considered poor soldiers, while the earliest evidence for *limitanei* owning land is from the mid-fifth century; furthermore, ownership of land need not imply that the soldiers themselves worked it, and even if they did, militias have often been highly effective fighting forces, as shown by the army of the Roman Republic.[21]

The creation of mobile field armies has also sometimes been seen as a weakness, on the assumption that the withdrawal of significant numbers of units from the frontier provinces reduced the empire's

18 Brennan 2007.
19 In addition to the overviews of the evolution of the army in late antiquity by Campbell (2005), Lee (1998), and Whitby (2000) previously noted, see also Whitby 2004; Elton 2007a; idem 2007c.
20 Tomlin 2000, 166-73.
21 Isaac 1988, 139-47; Whitby 1995, 110-16.

ability to turn back enemy invasions before they inflicted significant damage on provincial communities. Some of the units in the field armies were new creations, however, rather than being taken from the empire's perimeters. A dictum of Frederick the Great—"He who defends everything, defends nothing"—seems particularly relevant to the empire's situation in late antiquity when it regularly faced significant threats on more than one frontier. In light of these considerations, the principle of strategic reserves acquires greater cogency.[22]

More generally, the fact that the empire was on the back foot militarily throughout much of late antiquity and experienced major defeats and significant territorial losses should not be assumed automatically to mean that the army had declined in effectiveness. On the one hand, it is possible to point to many examples of success in battle—Strasbourg (357), Dara (530), the engagements which secured the reconquest of north Africa (533), Taginae (552), Heraclius' Persian campaign (627-8)—while on the other, the obvious cases of failure—Julian's Persian expedition (363), Adrianople (378)—were largely due to poor leadership and planning rather than any obvious deterioration in the quality of Roman forces. It also needs to be borne in mind that the loss of the western empire during the fifth century cannot be attributed primarily to military defeats. The only undoubted case of defeat in battle resulting directly in significant territorial losses was Heraclius' loss at the Yarmuk in 636, when Arab forces were able to capitalize on the empire still recovering after a quarter of a century's warfare with Persia.[23]

5. TACTICAL AND TECHNOLOGICAL CHANGE

Late antiquity saw a wide range of tactical and technological changes in the Roman army. Arising from the emergence of mobile field armies and then contact and interaction with nomadic peoples (Huns and Avars), cavalry played an increasingly significant role in the Roman army, with important sub-themes including the introduction of units of heavy armored cavalry inspired by Persian models (*cataphracti, clibanarii*), greater emphasis on mounted archers to counteract nomadic toxological expertise, and the adoption of the stirrup from the Avars in the later

---

22 Tomlin 2000, 168 (including the quotation from Frederick).
23 For positive assessments of the army's capabilities, see Elton 1996; Lee 1998; Nicasie 1998; Whitby 2004; idem 2007a. For the final war with Persia and the Islamic conquests, see Kaegi 1992; Howard-Johnston 1999; Kaegi 2003; Howard-Johnston 2010.

sixth century. At the same time, there were changes to the weaponry of infantry, especially the long, slashing *spatha* sword superseding the short, stabbing *gladius* in response to increasing engagement with spear-wielding Germanic warriors and the accompanying shift from the rectangular *scutum* to an oval shield which facilitated the use of the *spatha*, while the armor used by the majority of infantry appears to have become lighter by the sixth century. The late sixth century also witnessed the advent of traction-powered siege artillery, first used by the Avars drawing upon their knowledge of Chinese technology. These are all developments of which there has long been awareness, but current scholarship has helped to refine understanding of some of them and their significance.[24] They are also of relevance to Lendon's recent thesis that antiquarian respect for the past inhibited innovation in the Roman approach to warfare, suggesting as they do that, for late antiquity at least, a more complex array of factors was involved than his argument allows.[25]

In all this, important caveats need to be registered. The temptation to assume that cavalry superseded infantry as the most important element in Roman armies in late antiquity must be resisted: careful analysis of narrative accounts of battles in the classicizing historians confirms the continuing central importance of infantry, while the military treatises continue to devote significant space to the training of infantry.[26] At the same time, the role of infantry in battle shifted to a more defensive use—"away from the 'volley and charge' shock tactics of the earlier legion towards a less flexible and more compact deployment, which often remained stationary to receive the enemy attack while discharging a more sustained barrage of missiles."[27] Caution also needs to be exercised with regard to the extent of Germanic influence on infantry tactics, where the adoption of Germanic terminology for certain formations may reflect simple 'rebranding' rather than more fundamental tactical change.[28] Older skepticism about the utility of Roman units of heavy cavalry has also been well challenged.[29]

A related but somewhat different issue in the context of battle which has generated much recent debate has been the validity of attempts to

---

24 For an invaluable overview of these developments, see Rance 2007b.
25 Lendon 2005.
26 Haldon 1999, 191-7; Wheeler 2004a; idem 2004b; Rance 2005; idem 2007b, 349-59.
27 Rance 2007b, 352.
28 Rance 2004.
29 Speidel 1984; Nicasie 1998, 196-7.

apply the "face of battle" approach pioneered by the modern military historian John Keegan in relation to more recent historical periods.[30] The idea of exploring the experience of battle by the rank-and-file and the factors influencing morale has generated interest among historians of all the major periods of antiquity, including a number of studies relating to the late Roman period which have drawn their inspiration to varying degrees from Keegan's work.[31] At the same time, there have been other studies critical of this approach, whether skeptical about the validity of transferring modern insights to antiquity,[32] or arguing for the need for multiple perspectives.[33]

6. DEMOGRAPHICS, RECRUITMENT AND IDENTITY

As noted by Brent Shaw in a wide-ranging and stimulating essay on war in late antiquity, the fact that late antiquity did not witness any really major technological innovations in the military field meant that "the decisive forces were those of sheer size, combined with the intensive organization and deployment permitted by a bureaucratic infrastructure."[34] This means that the size of the army and its recruitment methods assume particular importance. As so often with ancient statistics, the surviving figures for the size of the army in late antiquity leave much scope for debate, but a figure of half a million is a reasonable compromise approximation, which it is broadly agreed represents a significant increase over the size of the army during the Principate.[35]

In principle, the larger number of troops required still ought not to have been an excessive burden on the empire's population, and yet it is apparent that in the aftermath of major military losses, the state struggled to find sufficient recruits. This is particularly apparent after the debacle of Julian's Persian expedition when, among other measures, the emperor Valentinian lowered the height requirement for recruits by three inches.[36] The efflorescence of paired units of *seniores* and *iuniores* at the start of his reign has also been persuasively interpreted as a

---

30 Keegan 1976.
31 Matthews 1989, 279-303; Lee 2007a, 123-33; Lenski 2007; Rance 2007b, 363-78 (including a caveat at 374 n.135).
32 Wheeler 1998; idem 2001.
33 Kagan 2006; Elton 2007b.
34 Shaw 1999, 134.
35 For overviews of the evidence and issues, see Treadgold 1995, 43-64; Lee 2007a, 74-7.
36 *Cod. Theod.* 7.13.3 (367).

strategy for restoring effective units as quickly as possible by dividing units into two and then filling them out with new recruits "who would mature more quickly side by side with old soldiers than if drafted into new regiments."[37] A crisis of a different sort with potentially significant implications for army recruitment was the great pandemic of the mid-sixth century, which has been the subject of increasing attention in recent years.[38] However, while this work on the pandemic has not addressed its demographic implications for the army directly, the overall size of armies in the later sixth century does not appear to have suffered any significant decline, and since cities were hardest hit by the pandemic, whereas the bulk of soldiers were recruited from rural areas, there is unlikely to have been any chronic deficiency of soldiers, whatever the immediate impact of the disease may have been.[39]

As for the mechanisms by which soldiers were recruited, conscription was the main method used during the fourth and fifth centuries. The tax system in kind formalized by the emperor Diocletian in the late third century (see further below under "The Economics of War") included a human element whereby landowners were required to provide suitable recruits, depending on the amount of land they owned, or money in lieu (the so-called *aurum tironicum* or "recruiting gold"). It has generally been assumed that conscription was abandoned in the sixth century, but this has been challenged more recently on the basis that it relies heavily on an argument from silence in the legal evidence and that "in practical terms conscription and volunteering are not such opposites as they might seem, since the former depends on a willingness to come forward, the latter on a degree of "encouragement" for the volunteers to emerge."[40]

During late antiquity the imperial authorities seem to have targeted population groups who were perceived as having particularly martial qualities. In the third century the Balkans became a major recruiting ground within the empire, while in subsequent centuries Isauria in south-eastern Anatolia filled a similar role. Both were rugged, relatively underdeveloped regions whose populations had a reputation for being doughty fighters—good examples of what one sociologist

---

37 Tomlin 1972, 264; with further discussion in Nicasie 1998, 24-33.
38 Hordern 2005; and Little 2007.
39 Whitby 1995, 100-103.
40 Whitby 1995, 68. Zuckerman (1998) has argued that there was a move away from conscription in the 370s, but this has been rejected independently by Carrié 2004; Whitby 2004, 170-2.

has referred to as the "Ghurka syndrome."[41] The significance of these regions is reflected in the fact that individuals from both gradually rose to high command in the army and even the imperial throne. "Martial races" also lived outside the empire and were drawn on by the Roman state as well, particularly from the various Germanic peoples beyond the Danube and Rhine in the third and fourth centuries. There is no doubt that recruits from these peoples made a significant contribution to the empire's military manpower in this period, reflected in the way that a notable number became generals in the Roman army: "for many Germans, the Roman empire was not an enemy, but a career."[42] Whether this development warrants the pejorative term "barbarization" or proved fatal to the survival of the empire in the west, however, is another matter. There is good reason to think that the proportion of barbarians was neither as large as sometimes assumed, nor increasing, that Germans in Roman employ did not have divided loyalties, and that their presence in the army did not have an adverse effect on its military effectiveness.[43]

The recruitment of barbarians is also relevant to the topical issue of identity. It has long been recognized that modern notions of national allegiance are unhelpful in assessing how Germanic tribesmen serving in the Roman army conceived of their identity; apart from anything else, they came from a range of loose tribal groupings and lacked any overarching sense of Germanic identity. Furthermore, it was quite possible for a barbarian to retain a sense of dual identity, as in the famous epitaph from Aquincum in which an individual identifies himself as both a Frankish citizen and a Roman soldier.[44] However, the more specific issue of their status vis-à-vis Roman citizenship

---

41 Enloe 1980, 23-49; with Lee 2007a, 83. Isaurians have received much attention: see Matthews 1989, 355-67; Shaw 1990; Lenski 1999; and a forthcoming study by Elton.

42 Whittaker 1983, 117 (citing Fustel de Coulanges).

43 On the proportion of Germans see Whitby 1995, 103-10; Elton 1996, 136-52; Lee 2007a, 85. On the loyalties of the Germans and their contribution to effectiveness see Lee 1998, 222-4, 232-7; and Nicasie 1998, 97-116. Surviving evidence for the eastern empire after 476 suggests that the proportion of foreigners in senior commands declined somewhat, see Lee 2007a, 85.

44 *ILS* 2814 (*Francus ego cives Romanus miles in armis...*); Rigsby 1999 has proposed different punctuation and the reading, "I, a Frank, a Roman citizen, a soldier in arms...", although this overlooks other cases where an individual is described as a *civis Alamanna* or a *civis Gothus* (details and discussion in Mathisen 2006, 1035-6). There is a substantial literature and debate about ethnic identity in the context of the emergence of the Germanic successor kingdoms during late antiquity: for an overview, see Halsall 2007, 35-62, 455-98.

has received less attention. A recent discussion of the subject puts forward the intriguing argument that by this period of Roman history "citizenship was a matter of participation and self-identification."[45]

7. The Military and Politics

Warfare and the army always had a symbiotic relationship with politics throughout Roman history, and the military upheavals of the mid-third century helped to continue, and even intensify, this link, instrumental as they were in changing the character of the imperial office and the political and administrative infrastructure of the empire. During the Principate, emperors were almost invariably men from the senatorial aristocracy, the extent of whose military experience was highly variable. However, the military crises of the mid-third century facilitated the emergence of a new kind of emperor—military men from less illustrious social backgrounds who, by the end of that era, had restored the empire's essential stability. Lacking the social connections and resources of the aristocracy, to maintain their position they relied closely on the army, whose loyalty they reinforced through a combination of material incentives and symbolic gestures. Material incentives often entailed the granting of tax privileges and the regular distribution of donatives to supplement soldiers' basic pay, while symbolic gestures included inviting the assent of troops in formal accession ceremonies and using language of identification and flattery when communicating with the army. Perhaps the most obvious instance of the latter is the expression *commilitones nostri* ("our fellow soldiers"), but there are a range of comparable phrases such as "our very valiant soldiers" and "very loyal army" which appear in official documentation from the period.[46]

These strategies for retaining the loyalty of the troops became even more important after emperors ceased to campaign in person in the fifth and sixth centuries, and therefore lost direct contact with soldiers in the field. That development came about in part because two emperors died on campaign in the second half of the fourth century—Julian in Persia (363) and Valens at Adrianople (378)—and partly because the sons and grandsons of Theodosius I who ruled the empire for the half century or so after his early death in 395 all acceded to the imperial throne while

---

45 Mathisen 2006; see also Garnsey 2004; Mathisen 2009.
46 Lee 2007a, 51-66.

still teenagers or younger. The emperors' lack of direct involvement in military affairs also made the propagation of the traditional ideology of victory even more important, despite there being fewer actual victories to celebrate.[47]

Regardless of their best efforts, even militarily active fourth-century emperors could not eliminate the risk of usurpation and civil war. These continued to be a problem, even if not with the frequency that had characterized the third century. The most famous and best documented episode from this century was that of Julian against Constantius II in 361. It is an episode of enormous interest because Julian's success briefly offered the prospect of the reversal of Constantine's religious policies, but it was also atypical insofar as Julian was not a professional general and was a member of the imperial family. Military commanders did, however, mount challenges at other points during the fourth century, notably Magnentius (350) and Magnus Maximus (383), with the "reluctant rebellions" of Silvanus (355) and Arbogast (392) providing further interesting instances; that of Procopius (365) was more akin to that of Julian in that he was a bureaucrat by background rather than a general, and had blood ties to Julian. Understanding of many of these individual episodes has been enhanced in recent years, but there remains scope for a focused study of usurpation and civil war in this period that, among other things, would seek to provide a convincing explanation as to why nearly all these usurpations occurred in the west.[48] Moreover, these episodes often had important wider consequences for military activity in the fourth century. The main battle between Constantius and Magnentius, at Mursa in 351, involved huge loss of life on both sides, with significant implications for recruitment which contemporaries themselves appreciated; Procopius' attempt to draw on Gothic manpower to bolster his challenge for the throne prompted Valens' campaigns against the Goths in the late 360s; and lack of recognition for the Gothic units which made such an important and costly contribution to Theodosius' victory over Arbogast at the Frigidus in 394 may well have helped to provoke the Gothic revolt led by Alaric in 395.

The advent of underage emperors from 395 increased the scope for generals to play an influential role in political life without having to resort to usurpation. Once again, this pattern was particularly evident

---

47 McCormick 1986.
48 Drinkwater 1994; idem 2000; Hunt 1999; Lenski 2002, 68-115.

in the west, where a succession of generals dominated the imperial court, notably Stilicho, Constantius, Aetius and Ricimer.[49] Stilicho and Ricimer were of Germanic origin, which explains their not attempting to seize the throne for themselves; Constantius did have himself promoted to be co-emperor of Honorius in 421, but he died unexpectedly after little more than six months; Aetius is perhaps the most puzzling of these figures, for although he was not handicapped by barbarian origin and was the most powerful person in the west during the 430s and 440s, he seems to have been content not to challenge Valentinian III, who nevertheless eventually saw Aetius as a sufficient threat to warrant murdering him in 454. In the east, civilian bureaucrats dominated the court until the middle of the fifth century when the general Aspar, an Alan, emerged as the key figure during the reign of Leo, before being challenged by another general, the Isaurian Zeno.[50] Aspar suffered the same fate as Aetius, but Zeno effectively succeeded Leo as emperor in 474. As with usurpation in the fourth century, there remains scope for analytical treatment of the phenomenon of dominant generals in the fifth century, as well as the absence of this phenomenon from the eastern empire in the sixth century, despite the military success enjoyed by a general like Belisarius.

8. THE ECONOMICS OF WAR

Certain elements of the economics of war remained constant from the earlier empire into late antiquity, such as the importance of booty as an incentive for soldiers, and the destruction that warfare brought to the communities on whom it impinged directly. However, the greater emphasis on defensive warfare in this period reduced the opportunities for booty, while the extent to which warfare had an impact upon the inhabitants of the empire and their livelihoods increased, due to the greater fragility of the frontiers and to the fact that sieges were such a common form of warfare during this period. Assessing the economic impact of this increased incidence of war within the empire is a forbidding task which needs to be done on a regional basis, with archaeological evidence to the fore. Clearly some regions were affected

---

49 O'Flynn (1983) provides an overview, while Lütkenhaus (1998), Stickler (2002), and MacGeorge (2002) present assessments of specific individuals.
50 Croke 2005.

much more severely than others, so caution needs to be exercised before generalizing.[51]

An important aspect of the economics of war is how the state organized the transfer of revenues to support the army effectively. One of the distinctive features of the fourth-century army was the way it was supplied in kind through a system formalized by Diocletian and known as the *annona militaris*. The fiscal system established by Diocletian involved peasants paying their taxes in grain and other forms of produce, much of which the state then distributed directly to military units. This system had developed in the later third century as a way of circumventing significant inflationary pressures. However, it also entailed certain disadvantages, most obviously the practical problem of transporting perishable foodstuffs in bulk. It is not surprising, therefore, that from the late fourth century onward, there was a gradual shift towards commuting taxes in kind to taxes in cash (the official term for which was *adaeratio*). Coin was easier to transport around the empire, and this revised system also allowed the imperial government to accumulate financial reserves more easily.[52]

Soldiers were equipped by the state, which had a network of state arsenals (*fabricae*) around the empire manufacturing weapons and armor. Their locations in the late fourth century are recorded in the *Notitia Dignitatum*, and reflect a high degree of central co-ordination.[53] Archaeological remains have been found of what must have been one of their major outputs—the so-called "ridge" helmet made of two simple halves fixed together. The dating of the first examples of this style of helmet to the late third century has been persuasively linked to the need for simpler and speedier methods of manufacture as the size of the army was expanded under Diocletian and his successors.[54]

Specific military expeditions made special demands on the empire's logistical capabilities, and it is increasingly apparent just how much the size of an expeditionary force was constrained by the terrain

---

51 See Lee (2007a, 106-17) for discussion of the issues, some case studies and further reading. Ward-Perkins 2005 is a more general study which emphasizes the destructive impact of the barbarian invasions in the west.

52 The most detailed study of the *annona militaris* is Mitthof 2001, but a convenient overview of it and of commutation remains Jones 1964, 448-62.

53 James 1988.

54 Bishop and Coulston (2006) include a chapter on military equipment in the fourth century; Rance (2007b) includes much incidental comment on military equipment throughout late antiquity.

through which it passed and by its make-up. In particular, a major cavalry presence in the expedition—which was a strong likelihood in late antiquity—increased the logistical pressures significantly, since horses required large quantities of fodder.[55] This in turn is relevant to a phenomenon which has attracted much comment—the relatively small size of expeditionary armies in late antiquity (typically never larger than about 50,000 men). This has often been seen as corroboration for lower estimates of the empire's total armed forces in late antiquity, but logistical constraints provide a more obvious explanation.[56]

The close relationship between revenues and military effectiveness is crucial to understanding the divergent fates of the eastern and western halves of the empire in the fifth century. In the west, the most economically productive region of the empire was North Africa (modern-day Tunisia and Algeria), rich in olive trees and in arable land suitable for grain production. This was a region of the empire which had never faced any serious military threat until, against all reasonable expectations, Germanic Vandals crossed from Spain in 429 and within the space of a decade gained control of it and its revenues. A number of attempts were made to regain it by military means, with the help of the eastern half of the empire, but when the last and most serious of these expeditions failed disastrously in 468, it is hardly surprising that the western empire effectively disappeared less than a decade later. Without North Africa's revenues, the western imperial court struggled to maintain its armed forces at the levels possible throughout the fourth century. By contrast, the eastern empire's most economically productive region—Egypt—never came under any serious military threat until the early seventh century when it was occupied briefly by the Persians and then permanently by the Arabs.

9. The Military and Society

Late antiquity is often seen as a period during which Roman society became more militarized and more exposed to the impact of the military. The best evidence for the first of these developments derives, somewhat surprisingly, from the imperial bureaucracy, where the work of civilians came to be referred to as a form of *militia* ("military service"), and where officials were often found wearing military-

---

55   Haldon 2005a; idem 2005b.
56   Nicasie 1998, 203-6.

style attire and received their *annona*.[57] The second point is related to the development of the mobile field armies. During the Principate, the overwhelming majority of troops were stationed on the empire's frontiers, removed for the most part from major urban centers. Mobile field armies, on the other hand, were often billeted in cities and towns, with householders required to surrender a part of their home to soldiers without recompense in an arrangement euphemistically referred to as *hospitalitas*. Almost inevitably, soldiers often took advantage of their monopoly of force to occupy more than their allotted third of the accommodation, to extract foodstuffs and other materials from householders, and sometimes to rape the women. Among a wide array of evidence, the *Chronicle* attributed to Joshua the Stylite provides a particularly vivid account of the frustrations and injuries experienced by the civilian inhabitants of Edessa while Roman troops were billeted on them in the early years of the sixth century.[58] A somewhat different picture emerges from evidence from Syria and Egypt in the late fourth century, where soldiers appear as patrons of peasants resisting the exactions of landlords and tax collectors, albeit in return for gifts from grateful clients. However, it remains unclear how common an occurrence this was.[59]

Despite service in the imperial bureaucracy being referred to as a form of *militia*, another distinctive feature of the late Roman world was the clear separation of military and civilian careers at the elite level, in contrast with earlier centuries when senatorial aristocrats had taken on roles which combined civilian and military duties (most obviously provincial governorships). Inevitably, late Roman arrangements encouraged the emergence of a military elite, but it has been recognized for some time that there were often close ties between members of this military elite and members of the civilian elite. Recent work has provided further insight into this, particularly through the study of correspondence from the latter to the former, including letters from bishops and clergy to military officers. While a certain amount of this correspondence is primarily concerned with demonstrating the cultural credentials of the author, some of it indicates the influence which

---

57   Jones 1964, 566.
58   Lee 2007a, 163-75.
59   Garnsey and Woolf 1989.

generals could have—or, at least, were thought to have—in areas of political and religious life far removed from military affairs.[60]

A distinctive feature of the social life of many ordinary Roman soldiers in late antiquity derives from the fact that from the beginning of the third century, they were officially allowed to marry. Although the previous prohibition on soldiers marrying had not prevented soldiers from cohabiting and having children, the change in the official stance removed uncertainty over the legal status and testamentary rights of their wives and children. The existence of soldiers' families occasionally emerges in the context of important events, such as the preliminaries to Julian's usurpation, when reluctance to leave wives and children became a major reason for the unwillingness of soldiers to accede to Constantius' request that they transfer eastwards, and the aftermath of the battle of Adrianople, when the trauma experienced by the wives of soldiers who did not return is movingly described by John Chrysostom. The problems of long-term separation and the inevitable uncertainties about the possible fate of their men was a more general problem which imperial laws addressed, although unsurprisingly they sided with the husband's interests by imposing very stringent conditions before allowing a likely widow to remarry. Epitaphs are another important potential source of evidence for this subject, but the families and family life of soldiers is one which is only beginning to receive attention, and offers scope for further work.[61]

10. RELIGION AND IDEOLOGY

The empire's religious allegiances underwent a fundamental shift during late antiquity as, starting with Constantine, Christianity began to receive official support and gradually became the religion of the empire. Just as in late antiquity when educated adherents of traditional religions saw a causal link between the abandonment of the old gods and the empire's growing military difficulties, so in more recent centuries some scholars—most famously, Edward Gibbon—have regarded the empire's embracing of Christianity as contributing significantly to the weakening of its military capabilities because of such factors as the strong pacifist strand in Christianity, as well as its encouragement of detachment from worldly values and priorities. Despite their intrinsic

---

60 Salzman 2006; Lee 2007a, 153-63.
61 For preliminary forays, see Pollard 2000, 152-9; Lee 2007a, 142-4, 147-53.

appeal to a modern mindset, such arguments prove less persuasive when subjected to close examination.[62]

With specific reference to the army, it is evident that the religious allegiances of most soldiers in the fourth-century army were flexible, well able to adapt to the unexpected twists and turns of a century which began with the resolutely pagan Diocletian and Galerius, followed by the Christian Constantine and his sons, followed by another resolute pagan in the person of Julian, before a return to Christian emperors.[63] This process of accommodation was facilitated by the fact that, apart from Diocletian's purge of Christians from the army at the start of the century, emperors generally did not force the issue. They were no doubt mindful that they could not afford to lose experienced soldiers over matters of principle. Moreover, it has increasingly been recognized that Christianity contributed positive benefits in the context of war through helping to maintain the morale of both soldiers and civilians, especially in the context of sieges, which were such a significant form of warfare in this period. This contribution sometimes took the practical form of local bishops organizing and inspiring defenders, and sometimes the more otherworldly form of reported sightings of divine helpers. The successful resistance of the important frontier fortress of Nisibis against the Persians in the fourth century illustrates both these features: during the siege of 338 the bishop Jacob was credited with reinvigorating flagging morale, while the Persian withdrawal from the siege of 350 was attributed to the appearance on the city walls of the figure of the emperor Constantius II when he was known to be elsewhere.[64]

There is also evidence for Christianity imparting a new ideological dimension to warfare, particularly against Persia, partly because Sasanian kings generally supported another theologically-developed religion in the form of Zoroastrianism, and partly because the inhabitants of Persia also included a substantial number of Christians. On one view, the campaign against Persia which Constantine was planning at the time of his death was envisaged as a sort of Christian crusade in defense of the interests of Persia's Christian population.[65] Theodosius II's war against Persia in the early 420s is said to have

---

62 Lee 2007a, 207-10.
63 Tomlin 1998; supplemented by Lee 2007a, 188-93 on the fifth and sixth centuries.
64 Whitby 1998; Lee 2007a, 193-205.
65 Barnes 1985.

been inspired by Persian persecution of Christians.[66] Heraclius tried to energize his troops during the lengthy war with Persia in the early seventh century by "portray[ing] the war as a religious one against a loathsome, pagan enemy."[67] The problem in these cases is knowing to what extent Christianity had permeated the ideology of war and to what extent it was being used as a convenient pretext to justify war or bolster flagging morale.

10. CONCLUSION

Late antiquity is a period rich in source material of relevance to military history, which is increasingly available in good English translations.[68] While the period has traditionally been viewed as one of defeat and decline, much recent scholarship in the field has brought a more positive perspective. Weaknesses have been highlighted in approaches which continue to emphasize "barbarization" and to present Christianity as having had a primarily negative impact on the empire's military capabilities. New avenues of research relating to the army beyond the battlefield have begun to be opened up. Finally, a number of studies in recent decades have argued that despite the defeats and setbacks which Roman armies undeniably suffered, and the trials, tribulations and upheavals which the empire experienced, the late Roman army nonetheless remained a largely effective fighting force—which means that answers to the perennial questions about decline and fall need to be sought elsewhere.

---

66   Holum 1977.
67   Howard-Johnston 1999, 39.
68   The *Translated Texts for Historians*, published by Liverpool University Press, deserves special mention in this respect; despite the general sounding nature of the series title, its focus is on texts of the period from AD 300 to 800, with more than forty volumes now in print.

BIBLIOGRAPHY

Abrahami, Ph. 2005. "Bibliographie sur les armées et les militaires au Proche-Orient ancien (I)." *Revue des études militaires anciennes* 2: 3-19.

———. 2009. "Bibliographie sur les armées et les militaires au Proche-Orient ancien (II)." *Revue des études militaires anciennes* 3: 3-12.

Adams, C. 2007. "War and Society." In *CHGRW*, 2: 198-232.

Adams, J. N. 1999. "The Poets of Bu Njem: Language, Culture, and the Centurionate," *JRS* 89: 109-34.

———. 2003. *Bilingualism and the Latin Language.* Cambridge: Cambridge University Press.

Addington, L. 1990. *The Patterns of War through the Eighteenth Century.* Bloomington, IN: Indiana University Press.

Ager, S. 1996. *Interstate Arbitrations in the Greek World, 337-90 B.C.* Los Angeles: University of California Press.

———. 2005. "Sacred Settlements: The Role of the Gods in the Resolution of Interstate Disputes." In Bertrand 2005: 413-29.

Ahmed Gouda, M. 2006. "The Roman Soldiers in Marriage in Egypt." *MEP* 11: 182-192.

Alföldy, G., B. Dobson, and W. Eck, eds. 2000. *Kaiser, Heer, und Gesellschaft in der römischen Kaiserzeit: Gedenkschrift für Eric Birley.* Stuttgart: F. Steiner.

Alger, J. 1982. *The Quest for Victory: The History of the Principles of War.* Westport: Greenwood Press.

Allason-Jones, L. 1999. "Women and the Roman Army in Britain." In Goldsworthy and Haynes 1999: 41-51.

Alston, R. 1995. *Soldier and Society in Roman Egypt.* New York: Routledge.

———. 1998. "Arms and the Man; Soldiers, Masculinity, and Power in Republican and Imperial Rome." In *When Men Were Men: Masculinity, Power, and Identity in Classical Antiquity.* ed. L. Foxhall and J. Salmon, 205-223. New York: Routledge.

———. 2007. "The Military and Politics." In *CHGRW*, 2: 176-97.

Amiri, B. 2007. "La condition servile dans l'armée romaine en Germanie: rupture et renouvellement culturels." *SHHA* 25: 435-450.

Anderson, J. K. 1970. *Military Theory and Practice in the Age of Xenophon.* Los Angeles: University of California Press.

———. 1974. *Xenophon.* London: Duckworth.

Ando, C. 2000. *Imperial Ideology and Provincial Loyalty in the Roman Empire.* Los Angeles: University of California.

———. 2007. "The Army and the Urban Elite: A Competition for Power." In *CRA*: 359-78.

Andreau, J., P. Briant, and R. Descat, eds. 2000. *Économie antique: La guerre dans les economies antiques. Entretiens d'archéologie et d'histoire.* Toulouse: Saint-Bertrand-de-Comminges, Musée archéologique.

Anson, E. 2009. "Philip II and the Creation of the Macedonian Pezhetairoi," In Wheatley and Hannah 2009: 88-98.

Aperghis, G. 2000. "War Captives and Economic Exploitation: Evidence from the Persepolis Fortification Tablets." Andreau, Briant, and Descat 2000, 128-44.

———. 2005. *The Seleukid Royal Economy: The Finances and Financial Administration of the Seleukid Empire.* Cambridge: Cambridge University Press.

———. 2007. "The Army and the Urban Elite: A Competition for Power." In *CRA*: 359-78.

Ardant du Picq, C. 1880. *Études sur le combat.* Paris: Dumaine & Hachette. Reprinted Paris: Éditions Champ Libre, 1978.

———. 1921. *Battle Studies: Ancient and Modern.* Tr. J. Greeley and R. Cotton. New York: Macmillan Co. Reprinted in *Roots of Strategy, Book 2*, 9-299. Mechanicsburg: Stackpole Books, 1987.

Armstrong, J. 2008. "Breaking the Rules? Irregularities in the Recruitment of the Early Roman Army (509-c.450 BC)." In Bragg, Hau, and Macaulay-Lewis 2008: 47-66.

Ash, R. 1999. *Ordering Anarchy: Armies and Leaders in Tacitus' Histories.* Ann Arbor, MI: University of Michigan.

Aubert, J.-J., and Z. Várhelyi, eds. 2005. *A Tall Order: Writing the Social History of the Ancient World.* München: F. G. Saur.

Aufrère, S. H. 2005. "La destruction des arbres et des cultures des villes à l'occasion d'un siège, le saccage des récoltes ete du couvert végé-tal lors des guerres." In *Encyclopédie religieuse de l'univers végétal. Croyances phytoreligieuses de l'Égypte ancienne*, ed. S. H. Aufrère, 49-57. *Orientalia Monspeliensia* 15. Montpelier: Université Paul Valery - Montpellier III.

Austin, M. 1986. "Hellenistic Kings, War and the Economy." *CQ* 80: 450-66.

―――. 2001. "War and Culture in the Seleucid Empire." In Bekker-Nielsen and Hannestad 2001: 90-109.

Austin, N. J. E., and N. B. Rankov. 1995. *Exploratio: Military and Political Intelligence in the Roman World from the Second Punic War to the Battle of Adrianople*. London & New York: Routledge.

Aymard, A. 1967. *Études d'histoire ancienne*. Paris: Presses universitaires de France.

Badian, E. 1979. "Alexander's Mules." *New York Review of Books* (20 December): 54, 56.

Bahrani, Z. 1995. "Assault and Abduction: The Fate of the Royal Image in the Ancient Near East," *Art History* 18.3: 363-83.

―――. 2001. *Women of Babylon: Gender and Representation in Mesopotamia*. London: Routledge.

―――. 2003. *The Graven Image: Representations in Babylonia and Assyria*. Philadelphia: University of Philadelphia Press.

―――. 2008. *Rituals of War: The Body and Violence in Mesopotamia*. New York: Zone Books.

Baker, Patricia A. 2004. *Medical Care for the Roman Army on the Rhine, Danube and British Frontiers in the First, Second, and Early Third Centuries A.D.* Oxford: Hedges.

Baker, Patrick. 2003. "Warfare." In *A Companion to the Hellenistic World*, ed. A. Erskine, 373-88. Malden, MA: Blackwell Publishing.

Bakewell, G. 2007. "Written Lists of Military Personnel in Classical Athens." In *Politics of Orality*, ed. C. Cooper, 89-101. *Mnemosyne*, Suppl. 280. Leiden: E. J. Brill.

Baltrusch, E. 1994. *Symmachie und Spondai. Untersuchungen zum griechischen Völkerrecht der archaischen und klassischen Zeit (8.-5. Jahrhundert v. Chr.* Berlin: Walter de Gruyter.

Bar-Kochva, B. 1976. *The Seleucid Army: Organization and Tactics in the Great Campaigns*. Cambridge: Cambridge University Press.

―――. 1989. *Judas Maccabaeus: The Jewish Struggle Against the Seleucids*. Cambridge: Cambridge University Press.

Barnes, T.D. 1985. "Constantine and the Christians of Persia." *JRS* 75: 126-36.

―――. 1998. *Ammianus Marcellinus and the Representation of Historical Reality*. Ithaca: Cornell University Press.

Barron, A. E. 2010. "Late Assyrian Arms and Armour: Art versus Artifact." Ph.D. Dissertation. Toronto: University of Toronto.

Barton, C. A. 2001. *Roman Honor: The Fire in the Bones*. Los Angeles: University of California.

———. 2007. "The Price of Peace in Ancient Rome." In Raaflaub 2007b: 245-255.

Bauman, R. 1996. *Crime and Punishment in Ancient Rome.* New York: Routledge.

Beal, R. H. 1995. "Hittite Military Rituals." In *Ancient Magic and Ritual Power*, ed. M. Meyer and P. Mirecki, 63-76. Leiden: Brill.

Beard, M. 2000. *The Invention of Jane Harrison.* Cambridge, MA: Harvard University Press.

———. 2008. *The Roman Triumph.* Cambridge, MA: Harvard University Press.

Bederman, D. 2001. *International Law in Antiquity.* Cambridge: Cambridge University Press.

Bekker-Nielsen, T. and Hannestad, L., eds. 2001. *War as a Cultural and Social Force: Essays on Warfare in Antiquity. Historisk-Filosofiske Skrifter*, 22. Copenhagen: Det kongelige danske videnskabernes Selskab.

Ben-Ezra, M. 2004. "Trauma in Antiquity: 4000 Year Old Post-Traumatic Reactions?" *Stress and Health* 20: 121-25.

———. 2010. "Traumatic Reactions from Antiquity to the 16th Century: Was there a Common Denominator?" *Stress and Health* 26. (http://dx.doi.org/10.1002/smi.1338), accessed September 1 2010.

Bernard, P. 1994. "L'Asie centrale et l'empire seleucide," *Topoi* 4.2: 473-511.

Bernard, A. 1999. *Guerre et violence dans le Grèce antique.* Paris: Hachette littératures.

Berry, W. D. 1996. "Roof Tiles and Urban Violence in the Ancient World." *GRBS* 37: 55-74.

Bersani, L. and U. Dutoit. 1985. The Forms of Violence: Narrative in Assyrian Art and Modern Culture. New York: Schocken Books.

Bertosa, B. 2003. "The Supply of Hoplite Equipment by the Athenian State down to the Lamian War." *JMH* 67: 361-79.

Bertrand, J.-M., ed. 2005. *La violence dans les mondes grec et romain.* Paris: Publications de la Sorbonne.

Berve, H. 1926. *Das Alexanderreich auf prosopographischer Grundlage.* 2 vols. Munich: C. H. Beck'sche Verlagsbuchhandlung. Reprinted Salem: Ayer Company, Publishers, Inc, 1988.

Beston, P. "Hellenistic Military Leadership." In van Wees, 2000a: 315-35.

Bettalli, M. 1995. *I mercenari nel mondo greco*, I. Pisa: Edizioni ETS.

———. 2002. "La disciplina negli eserciti delle *poleis*. Il caso di Atene." In Sordi 2002: 107-21.

———. 2009. "Ascesca e decadenza dell'oplita." ὅρμος 1: 5-12

Bichler, R. 2009. "Probleme und Grenzen der Rekonstruktion von Ereignissen am Beispiel antiker Schlachtenbeschreibungen." In *Das Ereignis. Geschichtsschreibung zwischen Vorfall und Befund*, ed. M. Fitzenreiter, 17-34. London: Golden House Publications.

Bickerman, 1938. E. *Institutions des Séleucides*. Paris: P. Geuthner.

Bielman, A. 1994. *Retour à liberté. Liberation et sauvetage des prisonniers en Grèce ancienne*. Athens: École Française d'Athènes.

Billows, R. 2010. *Marathon: The Battle That Changed Western Civilization*. Woodstock, NY: Overlook Press.

Bingen, J., et al., ed. 1992. *Mons Claudianus: ostraca graeca et latina I (O.Claud, 1 à 190)*. Cairo: Institut français d'archéologie orientale du Caire.

Bingham, S. 1997. "The Praetorian Guard in the Political and Social Life of Julio-Claudian Rome," PhD diss., University of British Columbia.

Birley, A. R. 1992. *Locus virtutibus patefactus?: zum Beförderungssystem in der Hohen Kaiserzeit*. Opladen : West-dt. Verlag.

―――. 2003. "The Commissioning of Equestrian Officers." In Wilkes 2003: 1-18.

―――. 2007. "Making Emperors: Imperial Instrument or Independent Force?" In *CRA*: 379-94.

Birley, E. 1988. *The Roman Army: Papers, 1929-1986*. MAVORS 4. Amsterdam: Gieben.

Bishop, M. C., and J. C. N. Coulston. 2006. *Roman Military Equipment: From the Punic Wars to the Fall of Rome*. 2nd ed. Oxford: Oxbow.

Black, Jeremy. 2004a. *Rethinking Military History*. New York: Routledge.

―――. 2004b. "Determinisms and Other Issues." *JMH* 68: 1217-32.

Bliese, John R. E. 1994. "Rhetoric Goes to War: The Doctrine of Ancient and Medieval Military Manuals" *Rhetoric Society Quarterly*, 24.3-4: 105-130.

Blois, L. de. 2000. "Army and Society in the Late Roman Republic: Professionalism and the Role of the Military Middle Cadre." In Alföldy, Dobson, and Eck 2000: 11-31.

―――. ed. 2001. *Administration, Prosopography, and Appointment Policies in the Roman Empire. Proceedings of the First Workshop of the International Network Impact of Empire (Roman Empire, 27 B.C. - A.D. 406), Leiden June 28-July 1 2000*. Amsterdam: Gieben.

―――. 2007. "Army and General in the Late Roman Republic." In *CRA*: 164-79.

Blois, L. de, and J. Rich, eds. 2002. *The Transformation of Economic Life under the Roman Empire : Proceedings of the Second Workshop of the International Network Impact of Empire (Roman Empire, c. 200 B.C.-A.D. 476), Nottingham, July 4-7, 2001*. Amsterdam: Gieben.

Blois, L. de, and E. Lo Cascio, eds. 2007. *Impact of the Roman Army (200 BC – AD 476): Economic, Social, Political, Religious, and Cultural Aspects.* Proceedings of the Sixth Workshop of the International Network Impact of Empire (Roman Empire, 200 B.C.-A.D. 476), Capri, March 29-April 2, 2005. Leiden: Brill.

Boëldieu-Trevet, 2007. J. *Commander dans le monde grec au Ve siècle avant notre ère.* Besançon: Presses universitaires de Franche-Comté.

Bois, J.-P, ed. 2004. *Dialogue militaire entre anciens et moderns.* Rennes: Presses universitaires de Rennes.

Bolmarcich, S. 2007. "Oaths in Greek International Relations." In *Horkos: The Oath in Greek Society,* ed. A. H. Sommerstein and J. Fletcher, 26-38. Exeter: Bristol Phoenix Press.

Bonneterre, D. 1997. "Surveiller, punir et se venger: la violence d'État à Mari." *Mari: Annales de Recherches Interdisciplinaires* 8: 537-62.

Bose, P. 2003. *Alexander the Great's Art of Strategy: The Timeless Leadership Lessons of History's Greatest Empire Builder.* New York: Penguin.

Bosworth, A. 1980-95. *A Historical Commentary on Arrian's History of Alexander.* 2 vols. Oxford: Clarendon Press.

———. 1996. *Alexander and the East: The Tragedy of Triumph.* Oxford: Oxford University Press.

———. 2002. *The Legacy of Alexander: Politics, Warfare, and Propaganda under the Successors.* Oxford: Oxford University Press.

Bourke, J. 1999. *Dismembering the Male: Men's Bodies, Britain, and the Great War.* Chicago: University of Chicago.

Bouvier, D. 2006. "De la plaine de Troie au champ de bataille hoplitique: la tradition d'une guerre sans ruse en Grèce ancienne." In Olivier *et al.* 2006: 27-50.

Bowman, A. K. 2003. *Life and Letters on the Roman Frontier: Vindolanda and its People.* London: British Museum.

———. 2006. "Outposts of Empire: Vindolanda, Egypt, and the Empire of Rome." *JRA* 19.1: 75-93.

Bradley, K. 2004. "On Captives Under the Principate." *Phoenix* 58.3-4: 298-318.

Bragg, E. 2008. "'Show us your scars, Manius Aquillius.' The Military Record of Magistrates in Defence Speeches During the Roman Republic." In Bragg, Hau, and Macaulay-Lewis 2008: 7-24.

Bragg, E., Lisa Hau and E. Macaulay-Lewis, eds. 2008. *Beyond the Battlefields: New Perspectives on Warfare and Society in the Graeco-Roman World.* Newcastle, UK: Cambridge Scholars.

Braudel, F. 1966. *La Méditerranée et le monde méditerranéen à l'époque de Philippe II².* Paris: A. Colin.

————. 1972. *The Mediterranean and the Mediterranean World in the Age of Philip II*. Tr. Siân Reynolds. New York: Harper & Row.

Breeze, D. J. 1969. "The Organization of the Legion: The First Cohort and the *equites legionis*." *JRS* 59: 50-55.

————. 1971. "Pay Grades and Ranks Below the Centurionate." *JRS* 61: 130-35. Reprinted in Breeze and Dobson 1993: 59-64.

————. 1974. "The Organisation of the Career Structure of the *immunes* and *principales* of the Roman Army." *BJ* 174: 245-92. Reprinted in Breeze and Dobson 1993: 11-58.

Breeze, D. J. and B. Dobson, eds. 1993. *Roman Officers and Frontiers*. *MAVORS* 10. Stuttgart: F. Steiner.

Brélaz, C., with J. Fournier. 2008. "Maintaining Order and Exercising Justice in the Roman Provinces of Asia Minor." In *The Province Strikes Back. Imperial Dynamics in the Eastern Mediterranean*, ed. B. Forsén and G. Salmeri, 45-64. Helsinki: Finnish Institute at Athens.

Brelich, A. 1961. *Guerre, agoni e culti nella Grecia antica*. Bonn: Habelt.

Brennan, P. 1996. "The *Notitia Dignitatum*." In *Les Litteratures techniques dans l'antiquité romaine*. ed. C. Nicolet, 153-69. Geneva: Fondation Hardt,.

————. 1998. "A User's Guide to the *Notitia Dignitatum*: The Case of the *dux Armeniae* (*ND Or. XXXVIII*)." *Antichthon* 32: 34-49.

————. 2007. "Zosimos 2.34.1 and 'the Constantinian reform': Using Johannes Lydos to Expose an Insidious Fabrication." In *The Late Roman Army in the Near East from Diocletian to the Arab Conquest : Proceedings of a Colloquium held at Potenza, Acerenza and Matera, Italy, May 2005*. ed. A.S. Lewin and P. Pellegrini, 211-18. Oxford: Archaeopress.

Brennan, S. 2008. "Chronological Pointers in Xenophon's *Anabasis*." *BICS* 51: 51-61.

Briant, P. 2002. *From Cyrus to Alexander: A History of the Persian Empire*. Winona Lake, IN: Eisenbrauns.

Brice, L. L. 2008. "Fog of War: The Roman Army in *Rome*." In *Rome, Season 1: History Makes Television*. ed. Monica Cyrino, 61-77. Malden, MA: Wiley-Blackwell.

————. 2011a. "Disciplining Octavian: A Case Study in Roman Military Culture, 44-30 BCE." In *Warfare and Culture in World History*, ed. W. E. Lee. forthcoming. New York: New York University Press.

————. 2011b. "Philip II, Alexander the Great, and the Question of a Macedonian RMA." *AncW* 42: forthcoming.

Brizzi, G. 2002. "Il guerriero e il soldato." In Sordi 2002b: 87-105.

Brodersen, K., ed. 2008. *Vincere Scis, Victoria Uti Nescis. Aspekte der Rückschauverzerrung in der Alten Geschichte.* Berlin: Lit Verlag Dr. W. Hopf.

Brulé, P. 1999. "La mortalité de guerre en Grèce classique: l'exemple d'Athènes de 490 à 322." In *Armées et sociétés de la Grèce classique. Aspects sociaux et politiques de la guerre aux Ve et IVe s. av. J.-C.*, ed. F. Prost, 51-68. Paris: Ed. Errance.

Brulé, P. and J. Oulhen, eds. 1997. *Esclavage, guerre, économie en Grèce. Hommages à Yvon Garlan.* Rennes: Presses universitaires de Rennes.

Brun, P. and R. Descat 2000. "Le profit de la guerre dans la Grèce des cités." In Andreau *et al.* 2000: 211-30.

Brunt, P. A. 1971. *Italian Manpower, 225 B.C.-A.D. 14.* Oxford: Oxford University Press.

———. 1975. "Did Imperial Rome Disarm her Subjects?" *Phoenix* 29: 260-270.

Bucholz, A. 1985. *Hans Delbrück & the German Military Establishment: War Images in Conflict.* Iowa City: University of Iowa Press.

Bugh, G., ed. 2006a. *The Cambridge Companion to the Hellenistic World.* Cambridge: Cambridge University Press.

———. 2006b. "Hellenistic Military Developments." In Bugh 2006a: 265-94.

Burckhardt, L. 1996. *Bürger und Soldaten. Aspekte der politischen und militärischen Rolle athenischer Bürger im Kriegswesen des 4. Jahrhunderts v. Chr. Historia Einzelschrift*, 101. Stuttgart: Franz Steiner Verlag.

———. 2001. Review of Hunt 1998. *Klio* 83: 236-37.

———. 2008. *Militärgeschichte der Antike.* Munich: Verlag C.H. Beck.

Burgière, A. 2009. *The Annales School: An Intellectual History.* Tr. J. Todd. Ithaca: Cornell University Press.

Burke, A. 2008. *"Walled Up To Heaven": The Evolution of Middle Bronze Age Fortification Strategies in the Levant.* Winona Lake, IN: Eisenbrauns.

Burrer, F. and H. Müller, ed. 2008. *Kriegskosten und Kriegsfinanzierung in der Antike.* Darmstadt: Wissenschaftliche Buchgesellschaft.

Cagniart, P. 2007. "The Late Republican Army (146-30 BC)." In *CRA*: 80-95.

Cairns, F. 1991. "The 'Laws of Eretria' (*IG* XII.9 1273 and 1274): Epigraphic, Historical and Political Aspects." *Phoenix* 45: 291-313.

Campbell, J. B. 1984. *The Emperor and the Roman Army.* Oxford: Clarendon Press.

———, ed. 1994. *The Roman Army, 31 BC – AD 337: A Sourcebook.* New York: Routledge.

———. 2002. *War and Society in Imperial Rome, 31 BC - AD 284.* New York: Routledge.

————, ed. 2004. *Greek and Roman Military Writers: Selected Readings.*
New York: Routledge.

————. 2005. "The Army." In *Cambridge Ancient History XII: The Crisis of
Empire, AD 193-337.* ed. A.K. Bowman, P. Garnsey, and A. Cameron,
110-30. Cambridge: Cambridge University Press.

Cancik-Kirschbaum, E. 1996. *Die mittelassyriachen Briefe aus Tall Åeh
Hamad.* Berlin: Dietrich Reimer.

Capdetrey, L. 2007. *Le pouvoir séleucide. Territoire, administration, finances
d'un royaume hellénistique (312-129 avant J.-C.).* Rennes: Presses universitaires de Rennes.

Carney, E. 2004. "Women and Military Leadership in Macedonia." *AncW* 35:
184-95.

Carrié, J.-M. 1993. "The Soldier." In *The Romans*, ed. A. Giardina, 100-137.
Tr. Lydia Cochrane. Chicago: University of Chicago Press.

————. 2002. "L'armée romaine tardive dans quelques travaux récents. 3e
partie: fournitures militaires, recrutement et archéologie des fortifications." *Antiquité tardive* 10: 427-42.

————. 2004. "Le systéme de recrutement des armées romaines de Diocétien
aux Valentiniens." In *L'Armée romaine de Dioclétien à Valentinien Ier.*
eds. Y. Le Bohec and C. Wolff, 371-88. Paris: Boccard.

Carrié, J.-M. and S. Janniard. 2000. "L'armée romaine tardive dans quelques
travaux récents. 1re partie: l'institution militaire et les modes de combat."
Antiquité tardive 8: 321-41.

Carroll, L. 1960. *Alice's Adventures in Wonderland* and *Through the Looking-
Glass.* New York: New American Library.

Cartledge, P. 2004. *Alexander the Great: The Hunt for a New Past.*
Woodstock, NY: Overlook Press.

Chambers, J.W. 1991. "The New Military History: Myth and Reality." *JMH*
55.3: 395-406.

Champion, C. B., ed. 2004. *Roman Imperialism: Readings and Sources.*
Malden, MA: Wiley-Blackwell.

Champlin, E. 1987. "The Testament of the Piglet." *Phoenix* 41: 174-83.

Chancey, M. 2005. *Greco-Roman Culture and the Galilee of Jesus.*
Cambridge: Cambridge University Press.

Chaniotis, A. 1996. *Die Verträge zwischen kretischen Poleis in der hellenistischen Zeit.* Stuttgart: Franz Steiner Verlag.

————. 2004. "Justifying Territorial Claims in Classical and Hellenistic
Greece." In *The Law and the Courts in Ancient Greece*, ed. E. Harris and
L. Rubinstein, 185-213. London: Duckworth.

————. 2005a. "Victory's Verdict: The Violent Occupation of Territory in
Hellenistic Interstate Relations." In Bertrand, 2005: 455-67.

————. 2005b. *War in the Hellenistic World.* Malden, MA: Blackwell Publishing.

Chaniotis, A. and P. Ducrey, eds. 2001. *Army and Power in the Ancient World.* Stuttgart: Franz Steiner Verlag, 2002.

Chapman, C. 2004. *The Gendered Language of Warfare in the Israelite-Assyrian encounter.* Winona Lake, IN: Eisenbrauns.

Charles, M.B. 2007. *Vegetius in Context: Establishing the Date of the 'Epitoma rei militaris'.* Stuttgart: Steiner.

Charpin, D. 2004. "Histoire politique du Proche-Orient Amorrite." In *Mesopotamien: Die altbabylonische Zeit,* ed. D. Charpin *et al.*, 25-480. Göttingen: Vandenhoeck & Ruprecht.

Chastagnol, A., ed. 1977. *Armées et fiscalité dans le monde antique.* Paris: Éditions du Centre national de la recherchre scientifique.

Chavalas, M., ed. 2006. *The Ancient Near East: Historical Sources in Translation.* Malden, MA: Blackwell.

Chrissanthos, S. 2001. "Caesar and the Mutiny of 47 B.C." *JRS* 91: 63-75.

————. 2004. "Freedom of Speech in the Roman Republican Army." In *Free Speech in Classical Antiquity*: ed. R. Rosen and I. Sluiter, 341-68. Leiden: Brill.

Christ. K. 1972. *Von Gibbon zu Rostovtzeff; Leben und Werk führender Althistoriker der Neuzeit.* Darmstadt: Wissenschaftliche Buchgesellschaft.

Christ, M. 2001. "Conscription of Hoplites in Classical Athens." *CQ* 51: 398-422.

————. 2006. *The Bad Citizen in Classical Athens.* New York: Cambridge University Press.

Christien, J. 2006. "The Lacedaemonian State: Fortifications, Frontiers and Historical Problems." In Hodkinson and Powell 2006: 163-83.

Cioffi-Revilla, C. 1996. "Origins and Evolution of War and Politics." *International Studies Quarterly* 40.1: 1-22.

————. 2000. "Ancient Warfare: Origins and Systems." In *Handbook of War Studies II,* ed. M. I. Midlarsky, 59-89. Ann Arbor: University of Michigan Press.

Citino, R. M. 2007. "Military Histories Old and New: A Reintroduction." *AHR* 112.4: 1070-90.

Clare, L. et al. 2008. "Warfare in Late Neolithic/Early Chalcolithic Pisidia, Southwestern Turkey." *Documenta Praehistorica* XXXV: 65-92.

Cline, E. 1997. "Review of R. Drews' *The End of the Bronze Age.*" *JNES* 56.2: 127-29.

Cohen, D., ed. 2002. *Demokratie, Recht und soziale Kontrolle im klassischen Athen.* Munich: Oldenbourg.

Cohen, E. 2000. *The Athenian Nation.* Princeton: Princeton University Press.

Cohen, J. J., ed. 1996. *Monster Theory: Reading Culture.* Minneapolis: University of Minnesota Press.

Coin-Longeray, S. 2006. "Ruse, tromperie et mensonge chez les historiens grecs: *dolos, apate, pseudos.*" In Olivier *et al.* 2006: 7-25.

Cole, S. W. and P. Machinist. 1998. *Letters from Assyrian and Babylonian Priests to Kings Esarhaddon and Assurbanipal.* Helsinki: University of Helsinki.

Colson, B. and Coutau-Bégarie, H., eds. 2000. *Pensée stratégique et humanisme. De la tactique des Anciens à l'éthique de la stratégie.* Paris: Economica.

Cooper, J. 1986. *Sumerian and Akkadian Royal Inscriptions: Presargonic Inscriptions.* New Haven: American Oriental Society.

Corbier, M. 1989. "The Ambiguous Status of Meat in Ancient Rome." *Food and Foodways* 3.3: 223-64.

Cordiano, G. 2007. "Entre *gymazein* et *hippeuein*: chevaux et "dressage" militaire de l'éphèbe Cyrène." In Sauzeau and Van Compernolle 2007: 563-84.

Corvisier, J.-N. 1994. "Médecine et demographie, l'exemple de Plutarque." *REG* 107: 129-57.

———. 1999. "Guerre et démographie en Grèce à la période classique." *Pallas* 51: 57-79.

———. 2005. "1985-2005: vingt ans de travaux sur la guerre grecque antique (I)." *Revue des études militaires anciennes* 2: 31-55.

———. 2006. "1985-2005: vingt ans de travaux sur la guerre grecque antique (II)." *Revue des études militaires anciennes* 3: 29-74.

Cosme, P. 2003. "Le châtiment des déserteurs dans l'armée romaine." *RD* 81.3: 287-307.

Coulston, J. C. N. 2004. "Military Identity and Personal Self-Identity in the Roman Army." In *Roman Rule and Civic Life: Local and Regional Perspectives.* Proceedings of the fourth workshop of the international network Impact of Empire (Roman Empire, c. 200 B.C. - A.D. 476), Leiden, June 25-28, 2003. ed. L. de Ligt, E. A. Hemelrijk, and H. W. Singor, 133-152. Impact of Empire , vol. 4. Amsterdam: Gieben.

Couvenhes, J.-C. 2004. "Les cités grecques d'Asie Mineure et le mercenariat à l'époque hellénistique." In Couvenhes and Fernoux 2004: 77-113.

———. 2005. "*De disciplina Graecorum*: les relations de violence entre les chefs militaries grecs et leur soldats." In Bertrand 2005: 431-54.

———. 2007. "La fourniture d'armes aux citoyens athéniens du IVe au IIIe siècle av. J.-C." In Sauzeau and Van Compernolle 2007: 521-40.

————. 2009. "L'armée de Mihridate VI Eupator d'après Plutarque, Vie de Lucullus, VII, 4-6." In *L'Asie Mineure dans l'Antiquité: Échanges, populations et territories*, ed. H. Bru, F. Kirbihler, and S. Lebreton, 415-38. Rennes: Presses universitaires des Rennes.

Couvenhes, J.-C. and H.-L. Fernoux, eds. 2004. *Les Cités grecques et la guerre en Asie Mineure à l'époque hellénistique.* Tours: Presses universitaires François-Rabelais.

Cozzo, A. 2009. "Come evitare le guerre e rendere amici i nemici. Forme della diplomazia nella Grecia antica." ὅρμος 1: 13-34.

Craig, G. 1986. "Delbrück: The Military Historian." In *Makers of Modern Strategy from Machiavelli to the Nuclear Age,* ed. P. Paret, 326-54. Princeton: Princeton University Press.

Crane, G. and M. Terras, eds. 2009. Changing the Center of Gravity: Transforming Classical Studies through Cyberinfrastructure. *Digital Humanities Quarterly* 3.1. http://digitalhumanities.org/dhq/vol/3/1/index. html (accessed 10/11/10).

Cresci, L. R., F. Gazzano, and D.P. Orsi, eds. 2002. *La retorica dell diplomazia nella Grecia antica e a Bisanzio.* Rome: L'Erma di Bretschneider.

Creasy, E. 1851. *Fifteen Decisive Battles of the World.* Reprinted New York: Dorset Press, 1987.

Croke, B. 2005. "Dynasty and Ethnicity: Emperor Leo I and the Eclipse of Aspar." *Chiron* 35: 147-203.

Crouch, C. L. 2009. *War and Ethics in the Ancient Near East: Military Violence in Light of Cosmology and History. Beihefte zur Zeitschrift für die alttestamentliche.* Wissenschaft 407. Berlin: Walter de Gruyter.

Curtis, J. E. and J. E. Reade. 1995. *Art and Empire: Treasures from Assyria in the British Museum.* London: British Museum Press.

Cuvigny, H., ed. 2003. *Praesidia du désert de Bérénice. 1, La route de Myos Hormos: l'armée romaine dans le désert oriental d'Egypte.* Cairo: IFAO.

Dalley, S. 1976. "An Assyrian Stela Fragment." *Iraq* 38.2: 107-111.

————. 1985. "Foreign Chariotry and Cavalry in the Armies of Tiglath-Pileser III and Sargon II." *Iraq* 47: 31-48.

Daly, G. 2002. *Cannae: The Experience of Battle in the Second Punic War.* New York: Routledge.

Dandeker, C. 2007."The End of War:—The Strategic Context of International Missions in the Twenty-First Century." In *Eight Essays in Contemporary War Studies,* ed, M. Christiansson, 19-45. Stockholm: Militärhögskolan Karlberg.

Darbo-Preschanski, C. 1994. "Le cité, 'l'oikoumene' et la guerre." *Métis* 9-10: 171-87.

Daverio Rocchi, G., ed. 2007. *Tra Concordia e pace: parole e valori della Grecia antica: giornata di studio, Milano, 21 ottobre 2005.* Milan: Cisalpino.

Davies, R. W. 1974. "The daily life of the Roman soldier under the Principate." *ANRW* 2.1: 299-338. In Davies 1989: 33-70.

———. 1989. *Service in the Roman Army.* ed. D. Breeze and V. A. Maxfield. New York: Columbia University Press.

Dayton, J. 2003. "'The Athletes of War': An Evaluation of the Agonistic Elements of Greek Warfare." *AJAH* N.S. 2.2: 17-97.

———. 2006. *The Athletes of War: An Evaluation of the Agonistic Elements in Greek Warfare.* Toronto: Edgar Kent, Inc. Publishers.

Debevoise, N. 1938. *A Political History of Parthia.* Chicago: University of Chicago Press. Reprinted New York: Greenwood Press, 1968.

De Graef, K. 2002. "An Account of the Redistribution of Land to Soldiers in Late Old Babylonian Sippar-Amnanum." *JESHO* 45: 141-78.

Delbrück, H. 1920. *Geschichte der Kriegskunst im Rahmen der politischen Geschichte*[3]. 4 vols. Berlin: Georg Stilke.

———. 1975-85. *History of the Art of War within the Framework of Political History.* 4 vols. Tr. W. Renfroe. Westport: Greenwood Press.

Dench, E. 1995. *From Barbarians to New Men: Greek, Roman, and Modern Perceptions of Peoples of the Central Apennines.* Oxford: Clarendon Press.

———. 1996. "Images of Italian Austerity from Cato to Tacitus." In *Les élites municipales de l'Italie péninsulaire des Gracques à Néron.* ed. M. Cébeillac-Gervasoni, 247-54. Rome: L'École française de Rome.

———. 1998. "Austerity, Excess, Success, and Failure in Hellenistic and Early Imperial Italy." In *Parchments of Gender: Deciphering the Bodies of Antiquity.* ed. Maria Wyke, 121-46. Oxford: Clarendon Press.

———. 2005. *Romulus' Asylum: Roman Identities from the Age of Alexander to the Age of Hadrian.* Oxford: Oxford University Press.

Dennis, G.T. 1985. *Three Byzantine Military Treatises.* Wasington DC: Dumbarton Oaks.

DeOdorico, M. 1995. *The Use of Numbers and Quantifications in the Assyrian Royal Inscriptions. = State Archives of Assyria Studies* 3. Helsinki: University of Helsinki.

de Souza, Ph., ed. 2008a. *The Ancient World at War: A Global History.* London: Thames and Hudson.

———. 2008b. "*Parta victoriis pax*: Roman Emperors as Peacemakers." In de Souza and France 2008, 76-106.

de Souza, Ph. and J. France, ed. 2008. *War and Peace in Ancient and Medieval History.* Cambridge: Cambridge University Press.

Detienne, M. and Vernant, J.-P. 1974. *Les ruses de l'intelligence: la mètis des Grecs.* Paris: Flammarion.

————. 1978. *Cunning Intelligence in Greek Culture and Society.* Tr. J. Lloyd. Atlantic Heights: Humanities Press.

Develin, R. 2005. "The Integration of Plebeians into the Political Order after 366 B.C." In Raaflaub 2005: 293-311.

Dewald, J. 2006. *Lost Worlds: The Emergence of French Social History, 1815-1970.* University Park: Penn State University Press.

Dewar, M. 2003. "Multi-Ethnic Armies in Virgil, Lucan, and Claudian." *SyllClass* 14: 143-159.

Dezsö, T. 2006. "Reconstruction of the Assyrian Army of Sargon II (721-705 BC) Based on the Nimrud Horse Lists." *State Archives of Assyria Bulletin* 15: 93-140.

Dietrich, M. 2003. *The Neo-Babylonian Correspondence of Sargon and Sennacherib.* Helsinki: University of Helsinki.

Dillon, S. 2006. "Women on the Columns of Trajan and Marcus Aurelius and the Visual Language of Roman Victory." In Dillon & Welch 2006: 244-271.

Dillon, S. and K. E. Welch, eds. 2006. *Representations of War in Ancient Rome.* Cambridge: Cambridge University Press.

Dobson, B. 1970. "The Centurionate and Social Mobility during the Principate." In *Recherches sur les structures sociales dans l'antiquité classique.* ed. C. Nicolet, 99-115. Paris: CNRS. Reprinted in Breeze and Dobson 1993: 201-17.

————. 1974. "The Significance of the Centurion and *'primipilaris'* in the Roman Army and Administration." *ANRW* 2.1: 392--434. Reprinted in Breeze and Dobson 1993:143-85.

————. 1986. "The Roman Army: Wartime Army or Peacetime Army?" In Eck and Wolff 1986: 10-25. Reprinted in Breeze and Dobson 1993: 113-28.

Dodgeon, M.H. and S. Lieu. 1991. *The Roman Eastern Frontier and the Persian Wars, AD 226-363.* New York: Routledge.

Dolce, R. 2004. "The 'Head of the Enemy' in the Sculptures from the Palaces of Nineveh: An Example of 'Cultural Migration?'" *Iraq* 66: 121-32.

Domaszewski, A. von. 1908. *Die Rangordnung des römischen Heeres.* Bonn: Marcus und Weber. 2nd ed. ed. B. Dobson. Köln, Böhlau 1967.

Downey, S. B. 2006. "Arms and Armour as Social Coding in Palmyra, the Palmyrène, and Dura-Europos." In Mode and Tubach 2006: 321-355.

Drijvers, J.W. and D. Hunt, eds. 1999. *The Late Roman World and its Historian: Interpreting Ammianus Marcellinus.* London: Routledge.

Drinkwater, J.F. 1994 "Silvanus, Ursicinus and Ammianus: fact or fiction?" In *Studies in Latin Literature and Roman History*, vol.7. ed. C. Deroux, 568-76. Brussells: Collection Latomus.

———. 2000. "The Revolt and Ethnicity of the Usurper Magnentius (350-353) and the Rebellion of Vetranio (350)." *Chiron* 30: 131-59.

———. 2007. *The Alamanni and Rome, 213-496: Caracalla to Clovis.* Oxford: Oxford University Press.

Drogula, F. K. 2005. "The Office of the Provincial Governor under the Roman Republic and Empire (to AD 235): Conception and Tradition." PhD diss., University of Virginia.

———. 2007. "*Imperium, potestas,* and the *pomerium* in the Roman Republic." *Historia* 56.4: 419-452.

Dubovsky, P. 2006. *Hezekiah and the Assyrian Spies.* Rome: Pontificio Instituto biblico.

Duby, G. 1973. *Le dimanche de Bouvines.* Paris: Gallimard.

———. 1990. *The Legend of Bouvines: War, Religion, and Culture in the Middle Ages.* Tr. C. Tihanyi. Los Angeles: Unversity of California Press.

Ducat, J. 2007. "L'arme des enfants spartiates." In Sauzeau and Van Compernolle 2007: 557-62.

Ducrey, P. 1997. "Aspects de l'historie de la guerre en Grèce ancienne, 1945-1996." In Brulé and Oulhen 1997: 123-38.

———. 1999a. "Prisonniers de guerre en Grèce antique 1968-1999." *Pallas* 51: 19-23.

———. 1999b. *La traitement des prisoniers de guerre dans la Grèce antique des origins à la conquête romaine².* Athens: École française de Athènes.

———. 2000. "Les aspects économiques de l'usage de mercenaries dans la guerre en Grèce ancienne: avantages et inconvénients du recours à une main-d'œuvre militaire rémunérée." In Andreau *et al.* 2000: 197-209.

Duncan-Jones, R. 1996. "The Impact of the Antonine Plague." *JRA* 9: 108-36.

———. 2006. "Roman Customs Duties: A Comparative View." *Latomus* 65.1: 3-16.

Durand, J.-M. 1991. "Espionnage et guerre froide." In *Florilegium marianum: Recueil d'études en l'honneur de Michel Fleury* (*Mémoires de N.A.B.U.* 1), ed. J.-M. Durand, Michel Fleury, 39-52. Paris: SEPOA.

Durry, M. 1935. "Juvénal et les prétoriens," *REL* 13: 95-106.

———. 1938. *Les cohortes prétoriennes.* Paris: De Boccard.

Earl, D. 1961. *The Political Thought of Sallust.* Cambridge: Cambridge University Press.

Eck, W. 2000. "Monumente der Virtus: Kaiser und Heer im Spiegel der epigraphischer Denkmäler." In Alföldy, Dobson, and Eck 2000: 483-96.

———. 2001. "Spezialisierung in der staatlichen Administration des römisch-en Reiches in der höhen Kaiserzeit." In Blois 2001: 1-23.

————. 2003. "Der Kaiser als Herr des Heeres: Militärdiplome und die kaiserliche Reichsregierung." In Wilkes 2003: 55-87.

Eck, W. and H. Wolff, eds. 1986. *Heer und Integrationspolitik: Die römische Militärdiplome als historische Quelle.* Köln: Böhlau.

Eck, W., A. Caballos, and F. Fernández. 1996. *Das senatus consultum de Cn. Pisone patre.* München: Beck.

Eckstein, A. 2005. "Bellicosity and Anarchy: Soldiers, Warriors, and Combat in Antiquity." *International History Review* 27: 481-97.

————. 2006a. *Mediterranean Anarchy, Interstate War, and the Rise of Rome.* Los Angeles: University of California Press.

————. 2006b. "Conceptualizing Roman Imperial Expansion under the Republic: An Introduction." In *A Companion to the Roman Republic,* ed. N. Rosenstein and R. Morstein-Marx, 567-89. Malden, MA: Wiley-Blackwell Publishing.

————. 2008. *Rome Enters the Greek East: From Anarchy to Hierarchy in the Hellenistic Mediterranean, 230-170 B.C.* Malden, MA: Wiley-Blackwell.

Edwards, C. 1993. *The Politics of Immorality in Ancient Rome.* Cambridge: Cambridge University Press.

————. 2003. "Incorporating the Alien: The Art of Conquest." In *Rome the Cosmopolis.* ed. C. Edwards and G. Woolf, 44-70. Cambridge: Cambridge University Press.

Edzard, D. O. 1997. *Gudea and His Dynasty.* Toronto: University of Toronto.

Ellis, M. DeJ. 1977. "The Land of Dead *redu*'s." In *Essays on the Ancient Near East in Memory of Jacob J. Finkelstein. Memoirs of the Connecticut Academy of Arts and Sciences* 19: 61-66.

Elton, H. 1996. *Warfare in Roman Europe, AD 350-425.* Oxford: Oxford University Press.

————. 2007a. "Military Forces." In *CHGRW*, 2: 270-309.

————. 2007b. "Cavalry in Late Roman Warfare." In *The Late Roman Army in the Near East from Diocletian to the Arab Conquest.* ed. A.S. Lewin and P. Pellegrini, 377-82. Oxford: British Archaeological Reports.

————. 2007c. "Army and Battle in the Age of Justinian (527-65)." In *CRA*, 532-50.

Engels, D. 1978. *Alexander the Great and the Logistics of the Macedonian Army.* Los Angeles: University of California Press.

————. 1980. "Alexander's Intelligence System." *CQ* 30: 327-40.

Engen, R. 2009. *Canadians under Fire: Infantry Effectiveness in the Second World War.* Montréal: McGill-Queen's University Press.

Enloe, C.H. 1980. *Ethnic Soldiers: State Security in Divided Societies.* Athens, GA: University of Georgia Press.

Eph ʿal, I. 2009. *The City Besieged: Siege and its Manifestations in the Ancient Near East.* Leiden: Brill.

Erdkamp, Paul, ed. 2002. *The Roman Army and the Economy.* Amsterdam: Gieben.

———. 2007. "War and State Formation in the Roman Republic." In *CRA*: 96-113.

Fagan, G. G. and M. Trundle, eds. 2010. *New Perspectives on Ancient Warfare.* Leiden: Brill.

Fales, F. M. and J. N. Postgate. 1995. *Imperial Administrative Records, Part II: Provincial and Military Administration.* Helsinki: University of Helsinki.

Fantham, E. 1991. "*Stuprum*: Public Attitudes and Penalties for Sexual Offences in Republican Rome." *EMC/CV* 35: 267-91.

Ferguson, R. B. 1999. "A Paradigm for the Study of War." In Raaflaab and Rosenstein 1999: 389-437.

Ferguson R. B. and L. Farragher, eds. 1988. *The Anthropology of War: A Bibliography.* New York: The Harry Frank Guggenheim Foundation.

Ferris, I. M. 2000. *Enemies of Rome: Barbarians through Roman Eyes.* Stroud, UK: Sutton.

Figueira, T. 206."The Spartan *hippeis.*" In Hodkinson and Powell 2006: 57-84.

Fink. R. O. 1971. *Roman Military Records on Papyrus.* Cleveland, OH: Case Western Reserve/APA.

Fink. R., A. Hoey, and W. Snyder. 1940. "The Feriale Duranum." *YCS* 7: 1-222.

Finley, M. 1973. *The Ancient Economy.* Los Angeles: University of California Press.

———. 1985. *Ancient History: Evidence and Models.* New York: Viking Penguin, Inc.

Flasher, M. 1996. "Die Sieger von Marthon—zwischen Mythisierung und Vorbildlichkeit." In *Retropektive. Konzepte von Vergangenheit in der griechische-römischen Antike*, ed. M. Flasher et al., 63-85. Munich: Biering & Brinkmann.

Flory, S. 2006. Review of Hanson 2005. *BMCR* 2006.03.40.

Flower, H. I. 1996. *Ancestor Masks and Aristocratic Power in Roman Culture.* Oxford: Clarendon Press.

Forni, G. 1953. *Il reclutamento delle legioni da Augusto a Diocleziano.* Rome: Bocca.

Forsythe, G. 2006. *A Critical History of Early Rome: From Prehistory to the First Punic War.* Los Angeles: University of California.

Foster, B. R. 1977. "Commercial Activity in Sargonic Mesopotamia." *Iraq* 39.1: 31-43.

———. 1982. "An Agricultural Archive from Sargonic Akkad." *Acta Sumerologica* 4: 7-52.

———. 1996. *Before the Muses: An Anthology of Akkadian Literature.* 2nd edition. Potomac, Maryland: CDL Press.

———. 2001. *The Epic of Gilgamesh: A New Translation.* New York: W.W. Norton.

Foulon, E. 1996a. "La garde à pied, corps elite de la phalange héllenistique." *BAGB* 1: 17-31.

———. 1996. "Hypaspastes, peltastes, chrysaspides, argyraspides, chalcaspides." *REA* 98: 53-63.

Frankena, R. 1966. *Briefe aus dem British Museum* (LIH und CT 2-33). Altbabylonische Briefe in Umschrift und Übersetzung, Heft 2 (Leiden: Brill).

Frayne, D. 1993. *Sargonic and Gutian Periods (2334-2113 BC).* Toronto: University of Toronto.

———. 1997. *Ur III Period (2112-2004 BC).* Toronto: University of Toronto.

———. 2008. *Presargonic Period (2700-2350 BC).* Toronto: University of Toronto.

Frazer, J. 1890. *The Golden Bough.* London: Macmillan and Co. Ltd.

French, S.E. 2003. *The Code of the Warrior: Exploring Warrior Values Past and Present.* Lanham, MD: Rowan and Littlefield.

Frölich, P. 2008. "Les magistrates militaires des cités grecques au IVe siècle a. C." *REA* 110: 39-55.

Fuchs, A. 2005. "War das Neuassyrische Reich ein Militärstaat?" In *Krieg - Gesellschaft - Institutionen: Beiträge zu einer vergleichenden Kriegsgeschichte,* ed. B. Meißner et al., 35-60. Berlin: Akademie-Verlag.

Fuchs, A. and S. Parpola. 2001. *The Correspondence of Sargon II, Part III: Letters from Babylonia and the Eastern Provinces.* Helsinki: University of Helsinki.

Fuhrmann, C. 2011. *Policing the Roman Empire,* Oxford: Oxford University Press.

Fuller, J.F.C. 1958. *The Generalship of Alexander the Great.* London: Eyre & Spottiswoode.

Fussell, P. 1975. *The Great War and Modern Memory.* Oxford: Oxford University Press.

Gabba, E. 2002. "Il generale dell'esercito romano nel I secolo a.C." In Sordi 2002b: 155-62.

Gabrielson, V. 2002a. "Socio-economic Classes and Ancient Greek Warfare."
In *Ancient History Matters: Studies Presented to Jens Erik Skydesgaard
on His Seventieth Birthday*, ed. K. Ascani, et al., 203-20. Rome: L'Erma
di Bretschneider.

————. 2002b. "The Impact of Armed Forces on Government and Politics in
Archaic and Classical Greek Poleis: A Response to Hans van Wees." In
Chaniotis and Ducrey 2002: 83-98.

————. 2007. "Warfare and the State." In *CHGRW*, 1: 248-72.

————. 2008. "Die Kosten der athenischen Flotte in klassischer Zeit." In
Burrer and Müller 2008: 46-73.

Gaibov, V. and G. Koselenko, 2008. "A Horseman Charging a Foot-Soldier: A
New Subject in Parthian Glyptic Art." *Parthica* 10: 99-107.

Garlan, Y. 1972. *La guerre dans l'antiquité.* Paris: F. Nathan.

————. 1975. *War in the Ancient World: A Social History.* Tr. J. Lloyd. New
York: W. W. Norton & Co.

Garnsey, P. 2004. "Roman Citizenship and Roman Law in the Late Empire."
In *Approaching Late Antiquity: The Transformation from Early to
Late Empire*. eds. S. Swain and M. Edwards 133-55. Oxford: Oxford
University Press.

Garnsey, P. and G. Woolf. 1989. "Patronage of the Rural Poor in the Roman
World." In *Patronage in Ancient Society*, ed. A. Wallace-Hadrill, 153-70.
New York: Routledge.

Garraffoni, R. 2004. "Robbers and Soldiers: Criminality and the Roman Army
in Apuleius' *Metamorphoses*." *Gerion* 22.1: 367-377.

Gat, A. 1989. *The Origins of Military Thought from the Enlightenment to
Clausewitz.* Oxford: Clarendon Press.

————. 2006. *War in Human Civilization.* Oxford: Oxford University Press.

Gaughan, J. 2009. *Murder Was Not A Crime: Homicide and Power in the
Roman Republic.* Austin, TX: University of Texas.

Gauthier, P. and M. Hatzopoulos. 1993. *La loi gymnasiarchique de Beroia.*
Paris: Diffusion de Boccard.

Gazzano, F. 2005. "Senza frode e senza inganno: formule 'pecauzionali' e
rapporti interstatali nel mondo greco." In Santi Amantini 2005: 3-33.

Gera, D. 1997. *Warrior Women: The Anonymous* Tractatus de Mulieribus.
Mnemosyne, Suppl. 162. Leiden: E. J. Brill.

Geroulanos S. and R. Bridler, eds. 1994. *Trama. Wund-Entstehung und Wund-
Pllege im antiken Griechenland* Mainz: von Zabern.

Gerlinger, S. 2008. *Römische Schlachtenrhetorik: Unglaubwürdige Elemente
in Schlachtendarstellungen, speziell bei Caesar, Sallust und Tacitus.*
Heidelberg: Universitätsverlag.

Gilliver, C. 1996b. "The Roman Army and Morality in War." In Lloyd 1996: 219-38.

———. 2007a. "Battle." In *CHGRW*, 2: 122-57.

———. 2007b. "Display in Roman Warfare: The Appearance of Armies and Individuals on the Battlefield." *War in History* 14: 1-21.

———. 2007c. "The Augustan Reform and the Structure of the Imperial Army." In *CRA*: 183-200.

Giovannini, A. 2007. *Les relations entre états dans la Grèce antique au temps d'Homère à l'intervention romaine (ca 700-200 av. Chr.). Historia Enzelschrift*, 193. Stuttgart: Franz Steiner Verlag.

Giuffre, V. 1974. *La letteratura de re militari: appunti per una storia degli ordinamenti militari*. Naples: Jovene.

———. 1983. *Il "diritto militare" dei Romani*. 2nd ed. Bologna: Patron.

———. 1996. *Letture e ricerche sulla "res militaris."* Naples: Jovene.

Gleason, M. W. 2001. "Mutilated Messengers: Body Language in Josephus." In *Being Greek Under Rome: Cultural Identity, the Second Sophistic and the Development of Empire,* ed. S. Goldhill, 50-85. Cambridge: Cambridge University Press.

Goldberg, S. 2005a. *Constructing Literature in the Roman Republic.* Cambridge: Cambridge University Press.

———. 2005b. "The Early Republic: The Beginnings to 90 BC." In *A Companion to Latin Literature*, ed. S. Harrison, 15-30. Malden, MA: Wiley-Blackwell.

Goldstein, J. S. 2001. *War and Gender: How Gender Shapes the War System and Vice Versa.* Cambridge: Cambridge University Press.

Goldsworthy, A. K. 1996. *The Roman Army at War 100 BC – AD 200.* Oxford: Clarendon Press.

———. 2000. *Roman Warfare.* London: Cassell.

———. 2003. *In the Name of Rome: The Men who Won the Roman Empire.* London: Orion.

———. 2007. "War." In *CHGRW*, 2: 76-121.

———. 2009. *How Rome Fell: The Death of a Superpower.* New Haven: Yale University Press.

Goldsworthy, A. K. and I. Haynes, eds. 1999. *The Roman Army as a Community.* Portsmouth, RI: Journal of Roman Archaeology.

Graf, D. 1994. "The Nabataean Army and the *Cohortes Ulpiae Petraeorum*." In *The Roman and Byzantine Army in the East*, ed. E. Dabrowa, 265-311. Cracow: Drukarnia Uniwersytetu Jagielloriskiego.

Grainger, J. 1997. *A Seleukid Prosopography and Gazetteer. Mnemosyne*, Suppl. 172. Leiden: E. J. Brill.

Grane, T., ed. 2007. *Beyond the Roman Frontier: Roman Influences on the Northern Barbaricum.* Rome: Quasar.

Grayson, A. K. 1975. *Assyrian and Babylonian Chronicles. Texts from Cuneiform Sources* 5. Locust Valley: J. J. Augustin.

————. 1987. *Assyrian Rulers of the Third and Second Millennia BC (to 1115 BC).* Toronto: University of Toronto Press.

————. 1991. *Assyrian Rulers of the Early First Millennium BC I (1114-859 BC).* Toronto: University of Toronto Press.

————. 1996. *Assyrian Rulers of the Early First Millennium BC II (858-745 BC).* Toronto: University of Toronto Press.

Greatrex, G. 1998. *Rome and Persia at War, 502-532.* Leeds: Francis Cairns.

Greatrex, G. and S. Lieu. 2002. *The Roman Eastern Frontier and the Persian Wars, AD 363-630.* London: Routledge.

Greatrex, G., H. Elton, and R. Burgess. 2005. "Urbicius' *Epitedeuma*: An Edition, Translation and Commentary." *ByzZ* 98: 35-74.

Greene, E.M. 2011. "Women and Children in Roman Military Communities and the Nature of Non-combatant Settlement in the Roman West." Ph.D. Dissertation, University of North Carolina at Chapel Hill, 2011.

Green, P. 1999. "War and Morality in Fifth-Century Athens: The Case of Euripides' *Trojan Women.*" *AHB* 13: 97-110.

Griffith, G. T. 1980. "Philip as a General and the Macedonian Army." In *Philip of Macedon*, ed. M. Hatzopoulos and L. Loukopoulos, 58-77. Athens: Ekdotike Athenon.

Groenman-van Waateringe, W. 1997. "Classical Authors and the Diet of Roman Soldiers: True or False?" In *Roman Frontier Studies 1995,* ed. W. Groenman-van Waateringe, 261-6. Oxford: Oxbow.

Gröschel, S. 1989. *Waffenbesitz und Waffeneinsatz bei den Griechen.* Frankfurt a.M.: Peter Lang.

Grotius, H. 1925. *The Law of War and Peace.* Tr. F. Kelsey. Indianapolis: The Bobbs-Merrill Company.

Gruen, E. 1992. *Culture and National Identity in Republican Rome.* Ithaca, NY: Cornell University Press.

Grünewald, T. 1999. *Räuber, Rebellen, Rivalen, Rächer: Studien zu Latrones im römischen Reich.* Stuttgart: F. Steiner. = *Bandits in the Roman Empire: Myth and Reality*, tr. J. Drinkwater. New York: Routledge, 2004.

Gunderson, E. 2003. *Declamation, Paternity. and Roman Identity.* Cambridge: Cambridge University Press.

Haas, J., ed. 1990. *The Anthropology of War.* Cambridge: Cambridge University Press.

Hahlweg, W. 1987. *Die Heeresreform der Oranier und die Antike*, rev. ed. Osnabrück: Biblio Verlag.

Haldon, J.F., ed. 2005a. *General Issues in the Study of Medieval Logistics: Sources, Problems and Methodologies.* Leiden: Brill.

————. 2005b. "Feeding the Army: Food and Transport in Byzantium, ca. 600-1100." In *Feast, Fast or Famine: Food and Drink in Byzantium.* ed. W. Mayer and S. Trzcionka, 85-100. Brisbane: Australian Association of Byzantine Studies.

Hale, J. 1983. *Renaissance War Studies.* London: The Hambledon Press.

Hale, John R. 2009. *Lords of the Sea: The Epic Story of the Athenian Navy and the Birth of Democracy.* New York: Viking.

Hallo, W. W., ed. 2003. *The Context of Scripture*, 3 vols. Leiden: Brill.

Halsall, G. 2007. *Barbarian Migrations and the Roman West, 376-568.* Cambridge: Cambridge University Press.

Hamblin, W. J. 2006. *Warfare in the Ancient Near East to 1600 B.C.: Holy Warriors at the Dawn of History.* New York: Routledge.

Hamel, D. 1998. *Athenian Generals: Military Authority in the Classical Period.* Leiden: E. J. Brill.

Hammond, N.G.L. 1983. "Army Transport in the Fifth and Fourth Centuries." *GRBS* 24: 27-31.

Hammond, N. G. L. and G. T. Griffith. 1979. *A History of Macedonia*, II. Oxford: Oxford University Press.

Hammons, M. B. 2008. "Before Joan of Arc: Gender Identity and Heroism in Ancient Mesopotamian Birth Rituals." Ph.D. Dissertation, Vanderbilt University.

Hannestad, L. "War and Greek Art." In Bekker-Nielsen and Hannestad 2001: 110-19.

Hansen, M. 1983. "The Athenian 'Politicians', 403-322 B.C." *GRBS* 24: 33-55.

Hanson, V. D. 1989 (2000). *The Western Way of War: Infantry Battle in Ancient Greece*, 2nd edition. Los Angeles: University of California Press.

————, ed. 1991a. *Hoplites: The Classical Greek Battle Experience.* London: Routledge.

————. 1991b. "Hoplite Technology in Phalanx Battle." In Hanson 1991a: 63-84.

————. 1995. *The Other Greeks: The Family Farm and the Agrarian Roots of Western Civilization.* New York: The Free Press.

————. 1998. *War and Agriculture in Classical Greece*, 2nd edition. *Biblioteca di Studi Antichi*, 40. Los Angeles: University of California Press.

————. 1999a. *The Wars of the Ancient Greeks.* London: Cassell.

————. 1999b. "Hoplite Obliteration: The Case of the Town of Thespiae."
In *Ancient Warfare: Archaeological Perspectives*, ed. J. Carmen and A.
Harding, 203-17. Stroud: Sutton.

————. 1999c. "The Status of Ancient Military History: Traditional Work,
Recent Research, and On-Going Controversies." *JMH* 63.2: 379-413.

————. 2005. *A War like No Other: How the Athenians and the Spartans
Fought the Peloponnesian War.* New York: Random House.

————. 2007. "The Modern Historiography of Ancient Warfare." In
CHGRW, 1: 3-21.

————. 2009. *Carnage and Culture: Landmark Battles in the Rise of Western
Power*. New York: Random House.

————, ed. 2010. *Makers of Ancient Strategy: From the Persian Wars to the
Fall of Rome*. Princeton: Princeton University Press.

Hanson, V.D. and B. Strauss. 1999. "Epilogue." In Raaflaab and Rosenstein
1999: 439-53.

Harl, K. 1996. *Coinage in the Roman Economy, 300 B.C. to A.D. 700.*
Baltimore, MD: Johns Hopkins University Press.

Harris, R. 1965. "The Journey of the Divine Weapon." In *Studies in Honor
of Benno Landsberger on his Seventy-fifth Birthday*, ed. H.G. Guterbock
and Th. Jacobsen, 217-25. Chicago: University of Chicago.

Harris, W. V. 1979. *War and Imperialism in Republican Rome.* Oxford:
Oxford University Press.

————. 1989. *Ancient Literacy*. Cambridge, MA: Harvard University Press.

————. 2006. "Readings in the Narrative Literature of Roman Courage." In
Dillon and Welch 2006: 300-320.

Hatzopoulos, M. 1996. *Macedonian Institutions under the Kings,* 2 vols.
Paris: Diffusion de Boccard.

————. 2001. *L'Organisation de l'armée macedonienne sous les
Antigonides. Problemes anciens et documents nouveaux*. Paris: Diffusion
de Boccard.

Heather, P. 1991. *Goths and Romans, 332-489*. Oxford: Oxford University
Press.

————. 1995. "The Huns and the End of the Roman Empire in Western
Europe." *EHR* 110: 4-41.

————. 2008. Review of Drinkwater 2007. *Nottingham Medieval Studies* 52:
243-5.

————. 2009a. "Why did the Barbarian Cross the Rhine?" *JLA* 2: 3-29.

————. 2009b. *Empires and Barbarians: The Fall of Rome and the Birth of
Europe*. Oxford: Oxford University Press.

Heather, P. and J. Matthews. 1991. *The Goths in the Fourth Century*.
Liverpool: Liverpool University Press.

Heckel, W. 1992. *The Marshals of Alexander the Great.* New York: Routledge.

———. 1994. Review of Sherwin-White and Kuhrt 1993. *BMCR* 1994.02.10.

———. 2003a. "King and 'Companions': Observations on the Nature of Power in the Reign of Alexander." In Roisman 2003: 197-225.

———. 2003b. "Alexander the Great and the 'Limits of the Civilized World'." In *Crossroads of History: The Age of Alexander,* ed. W. Heckel and L. Tritle, 147-74. Claremont: Regina Books.

———. 2006. *Who's Who in the Age of Alexander the Great: Prosopography of Alexander's Empire.* Malden, MA: Blackwell Publishing.

———. 2008. *The Conquests of Alexander the Great.* Cambridge: Cambridge University Press.

———. 2009a. "A King and His Army." In Heckel and Tritle 2009: 69-82.

———. 2009b. "The Asthetairoi: A Closer Look." In Wheatley and Hannah 2009: 99-117.

Heckel, W. and L. Tritle, eds. 2009. *Alexander the Great: A New History.* Malden, MA: Wiley-Blackwell.

Heimpel, W. 2003, *Letters to the King of Mari: A New Translation, with Historical Introduction, Notes, and Commentary.* Winona Lake, IN: Eisenbrauns.

Hekster, O. 2007. "The Roman Army and Propaganda." In *CRA*: 339-58.

Hellmann, O. 2000. *Die Schlachtszenen der Ilias. Das Bild des Dichters vom Kampf in der Heroenzeit.* Stuttgart: Franz Steiner Verlag.

Herz, P. 2007. "Finances and Costs of the Roman army." In *CRA*: 306-22.

Heuser, B. 2010. *The Evolution of Strategy: Thinking War from Antiquity to the Present.* Cambridge: Cambridge University Press.

Hingley, R. 2000. *Roman Officers and English Gentlemen: The Imperial Origins of Roman Archaeology.* New York: Routledge.

Hirt, A. M., ed. 2007. *Militärdiplome: die Forschungsbeiträge der Berner Gespräche von 2004.* Stuttgart: Steiner.

Hobbs, A. 2007. "Plato on War." In *Maieusis: Essays in Ancient Philosophy in Honour of Miles Burnyeat*, ed. D. Scott, 176-94. Oxford: Oxford University Press.

Hobsbawm, E. J. 1959. *Primitive Rebels: Studies in Archaic Forms of Social Movements in the 19th and 20th centuries.* Manchester: Manchester University Press.

Hodkinson, S. 2006. "Was Classical Sparta a Military Society?" In Hodkinson and Powell, 2006: 111-62.

Hodkinson, S. and A. Powell, eds. 2006. *Sparta and War.* Swansea: Classical Press of Wales.

Holder, P. A., ed. 2006. *Roman Military Diplomas 5.* London: Institute of Classical Studies, University of London.

Hollander, D. B. 2005. "Veterans, Agriculture, and Manpower in the Late Roman Republic." In Aubert and Várhelyi 2005: 229-39.

Hollard, D., ed. 2006. *L'armée et la monnaie : actes de la journée d'études du 10 décember 2005 à la Monnaie de Paris.* Paris: Séna.

Holleaux, M. 1926. "Ceux qui sont dans le bagage." *REG* 39: 355-66.

Holoka, J. 2006. Review of Hanson 2005. *Michigan War Studies Review* 2006.05.01

Hölscher, T. 2006. "The Transformation of Victory into Power: From Event to Structure." In Dillon and Welch 2006: 27-48.

Holt, F.L. 1999. "Alexander the Great Today: In the Interests of Historical Accuracy," *AHB* 13: 111-17.

———. 2000. "The Death of Coenus: Another Study in Method," *AHB* 14: 49-55.

Holum, K.G. 1977. "Pulcheria's Crusade AD 421-22 and the Ideology of Imperial Victory". *GRBS* 18: 153-72.

Hope, V. 2007. "Age and the Roman Army: the Evidence of Tombstones." In *Age and Ageing in the Roman Empire*, ed. M. Harlow and L. Ray, 111-29. Portsmouth, RI: Journal of Roman Archaeology.

Hopkins, K. 2009. "The Political Economy of the Roman Empire." In Morris and Scheidel 2009: 178-204.

Hopkins, K. and G. Burton. 1983a. "Ambition and Withdrawal: The Senatorial Aristocracy Under the Empire." In *Death and Renewal. Sociological Studies in Roman History*, volume 2, ed. K. Hopkins, 120-200. Cambridge: Cambridge University Press.

Hopkins, K. and G. Burton. 1983b. "Political Succession in the Late Roman Republic (249-50 BC)." In *Death and Renewal. Sociological Studies in Roman History*, volume 2, ed. K. Hopkins, 31-119. Cambridge: Cambridge University Press.

Hordern, P. 2005 "Mediterranean Plague in the Age of Justinian." In *The Cambridge Companion to the Age of Justinian.* ed. M. Maas, 134-60. Cambridge: Cambridge University Press.

Hornblower, S. 2007. "War in Ancient Literature." In *CHGRW*, 1: 22-53.

Horsfall, N. 2003. *The Culture of the Roman Plebs.* London: Duckworth.

Horsmann, G. 1991. *Untersuchungen zur militärischen Ausbildung im republikanischen und kaiserzeitlichen Rom.* Boppard am Rhein: H. Boldt.

Howard, M. 1978. *War and the Liberal Conscience.* New Brunswick: Rutgers University Press.

———. 2000. *The Invention of Peace.* New Haven: Yale University Press.

Howard-Johnston, J. 1999. "Heraclius' Persian Campaigns and the Revival of the East Roman Empire, 622-630." *War in History* 6: 1-44.

———. 2010. *Witnesses to a World Crisis: Historians and Histories of the Middle East in the Seventh Century.* Oxford: Oxford University Press.

Huizinga, J. 1950. *Homo Ludens.* New York: Roy Publishers.

Humble, N. 2006. "Why the Spartans Fight So Well, Even If They Are in Disorder—Xenophon's View." In Hodkinson and Powell 2006: 219-33.

Hunt, D. 1999. "The Outsider Inside: Ammianus on the Rebellion of Silvanus." In *The Late Roman World and its Historian: Interpreting Ammianus Marcellinus.* ed. J.W. Drijvers and D. Hunt, 51-63. New York: Routledge.

Hunt, P. 1997. "Helots at the Battle of Plataea." *Historia* 46: 129-44.

———. 1998. *Slaves, Warfare and Ideology in the Greek Historians.* Cambridge: Cambridge University Press.

Ilari, V. 1980. *Guerra e diritto nel mondo antico, I: Guerra e diritto nel mondo greco-ellenistico fino al III secolo.* Milan: Dott. A. Giuffre Editore.

———. 2002. "*Imitatio, restitutio, utopia*: la storia militare antica nel pensiero strategico moderno." In Sordi 2002: 269-381.

Irby-Massie, G. 1999. *Military Religion in Roman Britain.* Leiden: Brill.

Isaac, B. 1988. "The Meaning of the Terms *limes* and *limitanei*." *JRS* 78: 125-47.

———. 1992. *Limits of Empire: The Roman Army in the East.* 2nd ed. Oxford: Oxford University Press.

———. 2004. *The Invention of Racism in Classical Antiquity.* Princeton, NJ: Princeton.

Istasse, N. 2006. "Experts 'barbares' dans le monde politique séleucide." In *Transferts culturels et politique dans le monde hellénistique: actes de la table ronde sur les identités collectives, Sorbonne, 7 février 2004*, ed. J.-C. Couvenhes and B. Legras, 53-80. *Histoire ancienne et médievale*, 86. Paris: Publications de la Sorbonne.

Jackson, A. 1993. "War and Raids for Booty in the World of Odysseus." In Rich and Shipley 1993a: 74-76.

Jacobsen, T. 1943. "Primitive Democracy in Ancient Mesopotamia." *JNES* 2.3: 159-172.

Jacquemin, A. 2009. "La vente du butin dans le monde grec à l'époque hellénistique." In *Praeda: Butin de guerre et société dans la Rome républicaine/Kriegsbeute und Gesellschaft im republikanischen Rom*, ed. M. Coudry and M. Humm, 103-14. Stuttgart: Franz Steiner Verlag.

James, S. 1986. "Evidence from Dura-Europos for the Origins of Late Roman Helmets." *Syria* 63: 107-34.

————. 1988. "The *fabricae*: State Arms Factories of the Later Roman Empire." In *Military Equipment and the Identity of Roman Soldiers*. ed. J.C. Coulston, 257-331. Oxford: British Archaeological Reports.

————. 1999. "The Community of the Soldiers: A Major Identity and Centre of Power in the Roman Empire." In *TRAC 98: Proceedings of the Eighth Annual Theoretical Roman Archaeology Conference*. ed. Baker, P. et al., 14-25. Oxford: Oxbow.

————. 2002. "Writing the Legion: The Development and Future of Roman Military Studies in Britain." *ArchaeoJ* 159: 1-58.

————. 2006. "The Impact of Steppe Peoples and the Partho-Sasanian World on the Development of Roman Military Equipment and Dress, 1st to 3rd centuries AD." In Mode and Tubach 2006: 357-392.

Janniard, S. 2001. "L'armée romaine tardive dans quelques travaux récents. 2e partie: stratégies et techniques militaires." *Antiquité tardive* 9: 351-61.

Jeyes, U. 1989. *Old Babylonian Extispicy: Omen Texts in the British Museum*. Uitgaven van het Nederlands Historisch-Archaeologisch Instituut te Istanbul 64. Leiden: Historisch-Archaeologisch Instituut.

Joannès, F. 2006. *Haradum II: Les textes de la période paléo-babyloni-enne (Samsu-iluna - Ammi-saduqa)*. Paris: Éditions Recherche sur les Civilisations.

Jones, A.H.M. 1964. *The Later Roman Empire, 284-602: A Social, Economic and Administrative Survey*, 2 vols. Oxford: Basil Blackwell.

Joshel, S. 2010. *Slavery in the Roman World*. Cambridge: Cambridge University Press.

Jung, J.H. 1982. "Die Rechtsstellung der römischen Soldaten: Ihre Entwicklung von den Anfängen Roms bis auf Diokletian." *ANRW* 14.2: 882-1013.

Jung, M. 2006. *Marathon und Plataiai. Zwei Perserschlachten als "lieux de mémoire" im antiken Griechenland*. Göttingen: Vanderhoeck & Ruprecht.

Junkelmann, M. 1997. *Panis Militaris: Die Ernährung des römisch-en Soldaten oder der Grundstoff der Macht*. Mainz am Rhein: P. von Zabern.

Kaegi, W. 1981. "The Crisis in Military Historiography." *Armed Forces and Society* 7: 299-316.

————. 1992. *Byzantium and the Early Islamic Conquests*. Cambridge: Cambridge University Press.

————. 2003. *Heraclius, Emperor of Byzantium*. Cambridge: Cambridge University Press.

————. 2009. "Reassessing Late Antique Warfare" Presented as part of the panel "New Approaches to the Political and Military History of the Greek, Roman, and Late Roman Worlds" at the Annual Meeting of the

American Philological Association, January 9, 2009. http://apaclassics. org/images/uploads/documents/Kaegiapa2009.pdf

Kagan, K. 2006. *The Eye of Command*. Ann Arbor: University of Michigan Press.

Kah, D. and P. Scholz, eds. 2004. *Das hellenistische Gymnasium*. Berlin: Akademie Verlag.

Kaldellis, A. 2004. *Procopius of Caesarea: Tyranny, History and Philosophy at the End of Antiquity*. Philadelphia: University of Pennsylvania Press.

Kallett, L. 2001. *Money and the Corrosion of Power in Thucydides. The Sicilian Expedition and its Aftermath*. Los Angeles: University of California Press.

Kampen, N. B. 1995. "Looking at Gender: The Column of Trajan and Roman Historical Relief." In *Feminisms in the Academy*. ed. Donna C. Stanton, and Abigail J. Stewart, 46-73. Ann Arbor, MI: University of Michigan.

Kataja, L. and R. Whiting. 1995. *Grants, Decrees and Gifts of the Neo-Assyrian Period*. Helsinki: University of Helsinki.

Keaveney, A. 2007. *The Army in the Roman Revolution*. New York: Routledge.

Keegan, J. 1976. *The Face of Battle*. New York: Penguin.

————. 1987. *The Mask of Command*. New York: Penguin.

————. 1993. *A History of Warfare*. New York: Alfred A. Knopf.

Kehne, P. 2007. "War and Peacetime Logistics: Supplying Imperial Armies in East and West." In *CRA*: 323-38.

Kelly, C. 2004. *Ruling the Later Roman Empire*. Cambridge, MA: Harvard University Press.

Kelly, G. 2008. *Ammianus Marcellinus, the Allusive Historian*. Cambridge: Cambridge University Press.

Kelso, I. 2003: "Artillery as a Classicising Digression." *Historia* 52: 122-5.

Keppie, L. 1997. "The Changing Face of the Roman Legions (49 BC-AD 69)." *PBSR* 65: 89-102. Reprinted in *Legions and Veterans: Roman Army Papers 1971-2000*. ed. by M.P. Speidel. *Mavors* 12 (2000): 50-63.

————.1998. *The Making of the Roman Army: From Republic to Empire*. Rev. ed. Norman, OK: University of Oklahoma.

————. 2003. "'Having Been a Soldier,' The Commemoration of Military Service on Funerary Monuments of the Early Roman Empire." In Wilkes 2003: 31-54.

Keyser, P. 1994. "The Use of Artillery by Philip II and Alexander the Great." *AncW* 15: 27-49.

Klose, P. 1972. *Die völkerrechtliche Ordnung der hellenistisschen Staatenwelt in der Zeit von 280-168 v. Chr. Ein Beitrag zur Geschichte des Völkerrecht*. Munich: Beck.

Knapp, A. B. 1992. "Archaeology and *Annales*: Time, Space, and Change." In *Archaeology,* Annales, *and Ethnohistory*, ed. A.B. Knapp, 1-21. Cambridge: Cambridge University Press.

Knauf, E. A. 2009. Review of L. Burckhardt, K. Seybold, and J. von Ungern-Sternberg, eds., *Gesetzgebung in antiken Gesellschaften: Israel, Griechenland, Rom. RBL* 05.

Koehn, C. 2007. *Krieg–Diplomatie–Ideologie. Zur Aussenpolitik hellenistischen Mittelstaaten. Historia Einzelschrift*, 195. Stuttgart: Franz Steiner Verlag.

Kohn, R. 2009. "The Danger of Militarization in an Endless 'War' on Terrorism." *JMH* 73: 177-208.

Koortbojian, M. 2006. "The Bringer of Victory: Imagery and Institutions at the Advent of Empire." In Dillon and Welch 2006: 184-217.

Kouroumali, M. 2005. "Procopius and the Gothic War." D.Phil. diss., Oxford.

Kousser, R. 2006. "Conquest and Desire: Roman *Victoria* in Public and Provincial Sculpture." In Dillon and Welch 2006: 218-243.

Kraus, F. R. 1965. *Briefe aus kleineren westeuropäischen Sammlungen. Altbabylonische Briefe in Umschrift und Übersetzung,* Heft 10 (Leiden: Brill).

Krentz, P. 1985a. "The Nature of Hoplite Battle." *ClAnt* 4: 50-61.

———. 1985b. "Casualties in Hoplite Battles." *GRBS* 26: 13-20.

———. 1994. "Continuing the *othismos* on *othismos*." *AHB* 8: 45-49.

———. 1997. "The Strategic Culture of Periclean Athens." In *Polis and Polemos: Essays on Politics, War, and History in Ancient Greece in Honor of Donald Kagan*, ed. C. D. Hamilton and P. Krentz, 55-72. Claremont, CA: Regina Books.

———. 2000. "Deception in Archaic and Classical Greek Warfare." In van Wees 2000a: 167-200.

———. 2002. "Fighting by the Rules: The Invention of the Hoplite Agôn." *Hesperia* 71: 23-39.

———. 2007. "Warfare and Hoplites." In *The Cambridge Companion to Archaic Greece*, ed. H. Shapiro, 61-84. Cambridge: Cambridge University Press.

———. 2010. *The Battle of Marathon.* New Haven: Yale University Press.

Krieger, W. ed. 2005. *Und keine Schlacht bei Marathon. Große Ereignisse und Mythen der europäischen Geschichte.* Stuttgart: Klett-Cotta.

Kromayer, J. and G. Veith, eds. 1928. *Heerwesen und Kriegführung der Griechen und Römer.* Munich: Verlag C. H. Beck.

Krumeich, G. and S. Brandt, eds. 2003. *Schlachtenmythen: Ereignis—Erzählung—Erinnerung.* Cologne: Böhlau Verlag.

Kuhrt, A. 2001. "Women and War." *NIN: Journal of Gender Studies in Antiquity* 2: 1-26.

Kuijper, D. 1973. "De T. Vinii aetatis spatio et crimine." In *Archeologie en Historie: Opgedragen aan H. Brunsting*: 145-51. Bussum: Fibula-van Dishoeck.

Kulesza, R. 1999. "Population Flight: A Forgotten Aspect of Greek Warfare in the Sixth and Fifth Centuries B.C." *European Review of History* 6.2: 151-69.

Kulikowski, M. 2000. "The *Notitia Dignitatum* as a Historical Source." *Historia* 49: 358-77.

Laato, A. 1995. "Assyrian Propaganda and the Falsification of History in the Royal Inscriptions of Sennacherib." *Vetus Testamentum* 45/2: 198-226.

Láda, C. 2002. *Foreign Ethnics in Hellenistic Egypt. Prosopographia Ptolemaica*, 10. *Studia Hellenistica*, 38. Dudley, MA: Peeters.

Lafont, B. 2009. "The Army of the Kings of Ur." *Cuneiform Digital Library Journal* 5: 1-25.

Lanfranchi, G. B. and S. Parpola. 1990. *The Correspondence of Sargon II, Part II: Letters from the Northern and Northeastern Provinces*. Helsinki: University of Helsinki.

Lanfranchi, G. B., Michael Roaf, and Robert Rollinger, eds. 2003. *Continuity of Empire: Assyria, Media, Persia*. Padova: S.a.r.g.o.n. Editrice e Libreria.

Lange, C. H. 2008. "Civil War in the *Res Gestae Divi Augusti*: Conquering the World and Fighting a War at Home." In Bragg, Hau, and Macaulay-Lewis 2008: 185-204.

Larouge, C. 2007. *L'image des Parthes dans le monde gréco-romain. Du début du 1er siècle av. J.-C. jusqu'à fin du Haut-Empire romain*. Stuttgart: Fritz Steiner Verlag.

Launey, M. 1949-50/1987. *Recherches sur les armées hellenistiques*. 2 vols. Paris: de Boccard. Reprinted, Paris: de Boccard.

Lazenby, J. 1985. *The Spartan Army*. Warminster: Aris & Phillips.

———. 1994. "Logistics in Classical Greek Warfare." *War in History* 1: 3-18.

LeBlanc, S. with Register, K. 2003. *Constant Battles: Why We Fight*. New York: St. Martin's Griffin.

Le Bohec, Y. 1989. *La troisième légion Auguste*. Paris: CNRS.

———. 1994. *The Imperial Roman Army*. Tr. Raphael Bate. New York: Routledge.

———, ed. 1995. *La hiérarchie (Rangordnung) de l'armée romaine sous le haut-empire*. Paris: de Boccard.

———, ed. 2003. *Les légions de Rome sous le haut-empire : actes du congrès de Lyon (17-19 septembre 1998)*. Paris: Boccard.

———. 2006. *L'armée romaine sous le Bas-Empire*. Paris: Picard.

———. 2007. *L'armée romaine en Afrique et en Gaule*. MAVORS series. Stuttgart: Steiner.

Le Bohec, Y. and C. Wolff, eds. 2004. *L'armée romaine de Dioclétien à Valentinien Ier*. Paris: Boccard.

Lee, A.D. 1996. "Morale and the Roman Experience of Battle." In Lloyd 1996a: 199-217.

———. 1998. "The Army." In *Cambridge Ancient History XIII: The Late Empire, AD 337-425*. ed. A. Cameron and P. Garnsey, 211-37. Cambridge: Cambridge University Press.

———. 2007a. *War in Late Antiquity*. Malden, MA: Wiley-Blackwell.

———. 2007b. "The Later Roman Empire: Warfare and the State." In *CHGRW*, 2: 379-423.

Lee, J.W.I. 2004. "For There Were Many *Hetairai* in the Army: Women in Xenophon's *Anabasis*." *AncW* 35: 154-65.

———. 2005. "Xenophon's *Anabasis* and the Origins of Military Autobiography." In *Arms and the Self: War, the Military, and Autobiographical Writing*, ed. A. Vernon, 41-60. Kent, OH: Kent State University Press.

———. 2007. *A Greek Army on the March: Soldiers and Survival in Xenophon's Anabasis*. Cambridge: Cambridge University Press.

Lee, W. 2004. "Fortify, Fight, or Flee: Tuscarora and Cherokee Defensive Warfare and Military Cultural Adaptation." *JMH* 68: 713-70.

———. 2007. "Peace Chiefs and Blood Revenge: Patterns of Restraint in Native American Warfare, 1500-1800." *JMH* 71: 701-41.

Lehmann, B. 1982. "Das Eigenvermögen der römischen Soldaten unter väterlicher Gewalt." *ANRW* 2.14: 183-284.

Leitao, D. 2002. "The Legend of the Sacred Band." In *The Sleep of Reason: Experience and Sexual Ethics in Ancient Greece and Rome*, ed. M. Nussbaum and J. Silhvola, 143-69. Chicago: University of Chicago Press.

Lendon, J. E. 1997. *Empire of Honour: The Art of Government in the Roman World*. Oxford: Oxford University Press.

———. 1999. "The Rhetoric of Combat: Greek Military Theory and Roman Culture in Julius Caesar's Battle Descriptions." *CA* 18.2: 273-329.

———. 2000. "Homeric Vengeance and the Outbreak of Greek Wars." In van Wees 2000a: 1-30.

———. 2002. "Primitivism and Ancient Foreign Relations." *CJ* 97.4: 375-94.

———. 2004. "The Roman Army Now." *CJ* 99.4: 441-449.

———. 2005. *Soldiers and Ghosts: A History of Battle in Classical Antiquity*. New Haven, CT: Yale University Press.

————. 2006. "Xenophon and the Alternative to Realist Foreign Policy: *Cyropaedia* 3.1.14-31." *JHS* 126: 82-96.

————. 2007. "War and Society." In *CHGRW*, 1: 498-516.

————. 2010. *Song of Wrath: The Peloponnesian War Begins.* New York: Basic Books.

Lengauer, W. 1979. *Greek Commanders in the 5ᵗʰ and 4ᵗʰ Centuries. Politics and Ideology: A Study of Militarism.* Warsaw: Wydawnictwa Uniwersytetu Warszawskiego.

Lenski, N. 1999. "Romanization and Revolt in the Territory of Isauria." *JESHO* 42: 413-65.

————. 2002. *Failure of Empire: Valens and the Roman State in the Fourth Century AD.* Los Angeles: University of California Press.

————. 2007. "Two Sieges of Amida (AD 359 and 502-503) and the Experience of Combat in the Late Roman Near East." In *The Late Roman Army in the Near East from Diocletian to the Arab Conquest*, ed. A. Levin and P. Pellegrini, 219-36. Oxford: Archaeopress.

Lesquier, J. 1911. *Les institutions militaires de l'Égypte sous les Lagides.* Paris: Errnest Leroux.

Lévêque, P. 1968. "La guerre à l'époque hellénistique." In Vernant 1968: 261-87.

Levithan, J. 2008. "Emperors, Sieges, and Intentional Exposure." In Bragg, Hau, and Macaulay-Lewis 2008: 25-46.

Ligt, L. de. 2007. "Roman Manpower and Recruitment During the Middle Republic." In *CRA:* 114-31.

Ligt, L. de. and S. Northwood, eds. 2008. *People, Land, and Politics: Demographic Developments and the Transformation of Roman Italy, 300 BC-AD 14.* Leiden: Brill.

Linderski, J. 2007. *Roman Questions* II. Stuttgart: Franz Steiner Verlag.

Little, L.K., ed. 2007. *Plague and the End of Antiquity: The Pandemic of 541-750.* Cambridge: Cambridge University Press.

Lloyd, A., ed. 1996a. *Battle in Antiquity.* London: Duckworth.

————. 1996b. "Philip II and Alexander the Great: The Moulding of Macedon's Army." In Lloyd 1996a: 169-98.

Loman, P. 2004. "No Woman, No War: Women's Participation in Ancient Greek Warfare." *G&R* 51: 34-54.

————. 2005. "Mercenaries, their Women, and Colonisation." *Klio* 87: 346-65.

Lonis, R. 1969. *Les usages de la guerre entre grecs et barbares.* Paris: Les Belles Lettres.

Lonsdale, D. 2007. *Alexander the Great: Lessons in Strategy.* New York: Routledge.

Low, P. 2007. *Interstate Relations in Classical Greece: Morality and Power.* Cambridge: Cambridge University Press.

Luckenbill, D. D. 1927. *Ancient Records of Assyria and Babylonia.* Chicago: University of Chicago Press.

Luraghi. N. 2006. "Traders, Pirates, Warriors: The Proto-history of Greek Mercenary Soldiers in the Eastern Mediterranean." *Phoenix* 60: 21-47.

Lütkenhaus, W. 1998. *Constantius III: Studien zu seiner Tätigkeit und Stellung im Westreich, 411-421.* Bonn: Habelt.

Luttwak, E. 1976. *The Grand Strategy of the Roman Empire: From the First Century A.D. to the Third.* Baltimore, MD: Johns Hopkins.

Luukko, M. and G. Van Buylaere. 2002. *The Political Correspondence of Esarhaddon.* Helsinki: University of Helsinki.

Luvaas, J. 1964. *The Education of an Army: British Military Thought, 1815-1940.* London: Cassell.

Lynn, J. 2003. *Battle: A History of Combat and Culture.* Boulder: Westview Press.

———. 2005. "Discourse, Reality, and the Culture of Combat" *International History Review* 27: 475-80.

———. 2009. Review of Y. N. Harari, *The Ultimate Experience: Battlefield Revelations and the Making of Modern War Culture, 1450-2000. AHR* 114: 708-10.

McCormick, M. 1986. *Eternal Victory: Triumphal Rulership in Late Antiquity, Byzantium and the Early Medieval West.* Cambridge: Cambridge University Press.

McDonnell, M. 2003. "Roman Men and Greek Virtue." In Rosen and Sluiter 2003: 235-61.

———. 2005. "Aristocratic Competition, Horses, and the *spolia opima.*" In Aubert and Várhelyi 2005: 145-60.

———. 2006a. "Roman Aesthetics and the Spoils of Syracuse." In Dillon & Welch 2006: 68-90.

———. 2006b. *Roman Manliness: Virtue and the Roman Republic.* Cambridge.

McIvor, A. D., ed. 2005. *Rethinking the Principles of War.* Annapolis: Naval Institute Press.

Ma, J. 2000. "Fighting *Poleis of the Hellenistic World.*" In van Wees 2000a: 315-76.

MacGeorge, P. 2002. *Late Roman Warlords.* Oxford: Oxford University Press.

MacMullen, R. 1963. *Soldier and Civilian in the Later Roman Empire.* Cambridge, MA: Harvard.

———. 1984. "The Legion as a Society." *Historia* 33: 440-456. In MacMullen 1990: 225-35.

————. 1988. *Corruption and the Decline of Rome.* New Haven, CT: Yale University Press.

————. 1990. *Changes in the Roman Empire: Essays in the Ordinary.* New Haven, CT: Yale.

Maeda, T. 1992. "The Defense Zone During the Rule of the Ur III Dynasty." *Acta Sumerologica (Japan)* 14: 135-72.

Maidman, M. 2008. "Peace and War at Nuzi: A Prosopographical Foray." In *Treasures on Camels' Humps: Historical and Literary Studies from the Ancient Near East Presented to Israel Eph'al,* ed. M. Cogan and D. Kahn, 199-220. Jerusalem: Magnes Press.

Majno, G. 1975. *The Healing Hand: Man and Wound in the Ancient World.* Cambridge, MA: Harvard University Press.

Malitz, J. 2008. "Der Preis des Krieges. Thukydides und die Finanzen Athens." In Burrer and Müller 2008: 28-45.

Malkin, I. 2008. Review of H. Hurst and S. Owen, eds., *Ancient Colonizations. Analogy, Similarity & Difference. BMCR* 2008.11.08.

Mann, J. C. 1983. *Legionary Recruitment and Veteran Settlement during the Principate.* Ed. M. M. Roxan. London: University of London.

Marshall, A. 1975. "Tacitus and the Governor's Lady: A Note on *Annals* 3.33-4." *G&R* 22: 11-18.

Marshall, S. L. A. 1947. *Men against Fire: The Problem of Battle Command.* New York: William Morrow & Co., 1947. Reprinted Norman: University of Oklahoma Press, 2000.

Mathisen, R.W. 2006. "*Peregrini, barbari,* and *cives Romani*: Concepts of Citizenship and the Legal Identity of Barbarians in the Later Roman Empire." *AHR* 111: 1011-40.

————. 2009. "*Provinciales, gentiles,* and Marriages between Romans and Barbarians in the Late Roman Empire." *JRS* 99: 140-55.

Mattern, S. P. 1999. *Rome and the Enemy: Imperial Strategy in the Principate.* Los Angeles: University of California.

Matthew, C. 2009. "When Push Comes to Shove: What Was the *Othismos* of Hoplite Combat? *Historia* 58: 395-415.

Matthews, J. 1989. *The Roman Empire of Ammianus.* London: Duckworth.

————. 2000. *Laying Down the Law: A Study of the Theodosian Code.* New Haven: Yale University Press.

Matthews, R. 2007. *You Wouldn't Want To Be An Assyrian Soldier!* Danbury, CT: Children's Press.

————. 2008. *Alexander the Great at the Battle of the Granicus.* Stroud: Tempus Publishing Ltd.

Matthews, V. H. 1981. "Legal Aspects of Military Service in Ancient Mesopotamia. "*Military Law Review* 94: 135-51.

Mattingly, D. J. 1997. *Dialogues in Roman Imperialism : Power, Discourse, and Discrepant Experience in the Roman Empire*. Portsmouth, RI: JRA.

———. 2004. "Being Roman: Expressing Identity in a Provincial Setting." *JRA* 17.1: 5-25.

May, N. forthcoming. "Triumph as an Aspect of the Neo-Assyrian Decorative Program." In *Proceedings of the 54e Rencontre Assyriologique Internationale*. Würzburg: Universität Würzburg.

Meißner, B. 2007. "Die Kultur des Kreiges." In *Kulturgeschichte des Hellenismus. Von Alexander der Großen bis Kleopatra*, ed. G. Weber, 202-23. Stuttgart: Klett-Clotta.

Meißner, B., O. Schmitt, and M. Sommer, eds. 2005. *Krieg—Gesellschaft— Institutionen. Beiträge zu einer vergleichenden Kriegsgeschichte*. Berlin: Akademie Verlag, 2005.

Melville, S. C. 2011, *forthcoming*. "The Last Campaign: The Assyrian Way of War and the Collapse of the Empire." In: *Warfare and Culture in World History*, ed. W. E. Lee. New York: New York University Press.

Melville, S. C. and D. J. Melville. 2008. "Observations on the Diffusion of Military Technology: Siege Warfare in the Near East and Greece." In *From the Banks of the Euphrates: Studies in Honor of Alice Louise Slotsky*, ed. M. Ross, 145-68. Winona Lake, Indiana: Eisenbrauns.

Michalowski, P. 1989. *The Lamentation over the Destruction of Sumer and Ur*. Winona Lake, IN: Eisenbrauns.

———. 1993. *Letters from Early Mesopotamia*. Atlanta: Scholars Press.

Mielsczarek, M. 1993. *Cataphracti and Clibanarii: Studies on the Heavy Armoured Cavalry of the Ancient World*. Tr., M. Abramowicz. Lódz: Oficyna Naukowa MS.

———.1999. *The Army of the Bosporan Kingdom*. Tr., N. Sekunda. Lódz: Oficyna Naukowa MS.

Migeotte, L. 2000. "Les dépenses militaries de cités grecques." In Andreau *et al*. 2000: 145-76.

Milner, N.P. 1996. *Vegetius: Epitome of Military Science*. 2nd ed., Liverpool: Liverpool University Press.

Mitchell, S. 1976. "Requisitioned Transport in the Roman Empire: A New Inscription from Pisidia." *JRS* 66: 106-31.

Möbius, S. 2007. *Mehr Angst vor dem Offizier als dem Feind? Eine Mental- itätsgeschichtliche Studie zur preußischen Taktik im Siebenjährigen Krieg*. Saarbrücken: VDM Verlag Dr. Muller.

Mode, M., and J. von Tubach, eds. 2006. *Arms and Armour as Indicators of Cultural Transfer: The Steppes and the Ancient World from Hellenistic Times to the Early Middle Ages*. Wiesbaden: Reichert.

Moran, W. L. 1992. *The Amarna Letters*. Baltimore: The Johns Hopkins University Press.

Morgan, G. 2006. *69 A.D.: The Year of Four Emperors*. Oxford: Oxford University Press.

Morillo, S. 2006. *What Is Military History?* Malden, MA: Polity.

Morkot, R. G. 2007. "War and the Economy: The International 'Arms Trade' in the Late Bronze Age and After." In *Egyptian Stories: A British Egyptological Tribute to Alan B. Lloyd on the Occasion of His Retirement*, ed. Th. Schneider and K. Szpakowska, 169-96. =*AOAT* 347. Munster: Ugarit-Verlag.

Morley, N. 2007. "Civil War and Succession Crisis in Roman Beekeeping." *Historia* 56.4: 462-70.

Morris, I. and W. Scheidel, eds. 2009. *The Dynamics of Ancient Empires: State Power from Assyria to Byzantium*. Oxford: Oxford University Press.

Mossé, G. 1996. *The Image of Man: The Creation of Modern Masculinity*. Oxford: Oxford University Press.

Muccioli, F. 2008. Review of Capdetrey 2007. *BMCR* 2008.06.22.

Muscarella, O. 1966. "Hasanlu 1964." *The Metropolitan Museum of Art Bulletin* 25.3: 121-35.

Myerly, S. H. 1996. *British Military Spectacle: From the Napoleonic Wars through the Crimea*. Cambridge, MA: Harvard University Press.

Naiden, F. 2007. "The Invention of the Officer Corps." *Journal of the Historical Society* 7: 35-60.

Nicasie, M.J. 1998. *Twilight of Empire: The Roman Army from the reign of Diocletian until the Battle of Adrianople*. Amsterdam: Gieben.

Nippel, W. 1995. *Public Order in Ancient Rome*. Cambridge: Cambridge University Press.

Nissen, H. et al. 1990. *Archaic Bookkeeping: Early Writing and Techniques of Economic Administration in the Ancient Near East*. Chicago: University of Chicago.

Noelke, P. and B. Kibilka. 2005. "Zu den Grabreliefs mit Darstellung des *convivium coniugale* im römischen Germanien und im benachbarten Gallien." *BJ* 205: 155-241.

Nougaryol, J. 1968. "Textes Suméro-Accadiens des Archives et Bibliothèques Privées d'Ugarit." In *Ugaritica* V (=*Mission de Ras Shamra* XVI), 1-446. Paris: Librairie Orientaliste Paul Geuthner.

Noy, D. 2000. *Foreigners at Rome: Citizens and Strangers*. London: Duckworth.

O'Flynn, J.M. 1983. *Generalissimos of the Western Roman Empire*. Edmonton: University of Alberta Press.

Oates, J. et al. 2007. "Early Mesopotamian urbanism: a new view from the north." *Antiquity* 81: 585-600.

Ober, J. 1994. "Classical Greek Times." In *The Laws of War: Constraints on Warfare in the Western World*, eds. M. Howard, G. Andreopoulos, and M. Schulman, 2-26. New Haven: Yale University Press = *Id. The Athenian Revolution: Essays on Ancient Greek Democracy and Political Theory*, 53-71. Princeton: Princeton University Press, 1996 = "Les règles de guerre en Grèce classique." Tr. J. Odin. In Brulé and Oulhen 1997: 219-39.

Oded, B. 1979. *Mass Deportations and Deportees in the Neo-Assyrian Empire*. Wiesbaden: Ludwig Reichert Verlag.

———. 1997. "Cutting Down Orchards in Assyrian Royal Inscriptions – the Historiographic Aspect." *JAC* 12: 93-98.

Oestreich, G. 1982. *Neostoicism and the Early Modern State*. Ed. B. Oestreich and H. G. Koenigsberger. Tr. D. McLintock. Cambridge: Cambridge University Press.

Oliver, J. 1953. *The Ruling Power: A Study of the Roman Empire in the Second Century After Christ through the Roman Oration of Aelius Aristides*. Philadelphia, PA: American Philosophical Society.

Olivier, H., P. Giovannelli-Jouanna, and F. Bérard, eds. 2006. *Ruses, secrets et mensonges chez les historiens grecs et latins*. Paris: de Boccard.

Oman, C. 1939. *On the Writing of History*. London: Methuen & Co. Ltd.

Osgood, J. 2006. *Caesar's Legacy: Civil War and the Emergence of the Roman Empire*. Cambridge: Cambridge University Press.

Otterbein, K. 1999. "A History of Research on Warfare in Anthropology." *American Anthropologist* 101.4: 794-805.

———. 2004. *How War Began*. College Station: Texas A&M University Press.

Paret, P. 2009. "The Annales School and the History of War." *JMH* 73: 1289-94.

Parker, B. J. 1997. "Garrisoning the Empire: Aspects of the Construction and Maintenance of Forts on the Assyrian Frontier." *Iraq* 59: 77-87.

Parker, G. 1976. "The Military Revolution 1560-1660—A Myth?" Journal of Modern History 48: 195-214. Revised and reprinted In *Spain and the Netherlands 1559-1659: Ten Studies*, ed. G. Parker, 86-103. Short Hills, NJ: Enslow: 1979.

———. 1996a. *The Military Revolution: Military Innovation and the Rise of the West, 1500-1800*. 2nd ed. Cambridge: Cambridge University Press.

———. 1996b. "What Is the Western Way of War?" *Military History Quarterly* 8.2: 86-95.

Parpola, S. 1987. *The Correspondence of Sargon II, Part I: Letters from Assyria and the West.* Helsinki: University of Helsinki.

Partoens, G., G. Roskam, and T. Van Houdt, ed. 2004. *Virtutis imago: Studies on the Conceputalisation and Transformation of an Ancient Ideal.* Leuven: Peeters.

Patterson, J. 1993. "Military Organization and Social Change in the Later Roman Republic." In Rich and Shipley 1993b: 92-112.

Peachin, M. 2007. "Petition to a Centurion from the NYU Papyrus Collection and the Question of Informal Adjudication Performed by Soldiers (*P.Sijp.* 15)." In *Papyri in Memory of P.J. Sijpesteijn, American Studies in Papyrology* 40, ed. A. Sirks and K. A. Worp, 79-97. Chippenham: American Society of Papyrologists.

Peremans, W. and E. van 't Dack. 1950-91. *Prosopographia Ptolemaica.* 9 vols. Louvain: Bibliotheca universitatis.

Peretz, D. 2005. "Military Burial and the Identification of the Roman Fallen Soldiers." *Klio* 87.1: 123-138.

———. 2006. "The Roman Interpreter and his Diplomatic and Military Roles." *Historia* 55.4: 451-470.

Perrin-Saminadayar, E. 2007. *Éducation, culture et société à Athènes. Les acteurs de la vie culturelle athénienne (299-88).* Paris: de Boccard.

Petraccia Lucernoni, M. F. 2001. *Gli* stationarii *in età imperiale.* Rome: Bretschneider.

Phang, S.E. 2001. *The Marriage of Roman Soldiers (13 BC - A 235): Law and Family in the Imperial Army.* Leiden: Brill.

———. 2004. "Intimate Conquests: Roman Soldiers' Slave Women and Freedwomen." *AW* 35.2: 207-37.

———. 2005. "Soldiers' Slaves, 'dirty work,' and the Social Status of Roman Soldiers." In Aubert and Varhelyi 2005: 203-25.

———. 2007. "Military Documents, Languages, and Literacy." In *CRA*: 286-305.

———. 2008. *Roman Military Service: Ideologies of Discipline in the Late Republic and Early Principate.* Cambridge: Cambridge University Press.

Piccirilli, L. 1973-97. *Gli arbitrati interstatali greci.* 2 vols. Pisa: Marlin.

———. 2009. *L'invenzione della diplomazia nella Grecia antica.* Rome: L'Erma di Bretschneider.

Philip, T. 2002. "Woman in Travail as a Simile to Men in Distress in the Hebrew Bible." In *Sex and Gender in the Ancient Near East: Proceedings of the 47th Rencontre Assyriologique Internationale,* Helsinki, July 2-6, 2001, ed. S. Parpola and R. M. Whiting, 499-506. Helsinki; The Neo-Assyrian Text Corpus Project.

Pickford, K. L. 2005. "The Cruelty of Roman Military Punishments: Decimation in Practice." *AH* 35.2: 123-136.

Pirson, F. 1996. "Style and Message on the Column of Marcus Aurelius." *PBSR* 64: 139-79.

Pollard, N. 2000. *Soldiers, Cities, and Civilians in Roman Syria.* Ann Arbor: University of Michigan Press.

———. 2004. "Roman Material Culture across Imperial Frontiers? Three Case Studies from Parthian Dura-Europos." *YCS* 31: 119-144.

Popescu, M. 2004. *La religion dans l'armée romaine de Dacie.* Bucharest : Éditions de l'Académie roumaine.

Postgate, J. N. 1982. "*ilku* and Land Tenure in the Middle Assyrian Kingdom – A Second Attempt." In *Societies and Languages of the Ancient Near East: Studies in Honor of I. M. Diakonoff*, 303-312. Warminster: Aris & Philips.

———. 1992. *Early Mesopotamia: Society and Economy at the Dawn of History.* New York: Routledge.

———. 2000. "The Assyrian army in Zamua." *Iraq* 62: 89-108.

———. 2001. "Assyrian Uniforms." In *Veenhof Anniversary Volume: Studies Presented to Klaas R. Veenhof on the Occasion of His Sixty-Fifth Birthday*, ed. W. H. van Soldt, 373-88. Leiden: Nederlands Instituut voor het Nabije Oosten.

Potter, D. S. 1999. "Political theory and the *Senatus consultum de Cn. Pisone Patre*." *AJPH* 120.1: 65-88.

———. 2004. *The Roman Empire at Bay: AD 180--395.* New York: Routledge.

Prag, J. 2007. "*Auxilia* and *Gymnasia*: A Sicilian Model of Roman Imperialism." *JRS* 97: 68-100.

Prior, R. and T. Wilson. 1994. "Paul Fussell at War." *War in History* 1: 63-80.

Pritchett, W. K. 1971-91. *The Greek State at War.* 5 vols. Los Angeles: University of California Press.

Quillen, J. 2009. Review of Eckstein 2006a. *BMCR* 2009.06.44.

Raaflaub, K. A. 1987. "Die Militärreformen des Augustus und die politische Problematik des Frühen Prinzipats." In *Saeculum Augustum*, bd. 1: *Herrschaft und Gesellschaft.* Ed. Gerhard Binder, 246-307. Darmstadt: Wissenschaftliche Buchgesellschaft,.

———. 2004. *The Discovery of Freedom in Ancient Greece.* Tr. R. Franciscono. Chicago: University of Chicago Press.

———, ed. 2005. *Social Struggles in Archaic Rome: New Perspectives on the Conflict of the Orders.* Rev. ed. Malden, MA: Blackwell.

———. 2007a. "Searching for Peace in the Ancient World." In Raaflaub 2007b: 1-33.

————, ed. 2007b. *War and Peace in the Ancient World*. Malden, MA: Wiley-Blackwell.

Raaflaub, K. and N. Rosenstein, eds. 1999. *War and Society in the Ancient and Medieval Worlds*. Cambridge, MA: Harvard University Press.

Radner, K. 2010. "The Assyrian Army," *Assyrian Empire Builders*, University College London, 2010, (http://www.ucl.ac.uk/sargon/essentials/soldiers/ theassyrianarmy/) (accessed September 2010).

————. 2011. "Fame and prizes: competition and war in the Neo-Assyrian empire." In *Competition in the Ancient World*, ed. N. Fisher and H. van Wees, 37-57. Swansea: The Classical Press of Wales.

Rance, P. 2004. "The *fulcum*, the Late Roman and Byzantine *testudo*: The Germanization of Roman Infantry Tactics?" *GRBS* 44: 265-326.

————. 2005. "Narses and the Battle of Taginae (*Busta Gallorum*) 552: Procopius and Sixth-Century Warfare." *Historia* 54: 424-72.

————. 2007a. "The Date of the Military Compendium of Syrianus Magister (formerly the sixth-century Anonymus Byzantinus)." *ByzZ* 100: 701-37.

————. 2007b. "The Later Roman Empire: Battle." In *CHGRW*, 2: 342-78.

Rambaud, M. 1953. *L'art de déformation historique dans les Commenaires de Cèsar*. Paris: Les Belles Lettres.

Rankov, N. B. 1990. "*Frumentarii*, the *Castra Peregrina* and the Provincial *officia*." *ZPE* 80: 176-82.

————. 1994. "Die Beneficiarier in den literarischen und papyrologischen Texten." In *Der römische Weihebezirk von Osterburken II: Kolloquium 1990 und paläoboatische-osteologische Untersuchungen*, edd. E. Schallmayer et al., 219-32. Stuttgart: Theiss.

————. 1999a. "*Beneficiarii* (Military Staff Officers) and the Discoveries at Osterburken." *Journal of Roman Archaeology* 12.2: 675-81.

————. 1999b. "The governor's men: the *officium consularis* in provincial administration." In Goldsworthy and Haynes: 15-34.

————. 2002. "*Beneficiarii* and the Reality of Roman Bureaucracy." *JRA* 15.2: 524-27.

————. 2007. "Military Forces." In *CHGRW*, 2:30-75.

Rathbone, D. 2007. "Warfare and the State A: Military Finance and Supply." In *CHGRW* 2: 158-77.

Rausch, M. 1998. "Zeitpunkt und Anlaß der Einfuhrung der Phylenagone in Athen. *Nikophoros* 11: 83-105.

Rawlings, L. 2007. *The Ancient Greeks at War*. Manchester: Manchester University Press.

————. 2009. "Warfare." In *A Companion to Ancient History*, ed. A. Erskine, 531-44. Malden, MA: Wiley-Blackwell.

Rawson, E. 1971. "The Literary Sources for the Pre-Marian Army." *PBSR* 39: 13--31.

Reichel, C. 2009. "Beyond the Garden of Eden – Competition and Early Warfare in Northern Syria (4500–3000 B.C.)." In *Schlachfeldarchäologie (Battlefield Archaeology)*, ed. H. Meller, 17-30. =*Tagungen des Landesmuseums für Vorgeschichte Halle* 2. Halle: Landesdenkmalamt.

Reid, R.J. 2007. "Revisiting Primitive War: Perceptions of Violence and Race in History." *War & Society* 26: 1-25.

Revell, L. 2007. "Military Bath-Houses in Britain." *Britannia* 38: 230-237.

———. 2009. *Roman Imperialism and Local Identities*. Cambridge: Cambridge University Press.

Rey, Fernando E. "Weapons, Technological Determinism, and Ancient Warfare." In Fagan and Trundle 2010, 21-56.

Reynolds, F.S. 2003. *The Babylonian Correspondence of Esarhaddon and Letters to Assurbanipal and Sin-šarru-iškun from Northern and Central Babylonia*. Helsinki: University of Helsinki.

Ricci, C. 1994. *Soldati delle milizie urbane fuori di Roma: La documentazione epigrafica*. Rome: Quasar.

Rich, J.F. 1993. "Fear, Greed, and Glory: The Causes of Roman War-Making in the Middle Republic." In Rich and Shipley 1993b: 38-68.

Rich, J. and G. Shipley, eds. 1993a. *War and Society in the Greek World*. London: Routledge.

Rich, J. and G. Shipley, eds. 1993b. *War and Society in the Roman World*. London: Routledge.

Richardson, A. 2001. "The Order of Battle in the Roman Army: Evidence from Marching Camps." *OJA* 20.2: 171-185.

———. 2003. "Space and Manpower in Roman Camps." *OJA* 22.3: 303-313.

Richardson, S. 2005a. "The World of the Babylonian Countrysides." In *The Babylonian World*, ed. Gwendolyn Leick, 13-38. New York: Routledge.

———. 2005b. "Axes Against Eshnunna." *Orientalia* 74.1: 42-50.

———. 2007. "Death and Dismemberment in Mesopotamia: Discorporation between the Body and the Body Politic." In *Performing Death* (*OIS* 3), ed. N. Laneri, 189-208. Chicago: Oriental Institute.

———. 2010a. "On Seeing and Believing: Liver Divination and the Era of Warring States." In *Divination and Interpretation of Signs in the Ancient World* (*OIS* 6), ed. A. Annus, 225-266. Chicago: Oriental Institute.

———. 2010b. "Writing Rebellion back into the Record: A Methodologies Toolkit." In *Rebellions and Peripheries* (=*American Oriental Series* 91), ed. S. Richardson, 1-27. Ann Arbor, MI: American Oriental Society,

————. 2010c. *Texts of the Late Old Babylonian Period.* (=*Journal of Cuneiform Studies Supplemental Series* 2. Boston: American Schools of Oriental Research.

————. 2011, forthcoming. "The Presumptive State: Early Polity Formation in Mesopotamia." *Past & Present* 210/211.

Rigsby, K.J. 1999. "Two Danubian Epitaphs". *ZPE* 126: 175-6.

Rihill, T. 1993. "War, Slavery, and Settlement in Early Greece." In Rich and Shipley 1993a: 78-107.

Riess, W. 2001, *Apuleius und die Räuber: Ein Beitrag zur historischen Kriminalitätsforschung.* Stuttgart: F. Steiner.

————. 2000-01. "Between Fiction and Reality: Robbers in Apuleius' *Golden Ass.*" *Ancient Narrative* 1: 260-82.

————. 2007. "Hunting down Robbers in 3rd Century Central Italy." In *Les exclus dans l'Antiquité,* ed. C. Wolff, 195-213. Paris: De Boccard.

Rivière, Y. 1994. "*Carcer et uincula*: La détention publique à Rome (sous la République et le Haut-Empire)." *MÉFRA* 106: 579-652.

————. 2004a. *Le cachot et les fers: Détention et coercition à Rome.* Paris: Belin.

————. 2004b. "Les batailles de Rome: Présence militaire et guerrilla urbaine à l'époque impériale." *Histoire urbaine* 10: 63-87.

Roberts, M. 1956. *The Military Revolution, 1550-1660: An Inaugural Lecture Delivered before the Queen's University of Belfast.* Belfast: M. Boyd = *Essays in Swedish History*, 195-225. London: Weidenfeld & Nicolson, 1967.

Robinson, E. 2001. "Reading and Misreading the Ancient Evidence for Democratic Peace." *Journal of Peace Research* 38: 593-608.

Robinson, O. F. 2006. *Penal Practice and Penal Policy in Ancient Rome.* New York: Routledge.

Roebuck, D. 2001. *Ancient Greek Arbitration.* Oxford: Arbitration Press.

Rogers, C., ed. 1995. *The Military Revolution Debate. Readings on the Military Transformation of Early Modern Europe.* Boulder, CO: Westerview.

Roisman, J., ed. 2003. *Brill's Companion to Alexander the Great.* Leiden: E. J. Brill.

Romilly, J. de. 1968. "Guerre et paix entre cités." In Vernant 1968: 207-20.

Rosen, R. M., and I. Sluiter, ed. 2003. *Andreia: Studies in Manliness and Courage in Classical Antiquity.* Leiden: Brill.

Rosenstein, Nathan. 1990. *Imperatores Victi: Military Defeat and Aristocratic Competition in the Middle and Late Republic.* Los Angeles: University of California.

———. 1999. "Republican Rome. " In Raaflaub and Rosenstein 1999: 193-216.

———. 2004. *Rome at War: Farms, Families, and Death in the Middle Republic.* Chapel Hill, NC: University of North Carolina.

———. 2006. "Aristocratic Values." In *Companion to the Roman Republic*, ed. R. Morstein-Marx, and N. Rosenstein, 621-36. Malden, MA: Wiley-Blackwell.

———. 2007a. "Military Command, Political Power, and the Republican Elite." In *CRA:* 132-47.

———. 2007b. "War and Peace, Fear and Reconciliation at Rome." In Raaflaub 2007b: 226-244.

———. 2009a. "War, State Formation, and the Evolution of Military Institutions in Ancient China and Rome." In Scheidel 2009: 24-51.

———. 2009b. "New Approaches to Roman History," Presented as part of the panel "New Approaches to the Political and Military History of the Greek, Roman, and Late Roman Worlds" at the Annual Meeting of the American Philological Association, January 9, 2009. http://apaclassics. org/images/uploads/documents/RosensteinAPA2009.pdf

———. 2009c. Review of Phang 2008. *AHR* 114: 810-11.

Rosivach, V. 2002. "*Zeugitai* and Hoplites." *AHB* 16: 33-43.

Roth, J. 1999. *The Logistics of the Roman Army at War (264 BC - AD 235).* Leiden: Brill.

———. 2010. *Roman Warfare.* Cambridge: Cambridge University Press.

Roth, M.T. 1995. *Law Collections from Mesopotamia and Asia Minor.* 2nd edition. Society of Biblical Literature, *Writings from the Ancient World* Series 6. Atlanta, Georgia: Scholars Press.

Rubincam, C. 1991. "Casualty Figures in the Battle Descriptions of Thucydides." *TAPA* 121: 181-98.

———. 2003a. "Numbers in Greek Poetry and Historiography: Quantifying Fehling." *CQ* 53: 448-63.

———. 2003b. "Herodotus and his Descendants: Numbers in Ancient and Modern Narratives of Xerxes' Campaigns," *HSCPh* 104: 93-138.

Rüpke, J. 1990. *Domi Militiae: Die religiöse Konstruktion des Krieges in Rom.* Stuttgart: F. Steiner.

Russell, F. 1999: *Information Gathering in Classical Greece.* Ann Arbor, MI: University of Michigan Press.

Sabin, P. 2000. "The Face of Roman Battle." *JRS* 90: 1-17.

———. 2007a. "Land Battles," In *CHGRW*, 1: 399-433.

———. 2007b. *Lost Battles: Reconstructing the Great Clashes of the Ancient World.* London: Hambledon Continuum.

Sablayrolles, R. 1996. *Libertinus miles: Les Cohortes de vigiles. CÉFR* 224. Rome: École française de Rome.

———. 2000. "La rue, le soldat et le pouvoir: La garnison de Rome de César à Pertinax." *Pallas* 55: 127-53.

Sagan, E. 1979. *The Lust to Annihilate: A Psychoanalytic Study of Violence in Ancient Greek Culture.* New York: Psychohistory Publishers.

Salazar, C.F. 2000. *The Treatment of War Wounds* in *GraecoRoman Antiquity. Studies in Ancient Medicine* 21 Leiden: Brill.

Salonen, A. 1966. *Die Waffen der alten Mesopotamier. =Stmliu Orientaliu* 33. Helsinki: University of Helsinki.

Salzman, M.R. 2006. "Symmachus and the 'Barbarian' Generals." *Historia* 55: 352-67.

Sander, E. 1958. "Das Recht des römischen Soldaten." *RhM* 101: 152-234.

———. 1960. "Das römische Militärstrafrecht." *RhM* 103: 289-319.

Sanders, S. 2006. "Margins of Writing, Origins of Culture." In *Margins of Writing, Origins of Culture*, ed. S. Sanders, 3-11. Chicago: The Oriental Institute.

Santi Amantini, L., ed. 2005. *Dalle parole ai fatti: relazioni interstatali e communizione politica nel mondo antico.* Rome: L'Erma di Bretschneider.

Sarantis, A. 2005. "The Balkans During the Reign of Justinian: Barbarian Invasions and Imperial Responses." D. Phil. diss., Oxford.

Sartre, M. 2004. "Conclusions." In Couvenhes and Fernoux 2004: 249-55.

———. 2007, Review of Eckstein 2006a. *Topoi* 15: 619-25.

Sassmannshausen, L. 2001. *Beitrage zur Verwaltung und Gesellschaft Babyloniens in der Kassitenzeit (=Baghdader Forschungen*, 21). Mainz am Rhein: Verlag Philipp von Zabern.

Sasson, J. 1969. *The Military Establishments at Mari (=Studia Pohl*, 3). Rome: Pontificium Institutum Biblicum.

Sauzeau, P. and T. Van Compernolle, eds. 2007. *Les armes dans l'Antiquité: De la technique à l'imaginaire. Actes du colloque international du SEMA, Montpellier, 20 et 22 mars 2003*, 563-84. CERCAM—Université Paul-Valéry, Montpellier III: Presses universitaires de la Méditerranée.

Savalli-Lestrade, I. 1998. *Les* Philoi *royaux dans l'Asie hellénistique.* Geneva: Librairie Droz.

———. 2003. "La place des reines à cour et dans le royaume à l'époque hellénistique." In *Les femmes antiques entre sphère privée et sphère publique*, ed. R. Frei-Stolba, A. Bielman, O. Bianchi, 59-76. Bern: Peter Lang.

Schäfer, P., ed. 2003. *The Bar Kokhba War Reconsidered: New Perspectives on the Second Jewish Revolt against Rome.* Tübingen: Mohr.

Schaps, D. 1982. "The Women of Greece in Wartime." *CP* 77: 193-213.

Scheid, E. 2005. "Remarques sur les fondements de la vengeance en Grèce archaïque et classique." In Bertrand 2005: 395-410.

Scheidel, W. 1996a. "The Demography of the Roman Imperial Army." In Scheidel 1996b: 93-138.

———. 1996b. *Measuring Sex, Age and Death in the Roman Empire: Explorations in Ancient Demography.* Ann Arbor, MI: JRA.

———. 2003. "Germs for Rome." In *Rome the Cosmopolis*, ed. C. Edwards and G. Woolf, 158-76. Cambridge: Cambridge University Press.

———. 2006. "Stratification, Deprivation, and Quality of Life in the Roman World." In *Poverty in the Roman World*: ed. M. Atkins and R. Osborne, 40-59. Cambridge: Cambridge University Press.

———. 2007a. "Marriage, Families, and Survival: Demographic Aspects." In *CRA*: 417-34.

———. 2007b. "Roman funerary commemoration and the age at first marriage." *CPh* 102.4: 389-402.

———, ed. 2009a. *Rome and China: Comparative Perspectives on Ancient World Empires.* Oxford: Oxford University Press.

———. 2009b. "Sex and Empire: a Darwinian Perspective." In Morris and Scheidel 2009: 255-324.

———. 2010. "Real Wages in Early Economies: Evidence for Living Standards from 1800 BCE to 1300 CE." *JESHO* 53.3: 425-462.

Scheidel, W., and S. Friesen. 2009. "The Size of the Economy and the Distribution of Income in the Roman Empire." *JRS* 99: 61-91.

Schmitt, H. H. 1974. "Polybios und das Gleichgewicht der Mächte." In *Polybe*, ed. E. Gabba, *Entretiens Hardt*, 20, 65-102. Vandœuvres and Geneva: Fondation Hardt.

Schubert, C. and D. Laspe, 2009. "Perikles' defensiver Kriegsplan: Eine thukydideische Erfindung?" *Historia* 58: 373-94.

Schwartz. A. 2002. "The Early Hoplite Phalanx: Close Order or Disarray?" *C&M* 53: 31-63.

———. 2009. *Reinstating the Hoplite: Arms, Armour and Phalanx Fighting in Archaic and Classical Greece. Historia* Einzelschrift 207. Stuttgart: Franz Steiner Verlag.

Seibert, J. 1986. "Die Logistik der Feldzüge Alexanders des Großen." In *Die Bedeutung der Logistik für die militärische Führung von der Antike bis in die neueste Zeit*, 11-33. Bonn: Verlag E. S. Miller & Sohn.

Seitz, G., ed. 2006. *Im Dienste Roms: Festschrift für Hans Ulrich Nuber.* Remshalden: Greiner.

Sekunda, N. 2001a. *Hellenistic Infantry Reform in the 160s BC.* Lodz: Oficyna Naukowa MS. Reprinted Gdansk: Fundation for the Development of
Gdansk University, 2006.

————. 2001b. "The Sarissa." *Acta Universitatis Lodziensis. Folia
Archaeologica* 23: 13-41.

Serrati, J. 2007. "Warfare and the State." In *CHGRW*, 1: 461-97.

Shatzman, I. 1991. *The Armies of the Hasmonaeans and Herod: From
Hellenistic to Roman Frameworks. Texte und Studien zum antiken
Judentum*, 25. Tübingen: Mohr.

Shaw, B. 1983. "Soldiers and Society: The Army in Numidia." *Opus* 2.1: 133-
59.

————. 1984. "Bandits in the Roman Empire." *P&P* 105: 3-52.

————. 1990. "Bandit Highlands and Lowland Peace: The Mountains of
Isauria-Cilicia." *JESHO* 33: 199-233, 237-70.

————. 1999. "War and Violence." In *Late Antiquity: A Guide to the
Postclassical World.* ed. G. Bowersock, P. Brown, and O. Grabar, 130-69.
Cambridge, MA: Belknap.

————. 2003. "Judicial Nightmares and Christian Memory." *Journal of Early
Christian Studies* 11: 533-63.

Shay, J. 1994. *Achilles in Vietnam: Combat Trauma and the Undoing of
Character.* New York: Atheneum.

Sheets, G. 1994. "Conceptualizing International Law in Thucydides." *AJP*
115: 51-73.

Sherwin-White, S. and A. Kuhrt. 1993. *From Samarkhand to Sardis: A New
Approach to the Seleucid Empire.* Los Angeles: University of California
Press.

Shibano, H. 2002. "Soldier and Provincial Society in Roman Asia Minor."
JCS 50: 78-91.

Shils, E. A., and M. Janowitz. 1948. "Cohesion and Disintegration in the
Wehrmacht in World War II." *Public Opinion Quarterly* 12: 280-315.

Shipley, G. 1993. "Introduction: The Limits of War." In Rich and Shipley
1993a: 1-24.

————. 2006. "Recent Trends and New Directions." In Bugh 2006a: 315-26.

Showalter, Dennis. 1975. "A Modest Plea for Drums and Trumpets." *Military
Affairs* 39.2: 71-74.

Shy, John. 2008. "History, and the History of War." *JMH* 72: 1033-46.

Sidebottom, Harry. 2004. *Ancient Warfare: A Very Short Introduction.* Oxford:
Oxford University Press.

————. 2007. "International Relations." In *CHGRW*, 2:3-29.

Simons, A. 1999. "War: Back to the Future." *Annual Review of Anthropology* 28: 73-108.

Smith, R. E. 1958. *Service in the Post-Marian Roman Army*. Manchester: University of Manchester.

Smith, R. 2009. "The Construction of the Past in the Roman Empire." In *A Companion to the Roman Empire*, ed. D. Potter, 411-38. Malden, MA: Wiley-Blackwell.

Sonnabend, H. 1996. *Die Freundschaft der Gelehrten und die zwischen-staatliche Politik im klassischen und hellenistischen Griechenland*. Hildesheim: Olms-Weidmann.

Sordi, M. ed. 1990. *'Dulce et decorum est pro patria mori'. Le morte in com-battimento nell'antichità*. Milan: Vita e Pensiero.

Sordi, M. 2002a. "Bellum iustum ac pium." In Sordi 2002b: 3-11.

———, ed. 2002b. *Guerra e diritto nel mondo greco e romano*. Milan: Vita e Pensiero.

Southern, P. 2006. *The Roman Army: A Social and Institutional History*. Oxford: Oxford University Press.

Spann, P. 1999. "Alexander at the Beas: A Fox in Lion's Skin." In *The Eye Expanded: Life and Arts in Greco-Roman Antiquity,* ed. F. Titchener and R. Moorton, 62-74. Los Angeles: University of California Press.

Speidel, Michael A. 1992. "Roman Army Pay Scales." *JRS* 82: 87-106.

———. 1997. "Frauen und Kinder beim römischen Heer." *Pro Vindonissa*: 53-54.

———. 2000a. "Sold und Wirtschaftslage der römischen Soldaten." In Alföldy, Dobson and Eck: 65-94.

———. 2000b. "Geld und Macht : die Neuordnung des staatlichen Finanzwesens unter Augustus." In *La révolution romaine après Ronald Syme*, ed. Ph. Borgeaud and G. Rowe: 113-150. Geneva: Fondation Hardt.

———. 2001. "Specialisation and Promotion in the Roman Imperial Army." In Blois 2001: 50-61.

Speidel, M. A., and Hans Lieb, eds. 2007. *Militärdiplome: die Forschungsbeiträge der Berner Gespräche von 2004*. Stuttgart: F. Steiner.

Speidel, M. P. 1978a. *Guards of the Roman Armies: An Essay on the singula-res of the Provinces*. Bonn: Habelt.

———. 1978b. *The Religion of Iuppiter Dolichenus in the Roman Army*. Leiden: Brill.

———. 1984. "*Catafractarii clibanarii* and the Rise of the Later Roman Mailed Cavalry: A Gravestone from Claudiopolis in Bithynia." *EA* 3-4: 151-6.

————. 1989. "The Soldiers' Servants." *AncSoc* 20: 239-247.

————. 1991. "Swimming the Danube under Hadrian's eyes: A Feat of the Emperor's Batavian Horse Guards." *AncSoc* 22: 277-82.

————. 1992a. *The Framework of an Imperial Legion.* Cardiff: National Museum of Wales.

————. 1992b. *Roman Army Studies II* (MAVORS 8). Stuttgart : F. Steiner.

————. 1993. "Commodus the God-Emperor and the Army." *JRS* 83: 109-114.

————. 1994. *Riding for Caesar: The Roman Emperors' Horse Guards.* Cambridge, MA: Harvard University Press.

————. 2006. *Emperor Hadrian's Speeches to the African Army: A New Text.* Mainz: Römisch-Germanisches Zentralmuseum.

Spek, R. J. van der. 1993. "Assyriology and History: A Comparative Study of War and Empire in Assyria, Athens, and Rome." In: *The Tablet and the Scroll: Near Eastern Studies in Honor of W. W. Hallo,* ed. M. E. Cohen, Daniel C. Snell, David B. Weisberg, 62-70. Bethesda, MD: CDL Press.

Spiller, R. 1988. "S. L. A. Marshall and the Ratio of Fire." *Royal United Services Institute Journal* 133.4: 63-71.

————. 2006. "Military History and its Fictions." *JMH* 70: 1081-98.

Stäcker, Jan. 2003. *Princeps und miles: Studien zum Bindungs- und Nähverhältnis von Kaiser und Soldat im 1. und 2. Jahrhundert n. Chr.* Hildesheim: Olms.

Stallibrass, S. and R. Thomas, eds. 2008. *Feeding the Roman Army: the Archaeology of Production and Supply in NW Europe.* Oxford: Oxbow.

Starr, C. 1993. *The Roman Imperial Navy.* 3rd ed. Chicago: Ares.

Starr, I. 1990. *Queries to the Sungod: Divination and Politics in Sargonid Assyria.* Helsinki: University of Helsinki.

Stauner, K. 2004. *Das offizielle Schriftwesen des römischen Heeres von Augustus bis Gallienus (27 v. Chr.-268 n. Chr.)* Bonn: Habelt.

Stefan, A. 2005. *Les guerres daciques de Domitien et de Trajan: Architecture militaire, topographie, images et histoire. Collection de l'École Française de Rome,* 353. Rome: École Française de Rome.

Sternberg, R.H. 1999. "The Transport of Sick and Wounded Soldiers in Classical Greece." *Phoenix* 53: 191-205.

Stickler, T. 2002. *Aëtius: Gestaltungsspielräume eines Heermeisters im ausgehenden Weströmischen Reich.* Munich: Beck.

Stietencron, H. von and J. Rüpke, eds. 1995. *Töten im Krieg.* Munich: Verlag Karl Alber.

Stol, M. 1986. *Letters from Collections in Philadelphia, Chicago and Berkeley.* Altbabylonische Briefe in Umschrift und Übersetzung, Heft 11. Leiden: Brill.

————. 2004. "Wirtschaft und Gesellschaft in altbabylonischer Zeit." In *Mesopotamien: Die altbabylonische Zeit*, ed. D. Charpin et al., 643-975. Göttingen: Vandenhoeck & Ruprecht.

Stoll, O. 2001. *Zwischen Integration und Abgrenzung: Die Religion des Römischen Heeres im Nahen Osten*. St. Katharinen: Scripta Mercaturae Verlag.

————. 2007. "The Religions of the Roman Armies." In *CRA*: 451-76.

Stouder, G. 2006. "Πόλεμος ἀκήρυκτος: la guerre sans héraut." In *Guerre et diplomatie (IVᵉ-IIIᵉ siècles)*, eds. E. Caire and S. Pittia, 209-22. Aix-en-Provence: Publications de l'Université de Provence.

Strauss, B. 1996. "The Athenian Trireme, School of Democracy." In *Demokratia*, ed. J. Ober and C. Hedrick, 313-25. Princeton: Princeton University Press.

————. 2000. "Perspectives on the Death of Fifth-Century Athenian Seamen." In van Wees 2000a: 261-83.

————. 2003. "Alexander: The Military Campaigns." In Roisman 2003: 133-57.

Studevant-Hickman, B. 2008. "The Workforce at Umma: Some New Questions." In *The Growth of an Early State in Mesopotamia: Studies in Ur III Administration*, ed. S. J. Garfinkle and J. C. Johnson, 141-48. Madrid: Consejo Superior de Investigaciones Científicas.

Tadmor, H. 1994. *The Inscriptions of Tiglath-pileser III, King of Assyria*. Jerusalem: The Israel Academy of Sciences and Humanities.

Talbert, Richard J.A. 2010. "The Roman Worldview: Beyond Recovery?" In *Geography and Ethnography: Perceptions of the World in Pre-Modern Societies*, ed. K. Raaflaub and R. Talbert, 252-72. Malden, MA: Wiley-Blackwell.

Tarn, W.W. 1930. *Hellenistic Military and Naval Developments*. Cambridge: Cambridge University Press. Reprinted Chicago: Ares Publishers, 1984.

Tejeda, J. 2004. "Warfare, History and Literature in the Archaic and Classical Periods: The Development of Greek Military Treatises." *Historia* 53: 129-46.

Thomas, Y., ed. 1984. *Du châtiment dans la cité: supplices corporels et peine de mort dans le monde antique*. Rome: L'École française de Rome.

Thorne, J. 2007. "Battle, Tactics, and the Emergence of the *limites* in the West." In *CRA*: 218-34.

Tilly, Ch. 1985. "War Making and State Making as Organized Crime." In *Bringing the State Back In*, ed. D. Rueschemeyer and T. Skocpol, 169-91. Cambridge: Cambridge University Press.

Timpe, D. 2002. "Stadtstaat und Krieg in der Antike." In *Welt ohne Krieg?* ed. W. Böhm and M. Lindauer, 49-61. Stuttgart: Klett.

Tolstoy, L. 1966. *War and Peace. The Maude Translation, Background and Sources. Essays in Criticism.* ed. G. Gibian. New York: W. W. Norton.

Tomlin, R. 1972. "*Seniores-iuniores* in the Late-Roman Field Army." *AJP* 93: 253-78.

———. 1998. "Christianity and the Roman Army." In *Constantine: History, Hagiography and Legend.* ed. S.N.C. Lieu and D. Montserrat, 21-51. New York: Routledge.

———. 2000. "The Legions in the Late Empire." In *Roman Fortresses and their Legions.* ed. R.J. Brewer, 159-81. Cardiff: National Museums & Galleries of Wales.

———. 2008. "A.H.M. Jones and the Army of the Fourth Century." In *A.H.M. Jones and the Later Roman Empire.* ed. D.M. Gwynn, 143-65. Leiden: Brill.

Treadgold, W.T. 1995. *Byzantium and its Army, 284-1081.* Stanford: Stanford University Press.

———. 2007. *The Early Byzantine Historians.* London: Palgrave Macmillan.

Tritle, L. 2000. *From Melos to Mylai.* New York: Routledge.

Tritle, L. and J.B. Campbell, eds. 2011, forthcoming. *Oxford Handbook of Warfare in the Classical World.* Oxford: Oxford University Press.

Trombley, F.R., and J.W. Watt. 2000. *The Chronicle of Pseudo-Joshua the Stylite.* Liverpool: Liverpool University Press.

Trundle, M. 2004. *Greek Mercenaries: From the Late Archaic Period to Alexander.* New York: Routledge.

———. 2010 "Coinage and the Transformation of Greek Warfare." In Fagan and Trundle 2010: 227-252.

Tucci, Jim. 2010. "Historiographical Essay: Warfare in the Ancient World." *JMH* 74: 879-99.

Turney-High, H. 1971. Primitive War: Its Practice and Concepts, 2nd ed. Columbia: University of South Carolina Press.

———. 1981. *The Military: The Theory of Land Warfare as Behavioral Science.* West Hanover: The Christopher Publishing House.

Udwin, V. 1999. *Between Two Armies: The Place of the Duel in Epic Culture.* Leiden: Brill.

Urbainczyk, T. 2008. *Slave Revolts in Antiquity.* Los Angeles: University of California Press.

Vagts, A. 1959. *A History of Militarism: Civilian and Military,* rev. edition. New York: Meridian Books.

Van De Mieroop, M. 1999. *Cuneiform Texts and the Writing of History.* New York: Routledge.

———. 2005. *King Hammurabi: A Biography.* Malden, MA: Wiley-Blackwell.

van Driel, G. 2002. *Elusive Silver: In Search of a Role for a Market in an Agrarian Environment: Aspects of Mesopotamian Society*. Leiden: Nederlands Instituut voor het Nabije Oosten.

van Driel-Murray, C. 1995. "Gender in Question." *TRAC* 2, ed. P. Rush: 3-21. Avebury: Aldershot.

Vandkilde, H. 2003. "Commemmorative Tales: Archaeological Responses to Modern Myth, Politics, and War." *World Archaeology* 35.1: 126-44.

van Soldt, W. H. 1994. *Letters in the British Museum. Part 2*. Altbabylonische Briefe in Umschrift und Übersetzung, Heft 13. Leiden: Brill.

van Wees, H. 1992. *Status Warriors: Violence and Society in Homer and History*. Amsterdam: J.C. Gieben.

———. 1994. "The Homeric Way of War: The *Iliad* and the Hoplite Phalanx (I) and (II)." *G&R* 41: 1-18, 131-55.

———, ed. 2000a. *War and Violence in Ancient Greece*. London: Duckworth, 2000.

———. 2000b. "The Development of the Hoplite Phalanx: Iconography and Reality in the Seventh Century." In van Wees, 2000a: 125-66.

———. 2001. "The Myth of the Middle Class Army: Military and Social Status in Ancient Athens." In Bekker-Nielsen and Hannestad, 2001: 45-71.

———. 2004. *Greek Warfare: Myth and Realities*. London: Duckworth.

———. 2007. "War and Society." In *CHGRW*, 1: 273-99.

———. 2008. "'Diejenigen, die segeln, sollen Sold erhalten'. Seekriegführung und-finanzierung im archaischen Eretria." In Burres and Müller, 2008: 128-50.

———. 2010. "'Those Who Sail Are to Receive a Wage': Naval Warfare and Finance in Archaic Eretria." In Fagan and Trundle, 2010: 205-226.

van't Dack, E. 1988. *Ptolemaica Selecta. Études sur l'armée et l'administration lagides. Studia Hellenistica*, 29. Louvain: [s.n.].

Varhelyi, Z. 2007. "The Specters of Roman Imperialism: The Live Burials of Gauls and Greeks at Rome." *CA* 26.2: 277-304.

Vaughn, P. 1991. "The Identification and Retrieval of the Hoplite Battle-Dead," In Hanson 1991a: 38-62.

Veen, M. van der. 2003. "When is Food a Luxury?" *World Archaeology* 34.3: 405-427.

Vernant, J.-P., ed. 1968. *Problèmes de la guerre en Grèce ancienne*. Paris: Mouton & Co.

Versnel, H. 2002. "Writing Morals and Readings Gods. Appeal to the Gods as a Dual Strategy in Social Control." In *Demokratie, Recht und soziale Kontrolle im klassischen Athen*, ed. D. Cohen, 37-76. Munich: Oldenbourg.

Vidal, J., ed. 2010. *Studies on War in the Ancient Near East: Collected Essays on Military History* (AOAT 372). Münster: Ugarit-Verlag.

Visicato, G. 1999. "The Sargonic Archive of Tell el-Suleimah." *Journal of Cuneiform Studies 51*: 17-30.

Wallace-Hadrill, A. 2008. *Rome's Cultural Revolution.* Cambridge: Cambridge University Press.

Walters, J. 1997. "Invading the Roman Body: Manliness and Impenetrability in Roman Thought." In *Roman Sexualities*, ed. J. P. Hallett and M. B. Skinner, 29-43. Princeton: Princeton University Press.

Ward-Perkins, B. 2005. *The Fall of Rome and the End of Civilization.* Oxford: Oxford University Press.

Waterman, L. 1930. *The Royal Correspondence of the Assyrian Empire.* Ann Arbor: University of Michigan.

Watson, G. R. 1969. *The Roman Soldier.* Ithaca, NY: Cornell University Press.

Weber, J. A. and R. L. Zettler. 1998. "Tools and Weapons." In *Treasures from the Royal Tombs of Ur*, ed. R. L. Zettler and L. Horne, 163-74. Philadelphia: University of Pennsylvania Museum.

Webster, G. 1998. *The Roman Imperial Army of the First and Second Centuries A.D.* 3rd ed. Norman, OK: University of Oklahoma.

Webster, J. and N. Cooper, eds. 1996. *Roman Imperialism: Post-Colonial Perspectives.* Leicester, UK: Leicester University School of Archaeological Studies.

Wenger, R. 2008a. *Strategie, Taktik und Gefechtstechnik in der Ilias. Analyse der Kampfbeschreibung der Ilias.* Hamburg: Verlag Dr. Kovac.

————. 2008b. "Strategie, Taktik und Gefechtstechnik in der *Ilias.*" *WS* 121: 29-52.

Welch, K. E. 2006. "*Domi militiaeque*: Roman Domestic Aesthetics and War Booty in the Republic." In Dillon and Welch 2006: 91-161.

Welwei, K-W. 1988. *Unfreie im antiken Kriegsdienst, III : Rom.* Stuttgart: F. Steiner.

Wesch-Klein, G. 1998, *Soziale Aspekte des römischen Heerwesens in der Kaiserzeit.* Stuttgart: F. Steiner.

————. 2007. "Recruits and Veterans." In *CRA*: 435-50.

Westbrook, R. 2001. "Social Justice and Creative Jurisprudence in Late Bronze Age Syria." *JESHO* 44.1: 22-43.

Whately, C. 2009. "Descriptions of Battle in the *Wars* of Procopius," (Ph.D. diss., Warwick).

Whatley, N. 1964. "On the Possibility of Reconstructing Marathon and Other Ancient Battles." *JHS* 84: 119-39. Reprinted in Wheeler 2007b: 301-21.

Wheatley, P. and R. Hannah, eds. 2009. *Alexander & His Successors: Essays from the Antipodes.* Claremont: Regina Books.

Wheeler, E.L. 1978. "The Occasion of Arrian's *Tactica*." *GRBS* 19: 351-65.

———. 1979. "The Legion as Phalanx." *Chiron* 9: 303-18.

———. 1983. "The *Hoplomachoi* and Vegetius' Spartan Drillmasters." *Chiron* 13: 1–20.

———. 1984. "Sophistic Interpretations and Greek Treaties." *GRBS* 25: 253-74.

———. 1988a. *Stratagem and the Vocabulary of Military Trickery*. Leiden: E. J. Brill.

———. 1988b. "Πολλα κενα του πολεμου: The History of a Greek Proverb," *GRBS* 29: 153-84.

———. 1990. Review of Hanson 1989. *Journal of Interdisciplinary History* 21: 122–25.

———. 1991. "The General as Hoplite" In Hanson 1991a: 121-70.

———. 1993a. "Methodological Limits and the Mirage of Roman Strategy." *JMH* 57: 7-41 and 215-40.

———. 1993b. Review of Sherwin-White and Kuhrt 1993. *Journal of the Society for Armenian Studies* 6: 233-36.

———. 1993c. "Ruses and Stratagems." In *The International Military and Defense Encyclopedia*, ed. T. Dupuy, 5, 2330-34. Washington: Macmillan-Brassey's.

———. 1994. "Introduction." In *Polyaenus, Stratagems of War*, ed. and tr. P. Krentz and E. Wheeler, 1, vi-xxiv. Chicago: Ares Publishers.

———. 1996. "The Laxity of Syrian Legions." In *The Roman Army in the East*. ed. D. L. Kennedy, 229-76. *JRA* Suppl. 18. Ann Arbor, MI: Journal of Roman Archaeology.

———. 1998a. "Battles and Frontiers: A Review of A.K. Goldsworthy, *The Roman Army at War, 100 BC-AD 200* and Hugh Elton, *Frontiers of the Roman Empire*." *JRA* 11: 644-51

———. 1998b. Review of Ager 1996. *AJP* 119: 642-46.

———. 1999. "Krieg." In *Mensch und Landschaft in der Antike. Lexikon der Historische Geographie*, ed. H. Sonnabend, 272-80. Stuttgart und Weimar: Verlag J.B. Metzler.

———. 2001. "Firepower: Missile Weapons and the "*Face of Battle*." *Electrum* 5: 169-84

———. 2004a. "The Late Roman Legion as Phalanx in the Late Empire (I)." In *L'Armée romaine de Dioclétien à Valentinien Ier*. eds. Y. Le Bohec and C. Wolff, 309-58. Paris: Boccard.

———. 2004b. "The Legion as Phalanx in the Late Empire (II)." *Revue des études militaires anciennes* 1: 147-75.

———. 2006. Review of Hanson 2005. *JMH* 70: 816-18.

———. 2007a. "Land Battles." In *CHGRW*, 1: 186-223.

———, ed. 2007b. *The Armies of Classical Greece.* Aldershot and Burlington: Ashgate Publishing.

———. 2007c. "The Army and the *limes* in the East." In *CRA*, 235-66.

———. 2008. "Anti-Deceit Clauses in Greek Treaties: An Apologia." *Electrum* 14: 57-83.

———. 2009. Review of Sauzeau and Van Compernolle 2007. *AnTard* 17 (2009) 416-18.

———. 2010. "Polyaenus: *Scriptor Militaris.*" In *Polyainos. Neue Studien— Polyaenus. New Studies*, ed. K. Brodersen, 7-54. Berlin: Verlag Antike.

———. 2010b. "Rome's Dacian Wars: Domitian, Trajan, and Strategy on the Danube, Part I-II," *JMH* 74: 1185-1227, and 75: 191-219.

———. Forthcoming. "Present but Absent: Marathon in the Tradition of Western Military Thought." In *Marathon: The Day after....*, ed. K. Buresalis.

Whetham, D. 2009. *Just Wars and Moral Victories. Surprise, Deception and the Normative Framework of European War in the Later Middle Ages.* Leiden: Brill.

Whitby, M. 1988. *The Emperor Maurice and his Historian: Theophylact Simocatta on Persian and Balkan Warfare.* Oxford: Oxford University Press.

———. 1995. "Recruitment in Roman Armies from Justinian to Heraclius (*ca.* 565-615)." In *The Byzantine and Early Islamic Near East: III – States, Resources and Armies.* ed. Averil Cameron, 61-124. Princeton: Darwin Press.

———. 1998. "*Deus nobiscum*: Christianity, Warfare and Morale in Late Antiquity." In *Modus operandi: Essays in Honour of Geoffrey Rickman.* ed. M.M. Austin, J.D. Harries and C.J. Smith, 191-208. London: Institute of Classical Studies.

———. 2000. "The Army, c. 420-602." In *Cambridge Ancient History XIV: Late Antiquity – Empire and Successors, AD 425-600.* ed. A. Cameron, B. Ward-Perkins and M. Whitby, 288-314. Cambridge: Cambridge University Press.

———. 2004. "Emperors and armies, AD 235-395." In *Approaching Late Antiquity: The Transformation from Early to Late Empire.* ed. S. Swain and M. Edwards, 158-86. Oxford: Oxford University Press.

———. 2007a. "Army and Society in the Late Roman World: A Context for Decline?" In *CRA:* 515-31.

———. 2007b. "Reconstructing Ancient Warfare." In *CHGRW*, 1: 54-81.

Whitehead, D. 2008. "Fact and Fantasy in Greek Military Writers." *AAntHung* 48: 139-55.

Whitehorne, J. E. G. 2004. "Petitions to the Centurion: A Question of Locality?" *BASP* 41: 155-169.

Whitman, J. Q. 1995. "At the Origins of the Law and the State: Supervision of Violence, Mutilation of Bodies, or Setting of Prices?" *Chicago-Kent Law Review* 71: 41-84.

Whittaker, C.R. 1983. "Trade and Frontiers of the Roman Empire". In *Trade and Famine in Classical Antiquity*. ed. P. Garnsey and C.R. Whittaker , 110-27. Cambridge: Cambridge Philological Society.

———. 1994. *Frontiers of the Roman Empire: A Social and Economic Study*. Baltimore, MD: Johns Hopkins.

———. 2004. *Rome and Its Frontiers: The Dynamics of Empire*. New York: Routledge.

———. 2005. "The Roman Danube: An Archaeological Survey." *JRS* 95: 124-225.

Wiesehöfer, J. ed. 1998. *Das Partherreich und seine Zeugnisse. Historia Einzelschrift*, 122. Stuttgart: Franz Steiner Verlag.

Wilkes, J.J. 2003. *Documenting the Roman Army. Essays in Honour of Margaret Roxan*. London: Institute of Classical Studies.

Williams, C. 2010. *Roman Homosexuality: Ideologies of Masculinity in Classical Antiquity.* 2nd ed. Oxford: Oxford University Press.

Wilson, P. 2008. "Defining Military Culture." *JMH* 72: 11-41.

Woolf, G. 1993. "Roman Peace." In Rich and Shipley 1993b: 171-94.

———. 1998. *Becoming Roman.* Cambridge: Cambridge University Press.

Worthington, I. 1999a. "How 'Great' was Alexander?" *AHB* 13: 39-59.

———. 1999b. "Alexander and the Interests of Historical Accuracy: A Reply." *AHB* 13: 136-40.

———. 2008. *Philip II of Macedonia*. New Haven: Yale University Press.

Wyke, M. 2006. *Julius Caesar in Western Culture.* Malden, MA: Wiley-Blackwell.

Yarshater, E., ed. 1983. *The Cambridge History of the History of Iran,* III.1. Cambridge: Cambridge University Press.

Yoffee, N. 2005, *Myths of the Archaic State*. Cambridge: Cambridge University Press.

Young, A. 1995. *The Harmony of Illusions: Inventing Post-Traumatic Stress Disorder.* Princeton: Princeton University Press.

Zaccagnini, C. 1995. "War and Famine at Emar." *Orientalia* 64: 92-109.

Zanker, P. 1988. *The Power of Images in the Age of Augustus*. Tr. Alan Shapiro. Ann Arbor, MI: University of Michigan.

Ziegler, N. 1997. "L'armée, - quel monstre!" In *Recueil d'études à la mémoire de Marie-Térèse Barrelet* (=*Florilegium marianum* 3), ed. D. Charpin and J.-M. Durand, 145-52. Paris: SEPOA.

———. 2000. "Aspects économiques des guerres de Samsi-Addu." In Andreau, Briant, and Descat 2000: 13-33.

Zimmermann, M. 2007. "Antike Kriege zwischen privaten Kriegsherrn und staatlichem Monopol auf Kriegführung." In *Formen des Krieges. Von der Antike bis zur Gegenwart*, ed. D. Beyrau, M. Hochgeschwender, D. Langwiesche, 51-70. Paderborn: F. Schöningh.

Ziolkowski, A. 1993. "*Urbs direpta*, or How the Romans Sacked Cities." In Rich and Shipley 1993b: 69-91.

Zuckerman, C. 1990. "The Compendium of Syrianus Magister." *JÖByz* 40: 209-24.

———. 1998. "Two Reforms of the 370s: Recruiting Soldiers and Senators in the Divided Empire." *REByz* 56: 79-139.

———. 2004. "L'armée." In *Le monde byzantine, vol.1: L'empire romain d'orient, 330-641.* ed. C. Morrisson, 143-80. Paris: Presses universitaires de France.